THE
COMPLETE
POTATO
COOKBOOK

THE COMPLETE POTATO COOKBOOK

by

Ruth

Bakalar

PRENTICE-HALL, INC.
ENGLEWOOD CLIFFS
NEW JERSEY

The Complete Potato Cookbook by Ruth Bakalar

© 1969 by Ruth Bakalar

Printed in the United States of America

Prentice-Hall International, Inc., London
Prentice-Hall of Australia, Pty. Ltd., Sydney
Prentice-Hall of Canada, Ltd., Toronto
Prentice-Hall of India Private Ltd., New Delhi
Prentice-Hall of Japan, Inc., Tokyo

ACKNOWLEDGMENTS

The writer owes thanks for sound information and good ideas
to these energetic potato boosters:

  The United States Department of Agriculture
  The Department of Agriculture of Canada
  The National Potato Council
  Many associations of potato growers and purveyors,
  particularly those from California; Maine; New Brunswick
  Province, Canada; New Jersey; Oregon, and Pennsylvania

And most of all, many thanks to the cooks and recorders of
recipes, amateur and professional, who for more than a quarter
of a century have been an unfailing source of inspiration.

🌿 This book is dedicated to the potato-eating men in my life: husband, sons, and brothers.

CONTENTS

	Preface	1
1	Baked Potatoes and Stuffed Potatoes	7
2	Kettle-Frying	19
3	Skillet-Frying	28
4	Mashed Potatoes	36
5	Saucepan Potatoes, Creamed and Stewed	52
6	Oven Casseroles	62
7	New Potatoes	77
8	Stuffings and Dumplings	89
9	Potato Pancakes	103
10	Appetizers	109
11	Soups	121
12	Potato Salads	135
13	Potato Breads, Cakes, Cookies, Pies	155
14	Desserts	191
15	Garnishes	202
16	Main-Course Potatoes	209
17	Potatoes for the Barbecue	247
18	Choice for the Buffet	258
19	Profitable Potatoes for a Crowd	268
20	National Specialties	278
	Index	302

🌿 Preface
🌿

THE FACTS Our annual potato harvest in the United States adds up to some thirty billion pounds. Next to the Soviet Union, we are the largest producers in the world. This book is about how we eat potatoes, and how we can and should eat them.

PROCESSED POTATOES Some of our thirty billion pounds regularly go to the processors for nonfood uses and, more every year, to be frozen, dehydrated, or canned. You will find potatoes in dozens and dozens of forms at your supermarket. In the freezer case there are raw potato balls and grated potato patties, French and cottage fries, cooked and parcooked, stuffed baked potatoes, potato soup, and a wide variety of elaborate fried and baked specialties ready to reheat and eat. On the grocery shelves, bags and boxes of dehydrated potatoes appear as flakes, shreds, and granules for mashing; sliced or diced potatoes in cans, and potato chips and shoestring potatoes. Potato chips, in a variety of shapes and flavorings, are offered for sale in boxes and bags. And displayed among the fresh vegetables there will surely be plastic bags of peeled potatoes, some of them sliced for frying, some scooped into small balls. That is the lineup at this writing. Experience indicates that tomorrow, or the day after, there will be many more such preparations to add to the list.

However, it is with the rest of the potato crop—the seventy-five pounds per head that the processors do not scoop up—that this book is concerned. With a few exceptions, the recipes given here do not include prepared convenience foods among the ingredients. There are two reasons for this. First, the packers can be counted on to make perfectly adequate suggestions for their use. Just read the can or package label. And second, the readers of this book can be counted on to use the prepared or partly prepared product, rather than starting from scratch with fresh potatoes, whenever it is practical and economical to do so.

BUYING POTATOES Many different types of potatoes come to market, but most of them are multipurpose, which means that they can be cooked in many different ways with satisfactory results. But there are some potatoes that are especially good for boiling, baking, or potato salad. Growers who know the score—and most of them do—make a point of telling you the special talents of their potatoes on the potato bag or box. Use these special potatoes, and learn to recognize the brand names that belong to the types you like best. The varieties are rarely named, but state origins and brands are usually given. Whatever kind of potato you buy, it is foolish economy to buy anything but the best quality. You may see a government stamp of approval on the bag—the commercial U.S. No. 1 or U.S. Consumer Grade A—but there can be many a slip between grading and grating.

You can tell a good potato by its looks. Good potatoes are fairly clean, smooth, and bright-skinned. Do not buy soft-looking potatoes with obvious defects—soft spots, dark spots, or cuts. Potatoes with green spots on them have been exposed to light (this can happen if you're careless about how you store potatoes at home, too) and are likely to be bitter and even toxic. Never eat the green areas. Potatoes that have been around too long look wilted, wrinkled, leathery, and plain tired. If the potato has a great many deep-set eyes, or a very irregular shape, it will be wasteful and troublesome to peel. Size is a matter of choice. You may want larger potatoes for baking and stuffing and smaller ones for boiling. In either case it is a good idea to choose potatoes of uniform size so that they cook evenly. In this book most recipes specify medium potatoes, which run three to a pound, make one adequate serving, and are a convenient unit for measuring purposes.

STORING POTATOES When you get the potatoes home, store them in a cool, dark place. At temperatures between 50 and 60 degrees, with a relative humidity of 85 to 90, potatoes will keep well for months. At temperatures between 60 and 70 degrees, cool room temperature, they will keep for several weeks. New potatoes begin immediately to deteriorate in flavor, color, and texture, and should be purchased in small amounts and used quickly.

POTATO CALORIES A medium potato, an average serving of one-third pound, has a caloric value of less than 100, about the same as half a grapefruit, an apple, or two tablespoons of sugar. Common sense will tell you which of these 100-calorie packages, if you had to choose among them, would be the most satisfying choice for the dinner menu on your low-calorie diet. One of the great things about potatoes is that they are real food—hearty, satisfying, and bulky enough so that they give the calorie-counter a pleasant feeling of having dined, not dieted.

POTATO NUTRIENTS Potato calories have high nutritional value. This is more than can be said for sugar calories, which provide only fuel for energy. That potato you eat for dinner supplies half your body's daily Vitamin C requirement. It also contains large amounts of B Vitamins—as much thiamine, riboflavin, and niacin as two slices of whole wheat bread—plus Vitamin A and substantial totals of iron, calcium, and phosphorus. Potato protein is also present in a small amount, the kind readily assimilated by the body. But potatoes contain practically no fat, a fact which is earning them a place in medically approved low-cholesterol regimens as well as in reducing diets.

LOW-CALORIE POTATOES If you could develop a taste for raw potatoes (many children love them) you'd have the perfect low-calorie food—healthful, low in calories, high in chewing satisfaction and bulk. You probably can't learn to eat potatoes raw if you're already old enough to count calories, but the next best way to eat them is very easy to take. Enjoy a baked or boiled potato with salt, pepper, and a dash of lemon juice or a spoonful of yogurt or cottage cheese. It is the likes of butter that adds calories —100 to the tablespoon—and makes people say potatoes are fattening. Make a potato salad with low-calorie salad dressing, one of the fine new commercial products. Include cucumber, celery, and scallions, and the only thing missing—but not missed—will be the fat, and calories, usually added by mayonnaise or regular salad dressings. Make scalloped potatoes with mushrooms and fat-free bouillon instead of milk. With a sprinkling of chopped chives or parsley, this is a gourmet's delight—about 100 calories a serving!

All in all, the potato can be the dieter's best friend—low in calories, versatile enough to prepare in many ways and to avoid monotony, hearty and filling, and best of all, so good to eat that you can enjoy your meal and forget that you must count calories. You'll find an occasional recipe or tip in this book labeled "low calorie," but for the most part you can use your own judgment— and your detailed calorie chart—to tell you which potato dishes fit gracefully into your diet plan without taking more than their share of the day's calorie allowance.

THE RECIPES The potato has been called the world's most versatile vegetable, a fair enough description of this tuber that goes with everything and can be prepared in an almost endless variety of ways, with an almost endless variety of seasonings. This book gathers together a great many of these ways with the potato. Some of the recipes, long neglected, have been revived and brought up to date for modern use—the potato cakes and desserts, for instance. Some, like Pommes Duchesse, are part of the grand classic cuisine. Some are sturdy country fare and some were invented for kings. Some come from poverty-ridden countries where potatoes were the difference between life and death, as in Ireland, and some from hearty-eating countries like Germany. There is a chapter devoted to potatoes for the buffet, another to potatoes to cook outdoors, another to potatoes to cook for a crowd. There are potato dishes for every course of a meal, from soup to sweet. They are the best potato recipes we know—as many of them as would fit between these covers.

YIELDS A medium potato makes an average serving for an average eater, and unless otherwise stated, these recipes should provide enough for an average family of four to six. However, if your family consists of three teen-aged boys and a hearty-eating husband, or three picky small children and a husband on a diet, it is not average, so judge amounts accordingly.

SEASONING Salt tolerances differ widely, so salt (and pepper) should be used to suit your taste and your family's. Except in recipes where it is difficult or impossible to taste the mixture, no specific amount of salt is recommended.

OVEN TEMPERATURES In these recipes, oven temperatures are given in degrees. If your oven does not have a dependable thermostat control and you do not have an oven thermometer (you should—they are very inexpensive and almost indispensable if you use your oven frequently), read the temperature directions this way:

> 250°F. is slow
> 300°F. is moderately slow
> 325°F. is slow moderate
> 350°F. is moderate
> 375°F. is moderately hot
> 400°F. is hot
> 450°F. is very hot

POTATO CALORIE CHART

(U.S. DEPARTMENT OF AGRICULTURE)

Calorie Count

1 medium potato (5⅓ ounces)	96 calories
Baked, with one tablespoon sour cream	126 calories
Baked, with one tablespoon butter	196 calories
Boiled, with one tablespoon butter	196 calories
Boiled, with two tablespoons milk gravy	176 calories
Mashed, ⅔ cup serving with milk	97 calories
Mashed, ⅔ cup with milk and one tablespoon butter	197 calories
Mashed, ⅔ cup with milk, one tablespoon butter, and two tablespoons milk gravy	307 calories
Potato chips, ten chips, two-inch diameter	110 calories
French Fries, ten sticks, 2 by ½ by ½ inch	155 calories

Potato Chip on His Shoulder According to the story, a patron at one of the fashionable hotels in Saratoga Springs, New York, the famous nineteenth-century holiday resort, sent his French-fried potatoes back to the kitchen because he thought they were too thick. Chef George Crum angrily sliced potatoes paper thin, dropped them into hot fat, and scornfully had them served to the complaining guest—who loved them! Thus were born potato chips, originally called Saratoga chips.

❧ 1
❧

Baked
Potatoes
and
Stuffed
Potatoes

You can bake any kind or shape of potato in its skin, and enjoy it skin and all. But since potato texture figures so largely in potato taste, they will not all taste the same. The potato varieties known as "bakers" are favored for this use because of their long, oval shape and the fact that they bake dry and fluffy. The very largest of these species, sold like precious jewels in individual wrappings, are a dramatic choice for stuffing—half a potato to a serving. The skin of a baked potato is a great delicacy. Scrub it and coat it with fat before baking, and the skin will be soft and will taste of butter, or bacon fat, or good beef drippings. Just scrub and bake, and the skin will be crisp and brittle.

There is nothing simpler than baking a potato. Lay the potatoes on a baking sheet or directly on the oven rack. Bake them at any temperature, alone or along with the dinner roast, adjusting the baking time accordingly. A medium potato will bake at 450°F. in less than an hour, at 400°F. in a little over an hour, at 350°F. in an hour and fifteen or twenty minutes. It is impossible to be more definite than this, but you can tell when a potato is done by simply pressing it between thumb and fingers, to make sure that it is soft.

Serve them at once. Cut a cross in the center of one flat side and press firmly to force the pulp up through the gash. You can put a bit of butter in the gash, or let guests help themselves to butter, salt, and pepper. Freshly ground pepper has more flair, as well as more flavor, so pass the pepper grinder!

BAKED POTATO TOPPINGS

1. Instead of plain salt use the seasoned variety—garlic, onion, celery, or a mixture—and paprika instead of pepper.
2. Sprinkle the buttered potato with freshly grated Parmesan cheese.
3. Add a colorful sprinkle of chopped fresh parsley or chives. Frozen chives will do, too. Or add chopped scallion, with its greens.
4. Top with a little *maître d'hôtel* butter: one-half stick of butter creamed with two tablespoons of lemon juice, two tablespoons of chopped parsley, and salt and pepper to taste.
5. Slip a piece of Roquefort or blue cheese into the gash atop the potato. Return the potato to the oven for a moment to soften the cheese.
6. Sauté a finely chopped onion in butter, add salt, pepper, and paprika. Use as a hot sauce.
7. Pass a bowl of tart sour cream (heated, if you like, but not boiled)—or yogurt for dieters. Yogurt, plain or seasoned in any of the ways suggested for sour cream, adds a great deal of pleasure for a minimum of calories.
8. Flavor sour cream, or yogurt, with ground horseradish to taste. Add lemon juice, salt, and pepper if desired.
9. Mix sour cream with dehydrated onion soup mix (see the recipe on the package). This makes a deliciously savory topper with yogurt, too.
10. Stir sour cream with a spoonful of caviar, red or black. Luxury!

11. And of course, sour cream and chives, the specialty of many steak houses where a baked potato is the *pièce de résistance*.
12. Use your favorite salad dressing, or low-calorie dressing, as topping for a baked potato. Omit the butter, but more salt and pepper are probably in order.
13. Any of the dips served with potato chips—usually based on sour cream, cottage cheese, or cream cheese—makes a beautiful topping for a beautiful baked potato. Just make sure that the dip, which is probably highly seasoned and distinctively flavored, is compatible with the rest of the meal.

CREAM CHEESE TOPPING

½ *lb. cream cheese*
3 *Tbsp. lemon juice*
5 *scallions*
3 *hard-cooked egg yolks*
½ *cup light cream (or half-and-half)*
    Salt, pepper

Let a half-pound package of Philadelphia-type cream cheese soften at room temperature. With a fork, mash the cheese well. Gradually add 3 tablespoons lemon juice, blending well with the fork. Chop very finely 5 scallions, with the green parts, and mash the yolks of 3 hard-cooked eggs. Blend both into the cheese. Work in about ½ cup light cream or half-and-half, beating with the fork to make a light, smooth mixture. Season with salt and pepper to taste. Use as a topping for baked potatoes.

BAKED POTATOES ON THE HALF SHELL

It is possible to cut the baking time of potatoes almost in half by cutting the potatoes in half. Brush both sides with fat and bake, cut-side down, on a greased baking sheet, about half the usual time, at any temperature from 350°F. to 450°F.

BAKED POTATOES IN A HURRY

Scrub baking potatoes. Cook them, in their jackets, in boiling salted water to cover for about 5 minutes. Then bake as usual, but for about half the usual time.

> *The Railroads* Just before the turn of the century, when railroads were railroads and railroad dining cars were worthy of a gourmet's patronage, the Northern Pacific advertised itself as "The Line of the Great Big Baked Potato."

FRANCONIA POTATOES

Cook uniform-size potatoes in boiling salted water to cover for 10 minutes. Peel, drain, and dry. About an hour before the roast with which the potatoes will be served is due to be ready, put the potatoes in the roasting pan alongside the meat. Roll them in the drippings. If desired, salt and pepper or paprika may be sprinkled on them at this stage. Roast until brown and crusty, or until the meat is done, basting and turning occasionally.

OVEN-BROWNED POTATOES

  2 *lbs. potatoes*
  ¼ *cup bacon drippings or rendered poultry fat*
   Garlic salt, paprika, black pepper

Peel a strip from the middle of 6 medium potatoes (2 pounds). Cook in boiling salted water to cover, drain, and dry. Heat a baking dish in the oven and in it melt ¼ cup bacon drippings or rendered poultry fat. Roll the potatoes in the drippings and sprinkle them with garlic salt, paprika, and black pepper. Bake at 375°F. about 15 minutes, until the potatoes begin to glaze. The potatoes may be baked at any temperature, allowing for a difference in time, so put them in with the roast or the dinner biscuits or whatever is in the oven.

BAKED POTATOES OREGANO

¼ cup oil
1 clove garlic
1 tsp. oregano
2 lbs. baking potatoes
Salt, pepper

Heat ¼ cup oil in a baking pan with a clove of garlic, large or small depending on how well you like garlic. Crush 1 teaspoon dried oregano between your fingers and add it to the oil. Peel 6 medium or 3 large baking potatoes (2 pounds). Cut medium potatoes in half, or cut large ones in half lengthwise and then in half again crosswise. Roll the potatoes in the seasoned oil, sprinkle with salt and pepper, and arrange in an overlapping layer in the oil remaining in the pan. Cook in the oven, alone or along with a roast, until tender, about an hour at 350°F., 45 minutes or less at 450°F.

ALMOND BAKED POTATOES

2 lbs. potatoes
Salt
¼ cup melted butter
1 cup slivered almonds
1 cup bouillon

Peel 6 medium potatoes (2 pounds) and cut into thirds lengthwise. Season with salt. Roll first in ¼ cup melted butter, then in about 1 cup slivered almonds, blanched but not toasted. Lay potatoes side by side in a shallow oven-to-table casserole. Add 1 cup bouillon to the casserole, cover, and bake at 400°F. for about 40 minutes, until the potatoes are tender.

11

AROOSTOCK BAKED POTATOES

  3 *slices white bread*
½ *cup butter*
  Salt, pepper
  6 *medium potatoes*

Dry 3 slices bread in a slow oven (250°F.) and crush to make 1 cup fine crumbs. (Prepared crumbs may be used.) Melt ½ cup butter (¼ pound or 1 stick) and season well with salt and pepper. Peel 6 uniform potatoes (2 pounds) and dry them on paper towels. Roll the potatoes in the butter, then in the crumbs. Lay the potatoes side by side on a greased pan and bake at 375°F. about 50 minutes, until done. These potatoes may be baked with a roast, at lower or higher temperatures, by simply adjusting the time accordingly.

CRUNCHY BAKED POTATOES

  2 *lbs. potatoes*
½ *cup or more sour cream*
  1 *cup crushed cornflakes*
  Salt, pepper, paprika

Peel 6 uniformly shaped potatoes (2 pounds) and coat with dairy sour cream, using ½ cup or more (half an 8-ounce container). Roll in about 1 cup crushed cornflakes, measured after crushing (or use the prepared cereal crumbs) mixed with salt, pepper, and paprika to taste. Cover thickly. Lay the potatoes side by side on a foil-lined baking dish. Cover, bake at 425°F. about 45 minutes, until tender.

BAKED POTATOES SURPRISE

Scrub uniform oval baking potatoes, core with an apple corer, and remove the plug. Discard the center of the plugs, but reserve both ends, with about ½ inch of potato. Fill the hollow with any of the fillings below, replace the plugs to seal the ends closed, and bake as usual. Possible fillings include:

Bacon: Fry bacon until crisp, drain on paper towel, and crumble.

Sausage: Use parcooked link sausages, or put uncooked sausage in pan with water to cover and boil for a minute or two. Or brown the sausage, if you like. Canned Vienna sausages or cocktail franks may also be used as stuffers.

Sour Cream: Combine sour cream with chives, dill seed, or chopped fresh herbs.

Cheese: Soften Cheddar, Roquefort or Blue cheese. Combine with butter, if desired.

Herb Butter: Cream butter with basil, chives, dill, tarragon, rosemary, chervil, lovage, fennel tops, parsley of course—almost any herb you like and can grow or buy at the vegetable market.

Potato Publicist   When more conventional methods failed to persuade the people of France that potatoes were worth eating, promoter Parmentier invented press agentry. He arranged for Marie Antoinette to wear potato flowers in her hair, a sign of royal approval that was promptly imitated by all the courtiers. Then he made the potato into forbidden fruit. He protected the royally sponsored potato farms with armed soldiers during the day—and left them unguarded at night. The inevitable happily happened. The very people who had scorned to try the strange new potato when it was offered to them decided it was worth stealing! Soon potato patches flourished all over France, and a new, reliable source of food had been firmly established.

STUFFED BAKED POTATOES

2 *lbs. baking potatoes*
4 *Tbsp. butter*
   Salt, pepper
⅓ *cup hot milk or cream*

Bake 6 medium potatoes or 3 large bakers (2 pounds) until done. Cut a slice from the flat side of the medium potatoes and scoop out the pulp. If you use large oval potatoes, cut them in half lengthwise. In either case, leave the shells intact. Mash the pulp and season with 4 tablespoons butter and salt and pepper to taste. Add ⅓ cup hot milk or cream, to make a light and fluffy mixture. Pile back into the shells (for fancy effect, use a pastry bag) and return to the oven to heat at 350° to 400°F. for 15 to 20 minutes before serving. Stuffed potatoes can be prepared far ahead of time and reheated just before serving—a plus benefit!

VARIATIONS

1. Prepare as above and sprinkle with grated cheese before heating. Or sprinkle with slivered blanched almonds or with buttered bread crumbs.
2. Prepare as above and add 2 beaten eggs and a little grated onion or chopped chives, to taste. Or use just 2 yolks, or 2 whites, beaten stiff.
3. Chop a small onion and cook until translucent in ¼ cup rendered chicken fat. Mash the potato pulp, add the onion and fat, and season highly with salt and black pepper. A beaten egg or two is an optional addition.
4. Dice 3 slices of bacon and cook until crisp. Mash potato pulp and add the bacon with a little of the bacon drippings or butter to moisten. Season well with onion or garlic salt and pepper.
5. Add half a dozen sliced pimiento-stuffed olives to the mashed pulp. Or add a pimiento, cut fine, or some chopped parsley or chives.

6. Add ½ cup cottage cheese to the pulp—omit the milk if the cheese is sufficiently creamy—and a spoonful of finely chopped green pepper or scallion tops. No butter needed—low in calories!

VEGETABLE-STUFFED POTATOES

2 *lbs. baking potatoes*
3 *Tbsp. butter*
2 *Tbsp. chopped onion*
3 *Tbsp. flour*
1½ *cups milk*
1 *pkg. frozen mixed vegetables*
Salt, pepper

Bake 6 medium or 3 large oval baking potatoes (2 pounds) until tender. Meanwhile, melt 3 tablespoons butter in a saucepan. Add 2 tablespoons finely chopped onion and cook, stirring often, until the onion is translucent. Sprinkle with 3 tablespoons flour and cook, stirring, for a minute or two. Gradually add 1½ cups milk and continue to cook, stirring, until the sauce is thickened. Cook 1 package (about 10 ounces) frozen mixed vegetables until barely tender, as directed on the package. Drain well and combine with the cream sauce. Add salt and pepper to taste. (You may also use any leftover cooked vegetable or combination of vegetables.)

Split large potatoes in half and scoop out part of the pulp, leaving a thick shell. Or cut a large, wedge-shaped piece from the flat side of the smaller potatoes and scoop out evenly, leaving a thick shell. Mash the pulp with butter, salt and pepper, and a little milk. Fill the shells with the hot or reheated creamed vegetables, top with the mashed potato, and return to the oven to heat. A little grated cheese may be sprinkled on the potato topping if desired.

DILLED STUFFED POTATOES

2 *lbs. baking potatoes*
2 *Tbsp. butter*
⅓ *cup sour cream*
2 *egg yolks*
  Salt, pepper
2 *Tbsp. chopped dill*
2 *ozs. Swiss cheese (optional)*

Cook 6 medium oval baking potatoes (2 pounds) in boiling salted water to cover until just tender. Cool slightly, and carefully cut an oval wedge from the flat side of each. Scoop out the pulp and combine with the pulp attached to the wedge, leaving enough potato clinging to the skin to keep shell and top intact. Mash the pulp and combine it with 2 tablespoons butter, ⅓ cup dairy sour cream, 2 egg yolks, and salt and pepper to taste. Add 2 tablespoons chopped fresh dill and—if you like—about ½ cup grated Swiss cheese (2 ounces). Refill the shells, adjust the wedge-top as a cap, and brush the skin of the potato with oil. Sprinkle with salt and pepper. Bake at 400°F. until the filling is hot.

> *Shortcut* You can buy time when you bake potatoes if you pierce each with an aluminum skewer designed for just this purpose. The skewer conducts heat to the center of the potato and makes it cook more quickly.

HAM-STUFFED POTATOES

2 *lbs. baking potatoes*
2 *Tbsp. butter*
2 *Tbsp. minced onion*
¼ *lb. cooked ham*
⅓ *cup cream or milk*
  Salt, pepper
  Grated cheese for garnish

Bake 6 medium or 3 large oval potatoes (2 pounds). Cut a slice from the flat side of medium potatoes, or split large ones lengthwise. Scoop out the pulp, leaving a thin shell. Mash the pulp with 2 tablespoons butter and 2 tablespoons minced onion. Add ½ cup slivered cooked ham (¼ pound). Gradually add ⅓ cup cream or milk, using just enough to make a fluffy, light mixture. Add salt and pepper to taste. Pile the mixture into the potato shells, sprinkle with grated cheese, and return to the oven to bake until the top is brown and the potatoes are very hot.

SALMON PUFF POTATOES

2 lbs. baking potatoes
2 Tbsp. butter
2 Tbsp. milk
2 Tbsp. chopped parsley
1 can (8 ozs.) salmon
  Salt, pepper
  Mayonnaise

Bake 6 medium or 3 large oval baking potatoes (2 pounds). Scoop out, leaving the shells intact. Large potatoes should be split in half, small ones opened by removing a slice from the flat side. Mash the pulp with 2 tablespoons each butter, milk, and chopped parsley. Drain 1 can (about ½ pound) salmon and discard bones and skin. Flake the salmon coarsely and fold into the potatoes. Add salt and pepper to taste. Pile the mixture into the potato shells and coat each thickly with mayonnaise. Bake until the topping is puffed and slightly browned.

FOR VARIETY: Use chopped chives or green onion instead of parsley, or sprinkle the mayonnaise topping with grated cheese before reheating.

TUNA PUFF POTATOES

Substitute 1 can tuna (about 7 ounces) for the salmon. Serve with cheese sauce.

TURNIP-STUFFED POTATOES

2 *lbs. baking potatoes*
1 *pkg. mashed frozen turnips*
3 *Tbsp. butter*
  Milk
  Salt, pepper, paprika

Bake 6 medium or 3 large oval bakers (2 pounds). Split the large potatoes in half lengthwise, or cut a slice from the smaller potatoes, and scoop out the pulp. Heat 1 package (about 1½ cups) mashed frozen yellow turnips, or use about 1 pound freshly cooked, mashed turnips. Mash the potato pulp and blend with the turnips. Add 3 tablespoons butter, a little hot milk to make a fluffy mixture, and salt, pepper, and paprika to taste. Pile the turnip mixture high in the potato shells and return to the oven to brown.

GARDEN-STUFFED POTATOES

2 *lbs. baking potatoes*
2 *Tbsp. butter*
½ *cup cottage cheese*
1 *Tbsp. grated carrot*
1 *Tbsp. chopped chives*
2 *Tbsp. sour cream*
  Salt, pepper

Bake 6 medium potatoes or 3 large oval bakers (2 pounds). Cut a slice from flat side of the small potatoes or split the larger ones in half. Scoop out the pulp and mash it with 2 tablespoons butter, ½ cup cottage cheese, 1 generous tablespoon each grated carrot and chopped chives, and about 2 tablespoons sour cream, to make a fluffy mixture. If the cheese is dry, you may want to use more cream. Add salt and pepper to taste and pile the mixture into the potatoes. Reheat before serving.

❧ 2
❧

Kettle-Frying

When a French cook says *frites,* which is how he says fried, he means potatoes fried in deep fat. It is a safe guess that a majority, or at least a plurality, of American potatoes land in the deep fryer—some on the home kitchen range, a few in cans, and a huge and increasing volume in the scientifically efficient kitchens of the packers of frozen foods. Frozen French Fries are very good, and they can be seasoned in various ways to make them taste almost as they did when they first came out of the fat (more about them later). It is possible, however, for even an inexperienced cook to make her own perfect French Fries, with a minimum of mess and bother. There are two essentials to perfect French-frying: the proper fat and the proper temperature.

In the days when the temperature of fat was tested by dropping a one-inch cube of bread into it, every conscientious cook memorized the information that fat at about 360°F. would brown a bread cube in one minute, and was suitable for frying doughnuts. Fat at 370°F. would brown in forty seconds, and could be used for croquettes; for potatoes, the fat had to be hot enough, 380°F. or thereabouts, to brown the bread in twenty seconds.

When this system worked, it was satisfactory. But there were certain variables—the exact size, type, and staleness of the bread, and the fallibility of the cook's time-keeping or attention.

Therefore, if you plan to undertake any deep-frying at all, invest in a frying thermometer. You can also use it as a sugar thermometer in making jellies and candies, so it has a double use. And if you plan to do a considerable amount of deep-frying, invest in an electric fryer, which gives you a pot of the proper shape and depth, a frying basket, a thermostat to keep the fat at the correct temperature, and usually a chart to remind you of the correct temperature for various kinds of frying.

Choosing the proper fat is a simple matter of eliminating the unfit in favor of the fit: butter, ordinary lard, and bacon drippings cannot reach the necessary high temperatures without burning. Hydrogenated vegetable shortenings and peanut, corn, and soy bean oil are first choice. If you like flavored frying fat, a little olive oil or chicken fat can be added to the pot. The fat should be deep enough to cover the food well. Also, the pan should be deep enough to keep the fat at least three inches from the top of the pan—otherwise there is danger of the fat boiling over.

Make a practice of frying only a small amount of food at a time, to prevent crowding and prevent the temperature of the fat from dropping suddenly. Use a frying basket to make it easy to lower and raise the food without spattering and scalding yourself. You can hold the basket of fried food over the pot and shake it gently to drain away as much fat as possible before you empty it onto crumpled paper towels to blot up the excess. Transfer each batch of fried food to a slow oven (250°F.) to keep warm until all the frying is done.

Fat used for deep-frying can be used over and over again if it has not been allowed to burn. Let the sediment settle to the bottom of the kettle, and then pour the fat into a clean can through a fine sieve lined with several thicknesses of cheesecloth. Store the container in a cool place until the next time. Old-fashioned housewives drop a sliced potato in the hot fat used for frying breaded and crumbly foods; the potatoes attract and hold some of the burned bits that remain in the fat, and will absorb odors —as you know if you have eaten potatoes fried in the same kettle with fish. This is a good trick to use during the frying session, but not so effective as straining when the session is over.

FRENCH FRIES

Chill well-shaped, uniform potatoes (not the very moist and waxy new potatoes). Peel them and cut into sticks less than ½ inch thick and about 2 inches long. Plunge the sticks at once into cold water, partly to wash them and partly to keep them from turning brown. Heat deep fat in a frying kettle to 380°F. Leave the basket in the fat to heat.

Scoop up about a cup of sticks, drain well, and dry thoroughly in a towel. Remove the frying basket from the fat and drop into the basket a single layer of potatoes. Lower the basket and fry until the sticks are browned to your taste, at least 5 minutes. Lift the basket, hold it for a moment or two to drain off the fat, and shake gently. Empty the potatoes onto doubled paper toweling that will blot up the surface fat. Sprinkle with salt and keep hot in a slow oven (250°F.) until all the potatoes are fried.

TWICE-FRIED FRENCH FRIES

This method, the one used by professional chefs, has two advantages. First, it makes it possible to do the preparing, washing, and drying of the potato slices in advance, thus cutting down on last-minute chores. It also reduces actual last-minute frying time. Twice as many potatoes can be fried the second time as the first, since most of the moisture is expressed during the first frying. Fry the potatoes as for French Fries, above, but at 370°F., until they are cooked—do *not* allow them to brown. Drain and hold until wanted: an hour or two at room temperature, or for longer periods, covered, in the refrigerator, or even wrapped and stored in the freezer. At serving time, heat fat to 380°F. and fry the potatoes a minute or so until brown. If the potatoes have been frozen, they should be allowed to thaw before frying so that the temperature of the fat is not drastically lowered by the icy cold.

FRENCH FRIES IN VARIOUS SHAPES

Chips: Slice uniform, oval potatoes very, very thin, with a slicer.
Gaufrettes: Thinly slice uniform, oval potatoes with a rippled cutter designed for this purpose.
Balls: Use a melon-ball cutter to shape small potato balls. This is the most wasteful method of any, unless you have a pot of soup simmering on the stove and add the scraps to the broth.
Shoestrings: Cut into thin, matchlike sticks.
Crinkle Cuts: Use a rippled cutter to make slices the same length and width as classic French Fries.
Curls: Use a floating knife potato peeler to "peel" a thin, continuous strip around and around the potato. With practice, you may someday be able to "peel" a whole potato without breaking the spiral, but even if you don't, the broken curls make attractive French Fries.
Straws: Shred potatoes on a grater, drain, and dry. Stir with a two-pronged fork as they fry to keep the shreds separated. These are attractive as a nest for fried chicken.
Links and Bolts: Cut uniform, oval potatoes into crosswise slices about ¼-inch thick. With a cookie cutter of suitable size, cut out the center of each slice. Slit one ring and insert another to make a chain of links. Fry the cut-outs and serve chains and bolts together.

> *Pommes Soufflés*   Most of the stories about how *Pommes Soufflés* were invented are connected with railroading, naturally enough, since delay is the secret of their success. Our favorite version says that the train in question was on its initial run to Saint Germain en Laye, in France. The train carried a coach-load of dignitaries bound for an inaugural banquet celebrating the opening of the new extension. Difficulties developed and the Chef preparing the feast was informed that the train would be late. It was already too late for the French Fried potatoes, which were at that moment sizzling in the frying kettle. The Chef fished them out, half-cooked, and ordered his minions to prepare a fresh batch. But he had barely given the order when a second bulletin arrived. The train was pulling in. The Chef plunged the half-fried potatoes back into the hot fat. To his delight, they promptly puffed into the crisp ovals we call *Pommes Soufflés*.

POMMES SOUFFLES

Use long, oval baking potatoes, allowing at least one-fourth more than you would ordinarily prepare. There is considerable "waste" in the preparation and cooking of Pommes Soufflés. Peel the potatoes and trim them into flattened, slightly ovoid cylinders. The trimmings can be reserved for another use. Slice ⅛-inch thick—it is important that the slices be even in size and thickness—into cold water. Dry well before frying. Heat deep fat in a frying kettle to 325°F. Put a single layer of potato slices into the frying basket, lower into the fat, and cook 5 minutes. The potatoes will not brown, but they will cook slightly and lose some of their moisture. Remove them from the fat, drain, and transfer to doubled paper towels. Repeat until all the potatoes have been fried once.

The rest of the operation can be carried out as soon as the potatoes are cooled, or it can be postponed to a more convenient time. For the second frying, heat the fat to 425°F. Line the frying basket with par-fried potatoes and lower it into the very hot fat. The potatoes—or most of them—will pop as soon as they hit the hot fat. Let them brown a little (this happens very quickly at such high temperatures), lift them out of the fat, drain, and transfer to paper towels. The Pommes Soufflés will keep hot in the oven until all are ready to serve.

The slices that won't pop into little footballs, for whatever mysterious reasons, should not be served with the others, although they're perfectly good eating. The extra potatoes you start with are intended to provide for failures, as well as for potato sacrificed in trimming. Once the *pommes* have *souffléd,* they may deflate on standing, but will puff again in the hot fat.

MOCK POMMES SOUFFLES

2 lbs. potatoes
Onion salt, pepper
2 cups flour
½ cup sour cream

Cook 6 medium potatoes (2 pounds). Cool, peel, and mash. (Or use 4 cups rather dry leftover mashed potatoes.) Season very highly with onion salt and pepper or with your favorite seasoning salt mixture. Add 2 cups flour and mix well. Work in ½ cup dairy sour cream (half an 8-ounce container) or just enough to make a dough that can be kneaded. Knead the dough several times in the bowl. Pinch off pieces the size of a rounded half-teaspoon and dip into flour. Roll the pieces into a ball between your palms, then flatten the ball with your fingers to make a thin oval. The more regular the oval, and the more it looks like a crosswise slice of a small oval baking potato, the more closely the finished product will resemble the genuine pommes soufflés. Drop at once into very hot fat (390°F.), turn when the bottom browns, and remove to paper towels to drain. The mock souffléd potatoes cook in no time, so watch them carefully, and they deflate as they cool, so serve at once. If necessary to make in advance, drop them again into the hot fat and they will puff at once.

SOUTHERN FRIED POTATOES

Cut potatoes into uniform sticks as for French fried potatoes. Drop into cold water to prevent darkening. At cooking time, dip the slices into egg beaten with 1 tablespoon water, then into fine, dry bread crumbs. Fry in hot deep fat (380°F.) until brown. Drain and sprinkle with salt.

POTATOES TEMPURA

1 egg
⅞ cup water
½ tsp. salt
1 cup flour

Beat 1 egg with 1 cup water less two tablespoons (⅞ cup) and ½ teaspoon salt. Sift 1 cup flour directly into the liquid and stir it in gently with a long chopstick or a two-pronged fork. The batter will not be smooth, and it is not necessary that all the flour be moistened. The important thing is to avoid overmixing. Peel and slice potatoes, wash, dry, and dip into the batter. Drain off excess batter and drop potatoes into hot deep fat (380°F.) to fry until puffed and golden brown. Drain and serve at once.

NOTE: You will probably serve Potatoes Tempura with shrimp or fish fillets dipped in the same batter and fried; the amount of potatoes you use depends on the rest of the menu. If more batter is needed, make a second batch rather than doubling the recipe.

PENNSYLVANIA FRIES

Cut potatoes into uniform sticks as for French fried potatoes, wash, and dry well. Put 1 cup flour, seasoned with salt, into a brown paper bag. Add the potatoes, a handful at a time, and shake well to coat evenly. Fry as usual in hot deep fat (380°F.) until brown.

> *Strange Fruit* Like tomatoes, potatoes were first considered ornamental but probably poisonous. The first potato crop in New England was harvested in the early 18th century, but it was almost the end of the century before potatoes became a regular part of the American diet.

POMMES DAUPHINE
(Puffed Fritters)

½ cup water
6 Tbsp. butter
  Salt
½ cup flour
4 eggs
1 cup mashed potatoes
  Pepper

Bring ½ cup water to a boil with 4 tablespoons butter (¼ cup) and ½ teaspoon salt. Add ½ cup flour, all at once, and beat over low heat until the dough forms a ball that cleans the pan. Beat in 2 eggs, one at a time, beating well to combine after each. Season 1 cup mashed potatoes, freshly mashed or leftover, but very dry, with 2 tablespoons butter and salt and pepper to taste. Beat in 2 more eggs. Combine the two mixtures, beating well with a wooden spoon to blend. Scoop up small spoonfuls on a dessert spoon and push the fritters off into deep hot fat (380°F.) with a second spoon. Fry until brown. Drain on paper toweling and serve hot.

BAKED PUFFS

Drop the mixture for Pommes Dauphines on a baking sheet and bake at 400°F. until brown and dry. Serve to calorie-counters—omitting the frying cuts calories by about 75 percent. Or split the shells, fill with savory mixtures, and serve with cocktails.

Rejuvenation Tired old potatoes benefit greatly from a milk bath. Peel as thickly as necessary, cut into quarters, and cook covered with boiling salted half water, half milk.

OVEN FRIES

Peel and cut potatoes into uniform strips—the classic "frites," or French Fries, are about ½-inch thick. Choose a flat baking pan large enough to hold the strips in a single layer. Pour over them enough oil, melted bacon drippings, beef fat, or chicken fat to coat. Turn in the fat. Bake at 450°F. about 25 minutes, until tender, turning occasionally with a wide-bladed spatula so that they brown evenly. Sprinkle with salt and pepper or paprika. Garlic salt or another seasoned salt makes an interesting flavor change.

QUICK OVEN FRIES

A wonderful way to make "fried potatoes" with a minimum of fat and a maximum of flavor—quick, too. Scrub oval-shaped potatoes, but don't peel them. Cut crosswise into slices less than ¼-inch thick. Spread in a single layer on a baking dish covered with lightly oiled aluminum foil. Drizzle with a very little salad oil and season generously with salt (or with garlic or onion salt or any seasoned salt) and pepper. Bake at about 400°F. for 15 to 20 minutes, until just cooked through. As the tops begin to brown, at the half-way point, flip the discs to brown evenly. The peel adds interesting texture to these "fries."

OVEN-FRIED WEDGES

Peel potatoes and cut them into thick wedges. Coat the wedges with melted butter seasoned with salt and pepper. Dip into fine, dry bread crumbs, the packaged variety, seasoned if you like. Arrange side by side on a greased baking sheet, sprinkle with more melted butter, and bake at 400°F. about 40 minutes, until tender and brown.

℘ 3
℘

Skillet-Frying

Skillet-frying—cooking foods in a heavy, shallow pan in a small amount of fat—has always been a popular cooking method, both economical and easy, if not always of high quality. It naturally takes far less fat than is required for kettle-frying, and it involves comparatively little fuss and muss. Properly pan-fried potatoes are delicious, but quite different from French Fried potatoes. Do not confuse the two methods, or substitute one for the other without keeping the distinction in mind.

Note that the fat used in pan-frying affects the flavor of the food more extensively than the deep fat of kettle-frying. Use olive or salad oil, poultry fat, bacon drippings, beef fat, hydrogenated shortening, or butter, depending on what flavor (or absence of flavor) you want. If you have an electric skillet, this kind of frying is what it does best—use it!

BUTTER-FRIED POTATOES

Potatoes "fried" in butter—or more accurately, sautéed—have a subtle elegance that has earned them a place in the *haute cuisine*

28

of France, which most people agree is the most elegant cooking in the world. Plain butter tends to scorch easily, so it is helpful to clarify it for this kind of cooking.

Clarified Butter   Slowly melt the required amount of butter in a cup or small pan. The cloudy solids settle to the bottom of the cup and the clear golden liquid can be carefully poured off into another container. Discard the sediment. Any butter left after sautéing potatoes can be refrigerated and used again for the same purpose, or it can be used as a sauce for vegetables.

Tips on Butter-Frying   Use waxy potatoes for sautéing if you have a choice—others may not hold their shapes as well. Peel the potatoes and cut them into uniform shapes—anything from the olive shapes favored in professional kitchens to cubes or small balls scooped out with a melon-ball cutter. Very small, whole new potatoes make attractive sautéed potatoes. In any case, the shapes should not be more than one inch thick. Heat the clarified butter in a skillet to the foaming point and add the potatoes in a single layer. Cook until brown, turning often and shaking the pan very frequently over the heat at first to prevent sticking. The trick is to have the butter as hot as possible without browning it, so regulate the heat accordingly. It will take about ten minutes to brown the potatoes. Cover the skillet and continue to cook over low heat until tender, about ten to fifteen minutes longer. Shake the pan occasionally and add more clarified butter as needed. Sprinkle with salt, pepper, and chopped herbs—parsley, chives, or a mixture of your favorites—and serve.

For the record, and for your information in reading a menu, olive-shaped potatoes cooked this way are called Potatoes Château, ball-shapes are Potatoes Parisienne, and cubes are Potatoes Sautées en Dès. Small potato shapes that have first been parboiled and then sautéed in butter are called Rissolées.

LYONNAISE POTATOES

2 lbs. potatoes
5 Tbsp. butter
3 onions, chopped
Salt, pepper
Chopped parsley for garnish

Cook 6 medium potatoes (2 pounds) in boiling salted water to cover. Peel and slice. Leftover cooked potatoes may also be used. Melt 3 tablespoons butter in a large skillet, add the sliced potatoes, and cook until brown on both sides, turning often. In a smaller skillet, melt 2 tablespoons butter and cook 3 medium onions, chopped, until translucent. Add the onions to the potatoes, season with salt and pepper, and cook, stirring gently with a fork, for a minute or two. Serve sprinkled with chopped parsley.

POTATOES LANDAISE

Rendered fat for frying
1 onion
1 cup diced cooked ham
2 lbs. potatoes
Salt, pepper
1 garlic clove
Chopped parsley for garnish

Heat a quarter-inch layer of rendered chicken fat or bacon fat in a large skillet. Dice a large onion and add with 1 cup diced cooked ham (½ pound). Use leftover cooked ham or a thick slice, not the thin sandwich slices. Cook the onion and diced ham until the onion is golden, turning often with a spatula. Peel 6 medium potatoes (2 pounds) and dice them directly into the pan. Stir to coat well with the onion and ham mixture, and season with salt and pepper to taste. Cover the pan and simmer about 20 minutes, until the potatoes are tender, turning occasionally with a spatula and adding a little more fat if necessary to prevent the mixture from becoming too dry. Just before serving, chop 1 small clove garlic very fine and mix through the potatoes. Serve sprinkled with chopped parsley. Good with a plain or cheese omelette.

O'BRIEN POTATOES

2 Tbsp. butter
1 small onion
1 small green pepper
1 can (8 ozs.) pimientos
  Fat for frying
2 lbs. potatoes
  Salt, pepper

Melt 2 tablespoons butter in a saucepan. Dice finely a small onion and a small green pepper, and cook in the hot butter until the onion is translucent. Drain and dry 1 can pimientos, sliver finely (or use only part of the can), and add to the pan. Meanwhile, heat ½ inch of fat in another skillet. Peel and dice 6 medium potatoes (2 pounds). Fry the diced potatoes in the hot fat until brown and tender. Drain, salt lightly, combine with the vegetables, and toss together over the heat for a minute or two. Add salt and pepper and serve very hot.

FORESTER'S POTATOES

Prepare potatoes as for O'Brien Potatoes, above, but omit green pepper and pimiento and sauté 1 cup sliced mushrooms with the onion.

COTTAGE-FRIED POTATOES

2 lbs. potatoes
  Bacon or beef drippings or rendered poultry fat
  Salt, pepper, paprika

Cook 6 medium potatoes (2 pounds) in boiling salted water to cover. Peel and slice. Leftover baked or boiled potatoes may also be used. Heat a quarter-inch layer of fat in a large skillet—use bacon or beef drippings, or rendered poultry fat, for flavor. Brown the slices on both sides, sprinkle with salt, pepper, and paprika, and serve very hot.

PROVENCALE POTATOES

 2 *lbs. potatoes*
   Olive oil
   Salt, pepper
   Garlic cloves
 ¼ *cup chopped parsley for garnish*

Peel 2 pounds (6 medium) potatoes and cut into uniform quarter-inch discs, or into balls, olives, or cubes. Heat a thin layer of olive oil (a neutral oil will not give the Provençale flavor) in a large skillet and brown the potatoes rather slowly on all sides. Season with salt and pepper. Reduce the heat, cover the skillet, and cook until the potatoes are tender. Shake the skillet often to prevent sticking. Chop very finely one or two cloves of garlic, depending on your fondness for garlic, and add. Cook a minute or two longer. Sprinkle with ¼ cup chopped parsley and serve. Particularly good with steak or lamb chops.

SOUR-CREAM FRIES

 4 *Tbsp. butter*
 2 *lbs. potatoes*
 1 *large onion*
   Salt, pepper
   Sour cream

Melt 4 tablespoons butter, preferably clarified butter, in a heavy skillet equipped with a cover. Peel and thinly slice 6 medium potatoes (2 pounds) and cook them gently in the butter for 5 minutes, turning often with a spatula to coat all sides well. Slice a large onion thinly, add it to the pan, and cook a few minutes longer until the onion is translucent. Be very careful not to let the mixture scorch. Add salt and pepper to taste. Add just enough dairy sour cream to show through the slices. Cover the pan and cook, very gently, until the potatoes are tender. Just before serving, increase the heat, remove the cover, and let the potatoes brown a little. Particularly good with chicken.

SWEET AND SOUR FRIES

5 *slices bacon*
2 *lbs. potatoes*
½ *onion, chopped*
  Salt
1 *Tbsp. sugar*
½ *cup water*
¼ *cup vinegar*

Cook 5 slices bacon until crisp. Drain and crumble, leaving 3 tablespoons fat in the skillet and reserving the rest. Peel and cut 6 medium potatoes (2 pounds) into uniform cubes. Press the potatoes into the hot fat in the skillet and cook over moderate heat until the bottom is brown and crisp. Sprinkle the top with half an onion, finely chopped, and a little salt. Cut the cake into wedges and turn each wedge separately, retaining the shape of the cake. Cook until the bottom is brown, adding more bacon fat, if necessary, to prevent sticking. Add 1 tablespoon sugar and ¾ teaspoon salt to ½ cup water. Pour this over the potato wedges, cover the skillet, and simmer about 10 minutes, until the potatoes are tender. Remove the pan from the heat and sprinkle the potatoes with ¼ cup mild vinegar. Cover the pan and let the potatoes absorb the vinegar for 15 minutes. Remove the cover, sprinkle with the crumbled bacon, reheat quickly, and serve very hot.

The Irish In eighteenth-century Ireland, potatoes and buttermilk were mainstays of the diets of peasants, if not the only food they had. And they thrived on it. An English commentator was baffled: "When I see the people with well-formed vigorous bodies . . . their cottages swarming with children . . . their beautiful women, I do not know how to believe them subsisting on unwholesome food."

CREAM FRIES

    2 lbs. potatoes
    ¼ cup butter
        Salt, white pepper
    1 Tbsp. flour
    ¼ cup half-and-half or light cream
        Paprika for garnish

Cook 6 medium potatoes (2 pounds) in boiling salted water to
cover. (Or use leftover boiled or baked potatoes.) Peel and cut
into thin uniform slices. Melt ¼ cup butter in a skillet and brown
the slices lightly on both sides. Season with salt and white pepper
to taste and sprinkle with 1 tablespoon flour. Toss carefully with
a spatula to distribute the flour without breaking the potato slices.
Add ¼ cup half-and-half or light cream, stir gently with the spatula over the heat for a minute, and serve sprinkled with paprika. Especially dry potatoes may require more cream to moisten
them sufficiently. Fine with steak or hamburgers.

ONION CAKE

    2 lbs. potatoes
    4 onions
    6 Tbsp. butter
        Salt, pepper
        Fine, dry bread crumbs

Peel 6 medium potatoes (2 pounds) and slice very thinly, on
a slicer if possible. Slice 4 onions thinly and separate the rings.
Melt 4 tablespoons (¼ cup) butter in a heated heavy skillet.
Fill the skillet with alternate layers of potatoes and onions, seasoning each layer generously with salt and pepper. Sprinkle the
top with fine, dry bread crumbs. Cook slowly until the bottom of
the cake is well browned. Loosen occasionally with a spatula,
and add more butter if necessary to keep from sticking. Cover
the skillet with a large plate and invert it to unmold the cake.
Add 2 more tablespoons butter (6 tablespoons used in all) to
the pan and slide the cake back into the skillet, browned side up.
Cook slowly until the bottom is browned, about 45 minutes in all.

POTATO PATTIES

Fat for pan-frying
½ *small onion*
1 *tsp. salt*
Pepper
2 *lbs. potatoes*
¼ *cup water*

Heat a quarter-inch thick layer of chicken fat or bacon or ham drippings in a large, heavy skillet over moderate heat. Grate half a small onion. Add 1 teaspoon salt and a generous dash of pepper. Peel 6 medium potatoes (2 pounds) and grate into cold water. Drain and press out excess liquid. Blend with onion, shape into 10 or 12 flat patties, and put at once in the hot fat in the skillet. Cook over moderate heat, turning to brown both sides. Add ¼ cup hot water. Reduce the heat and cook slowly 5 to 10 minutes longer, until the patties are cooked through. Turn as necessary to prevent them from getting too brown, and test after 5 minutes.

HASHED BROWN POTATOES

2 *lbs. cooked potatoes*
2 *tsp. finely grated onion*
1 *Tbsp. chopped parsley*
Salt, pepper
¼ *cup bacon drippings or rendered fat*

Chop by hand 6 medium potatoes, freshly cooked or leftover, to make 4 cups. Toss with 2 teaspoons finely grated onion or with a little onion juice, to taste, 1 tablespoon finely chopped parsley, and salt and pepper to season well. Heat ¼ cup bacon drippings in a large skillet, or use beef or rendered chicken fat. Spread potatoes in the fat and cook over moderate heat until the bottom is crisp and brown and the potatoes are hot throughout. Fold in half, like an omelette, to serve. Or cut the cake in half with the spatula and turn each half separately, add a little more fat if necessary, and cook until brown and crisp.

4

Mashed Potatoes

Perfect mashed potatoes begin with the right kind of potato—new potatoes, which tend to be waxy and moist, will not do, but old-crop all-purpose or baking potatoes can make light, puffy mashed potatoes every time, if you give them a chance.

Scrub the skins and cook the potatoes until soft in boiling salted water to cover, allowing two teaspoons salt for six potatoes. Test potatoes with a skewer after twenty-five minutes; medium potatoes can take as long as thirty-five minutes.

If you are in a hurry, you can peel the potatoes and cut them into quarters, thus reducing the cooking time by half, or at least by one-third. But this method also robs you of some of the important mineral and vitamin content. You will lose a little less nutritional value if you thoroughly chill the potatoes before you peel, quarter, and cook them.

Drain the cooked potatoes well and shake the pan over the heat, uncovered, for a few minutes to allow them to dry thoroughly. To peel cooked potatoes, hold them one at a time on a two-pronged fork, or wrap your hand in a towel to protect it, and peel quickly with a sharp knife. Keep the waiting potatoes in the pan, and cover them *not* with the lid but with a towel, which will absorb steam and keep the potatoes from getting soggy.

POTATO MASHER, FORK, OR ELECTRIC BEATER Mash the potatoes in the still-warm cooking pan, over very low heat, until they are perfectly smooth. Push the potatoes to the edges of the pan, leaving a clear space in the middle. Pour the milk, about one-fourth to one-half cup, into the center of the pan and heat it well. Then blend it into the potatoes. Add butter, two to four tablespoons, and salt and pepper to taste. Work as quickly as possible and serve at once; or set the pan in a larger pan of hot water. If the potatoes must be prepared in advance and re-heated, spread them on a heat-proof serving dish, add an extra dab of butter, and brush with hot milk or cream. Brown and heat quickly under the broiler.

POTATO RICER Potatoes forced through a ricer, or through a food mill or a coarse sieve, are more uniformly mashed than with a potato masher, a fork, or the electric mixer. Return the riced potatoes to the cooking pan and stir over low heat for a moment. Then add milk, butter, and salt and pepper as directed.

WHIPPED POTATOES

Mash or rice 6 medium potatoes, as directed, and add 2 table-spoons butter. With a heavy sauce whisk or an electric mixer, begin to whip the potatoes hard, gradually adding up to 1 cup hot half-and-half or light cream to make a very light mixture. The amount of cream the potatoes will take varies with their natural moisture content. Season with salt and pepper to taste and reheat quickly. Top with a dab of butter and sprinkle with paprika or parsley. This preparation is also known as Potatoes Mousseline, a compliment to its creamy mousse-like texture.

MASHED POTATO VARIETIES

1. *Add a seasoning extra:* In addition to salt and pepper, add horseradish, mustard, onion juice or grated onion, celery or dill seed, finely crushed dried marjoram or basil, or grated cheese. Instead of milk or cream to soften, choose broth or diluted cream soup. Or use bacon drippings or chicken fat instead of butter, and omit the milk and butter.

2. *Add contrast in color and texture:* Send the mashed potatoes to the table with a colorful topping—a sprinkle of paprika, chopped fresh parsley or chives, watercress leaves, green onion circles or slivered red onion, pimientos or pimiento-stuffed olives. Shredded almonds or bread crumbs, toasted in butter, make an attractive topping and also add crunch, as do a handful of potato chips crushed to small fragments, and crisp crumbled bacon.

POTATO SNOW

Force hot cooked potatoes through a ricer or food mill directly onto a heated serving platter. Melt ¼ cup butter and drizzle the potatoes with it. Sprinkle with salt and paprika. Do not attempt to mix in the seasonings.

POTATOES CHANTILLY

Mash and season potatoes as directed. For 6 potatoes, whip stiff ½ cup heavy cream. Spread the potatoes on a heat-proof serving dish, cover them with whipped cream, and brown under the broiler. If desired, grated cheese may be sprinkled on the whipped cream before browning.

POTATOES A LA CREME

Follow the recipe for Potatoes Chantilly, but use unwhipped heavy cream instead of whipped cream, and add cheese or not, as you like.

MASHED POTATOES WITH
OTHER VEGETABLES

Combine mashed potatoes with approximately an equal volume of hot mashed carrots, turnips or parsnips, cabbage cooked seven minutes and coarsely chopped, well-drained chopped spinach or other greens, riced fresh lima beans. Strong-flavored vegetables soften their personalities when they are combined with potatoes. Adjust amounts of seasoning and milk to make a light, fluffy mixture to your taste. Other cooked vegetables also combine beautifully and deliciously with mashed potatoes: cooked, frozen, or canned corn kernels; green peas; green beans; mixed carrots and peas; mixed vegetables; sautéed mushrooms or onions, or pimientos. Fold in a few chopped nut meats or sliced pitted black olives for good texture contrast as well as an attractive garnish.

MONT D'OR

1½ lbs. potatoes
1 lb. carrots
3 Tbsp. light cream
2 Tbsp. butter
1 egg
Salt, pepper, sugar
2 Tbsp. grated cheese

Cook separately, in boiling salted water to cover, 4 medium-large potatoes (1½ pounds) and 4 medium carrots (1 pound). Peel and mash together. Beat in 3 tablespoons cream, 2 tablespoons butter, and 1 egg, to make a light and fluffy mixture. Season with salt and pepper and a little sugar to taste. Pile on a heat-proof serving dish, sprinkle with 2 tablespoons grated Cheddar or other yellow cheese, and bake or broil for a few minutes to melt the cheese.

VINTNER'S MASHED POTATOES

2 *lbs. potatoes*
1 *can condensed bouillon*
½ *tsp. monosodium glutamate*
1 *stalk celery, 1 sprig parsley, bit of bay leaf*
3 *Tbsp. butter*
¼ *cup dry white wine*
  Salt, pepper
2 *Tbsp. chopped chives*

Peel 6 medium potatoes (2 pounds) and cut into small pieces directly into a pan containing 1 can condensed undiluted bouillon or consommé (or use 1½ cups boiling water and 2 bouillon cubes). Add sufficient boiling water barely to cover the potatoes. Season with ½ teaspoon monosodium glutamate and top with a stalk of celery, a sprig of parsley, and a bit of bay leaf, tied with string. Cover and cook until tender. Discard the herbs and strain the bouillon. Drain and mash the potatoes and season with 3 tablespoons butter. Add ¼ cup heated dry white wine and enough strained bouillon to make a very light and creamy mixture. Adjust the seasoning with salt and pepper and sprinkle with 2 tablespoons chopped chives.

MASHED POTATOES SMETANA

2 *lbs. potatoes*
1 *cup sour cream*
1 *Tbsp. grated onion*
  Salt, pepper
2 *Tbsp. butter*

Cook 6 medium potatoes (2 pounds) in boiling salted water to cover. Peel and mash. Add 1 cup sour cream and 1 tablespoon grated onion, with salt and pepper to taste. Pile lightly in an ovenproof serving dish and dot with 2 tablespoons butter. Bake at 375°F. until the top browns lightly.

MASHED POTATOES WITH
EGG MAYONNAISE

2 *lbs. potatoes*
2 *Tbsp. butter*
3 *hard-cooked egg yolks*
2 *Tbsp. mayonnaise*
¼ *cup milk*
  Salt, pepper
1 *center stalk, heart of celery*
  Paprika

Cook 6 medium potatoes (2 pounds). Peel and mash with 2 table-spoons butter. Mash or grate the yolks of 3 hard-cooked eggs, mix to a paste with 2 tablespoons mayonnaise, and add to the mashed potatoes. Beat in ¼ cup hot milk or more, to make a light, smooth mixture, and salt and pepper to taste. Sprinkle with 2 tablespoons very finely chopped celery with some of the leaves and a dash of paprika, and serve at once.

PEANUTTY POTATOES

2 *lbs. potatoes*
2 *Tbsp. milk*
¼ *cup peanut butter*
2 *Tbsp. grated onion*
  Salt, pepper
1 *Tbsp. melted butter*
1 *Tbsp. chopped salted peanuts*

Cook 6 medium potatoes (2 pounds). Peel and mash, adding 2 tablespoons hot milk. Blend in ¼ cup chunky-style peanut butter and 2 tablespoons finely grated onion. Season with salt and pepper to taste and pile on a heat-proof serving dish. Melt 1 table-spoon butter in a small pan, add 1 tablespoon chopped salted peanuts, and stir until lightly brown. Sprinkle butter and nuts on the potatoes and bake at 400°F. to reheat and brown the top lightly.

HERB GARDEN MASH

   2 *lbs. potatoes*
   2 *Tbsp. butter*
   ½ *cup half-and-half or light cream*
      Salt, pepper
   2 *tsp. finely chopped fresh herbs*
   1 *egg*
   ¼ *cup milk*

Cook 6 medium potatoes (2 pounds) in boiling salted water to
cover. Peel and mash. Add 2 tablespoons butter, ½ cup half-and-
half or light cream, and salt and pepper to taste. Beat until light
and fluffy. Add 2 teaspoons or more of your favorite fresh herb
leaves, finely chopped. Basil, dill weed, marjoram or oregano,
chives, savory and fennel tops are all delicious with potatoes. Pile
in a buttered baking dish. Beat 1 egg with ¼ cup milk and a little
salt and pour over potatoes. Bake at 350°F. until brown.

MASHED POTATO CAKES

Shape well-seasoned, cold mashed potatoes into oval patties, roll
in flour, and brown on both sides in butter or bacon drippings.
Add any of the seasonings suggested below for a welcome change.
OR dip the patties into an egg beaten with 2 tablespoons water,
then into crushed cereal flakes or potato chips, and bake at 375°F.
until hot and browned.

SEASONINGS: Chopped parsley, dill, onion salt, celery salt,
seasoned salt, celery seed, finely slivered celery or green pepper,
minced scallion tops or chives, chopped onion sautéed in butter,
or caraway seed.

HASH CAKES

Combine leftover or freshly mashed potatoes with cooked leftovers—meat, chicken, or fish cut into small pieces or chopped.
Season appropriately (see the preceding recipe for Mashed Potato Cakes for suggestions) and brown in a skillet or in the oven.

SALMON PATTIES

1 *can (1 lb.) salmon*
2 *cups mashed potatoes*
2 *cups soft bread crumbs*
2 *eggs*
  Salt, pepper

Coarsely flake a 1-pound can of salmon, discarding skin and bones. Blend 2 cups mashed potatoes, 2 cups soft bread crumbs, and 2 eggs, beating well. Add a little salt and pepper. Carefully stir in the salmon, trying not to break it up too much. Shape into cakes ½-inch thick and brown on both sides in a skillet in hot melted butter. Serve with chili sauce.

TUNA CROQUETTES

1 *can (about 15 ozs.) grated tuna*
1½ *cups mashed potatoes*
1 *Tbsp. chopped parsley*
½ *tsp. lemon juice*
½ *tsp. onion juice*
1 *egg*
  Salt, pepper, celery salt
  Fine dry bread crumbs

Mix a large can of grated tuna—the least expensive pack is fine for this purpose—with 1½ cups mashed potatoes and 1 tablespoon chopped parsley. Add ½ teaspoon each lemon juice and onion juice, or a little onion, freshly grated on the finest side of the hand grater. Add an egg and seasonings to taste: salt, pepper, celery salt. Mold the mixture into balls or pear-shaped croquettes and roll in fine dry bread crumbs or cracker crumbs. Fry in deep hot fat or in a skillet until crisp and brown.

CLAM CAKES

4 cups mashed potatoes
4 egg yolks
1 Tbsp. chopped parsley
   Salt, pepper
1 cup drained chopped clams
   Flour for dredging

Blend 4 cups dry mashed potatoes with 4 egg yolks, 1 tablespoon chopped parsley, and salt and pepper to taste. Add 1 cup (or more) very well-drained chopped clams. Cool until firm. Shape into small cakes, dredge with flour, and fry in a generous amount of hot fat until crisp and brown on both sides. Serve very hot, with cold seafood cocktail sauce.

HAM PATTIES

1 lb. potatoes
¼ lb. cooked ham
1 egg
¼ tsp. prepared mustard
   Salt, pepper
   Bacon drippings or shortening

Cook, peel, and mash 3 medium potatoes (1 pound), or use 2 cups leftover mashed potatoes. Chop or grind ¼ pound or more cooked ham. Blend ham and potatoes and add 1 egg. Season with ¼ teaspoon prepared mustard, or more to taste, and salt and pepper. Shape into cakes and brown on both sides in hot bacon drippings or shortening. Serves 3.

Sweet Touch A teaspoonful of sugar added to the water in which you boil the last of the week's potatoes will brighten their flavor.

CHICKEN LIVER PATTIES

½ lb. chicken livers
2 Tbsp. bacon drippings
½ onion
1½ cups mashed potatoes
2 Tbsp. parsley
Salt, pepper
1 egg
Fine dry bread crumbs

Wash and dry ½ pound chicken livers and cut them into small pieces. Simmer chicken livers in 2 tablespoons bacon drippings, rendered chicken fat, or butter until nearly cooked. Mince half a small onion and cook it with the livers until the onion is translucent and the livers are cooked through. Add 1½ cups mashed potatoes, 2 tablespoons chopped parsley, and salt and pepper to taste. The mixture should be highly seasoned. Mold into small cakes of any desired shape. Beat an egg lightly in a shallow soup plate and spread fine dry bread crumbs in a second plate. Dip each liver patty into the egg, then coat it with crumbs. Fry in ½ inch hot fat in a skillet until brown on all sides. Serves 3.

GRIDDLE CRUMB CAKES

½ medium onion
2 cups mashed potatoes
2 slices bread
⅓ cup milk
2 eggs
Salt, pepper

Grate half an onion and blend with 2 cups mashed potatoes. Crumble 2 slices bread into ⅓ cup milk and soak 5 minutes. Add to potatoes. Add 2 eggs and beat well. Season with salt and pepper to taste. Drop by tablespoons on a hot greased griddle. Flatten the cakes slightly with a spatula. Turn once to brown both sides.

SEEDY PUFFS

1 lb. potatoes
1 Tbsp. butter
2 egg yolks
¼ cup milk
1 tsp. salt
½ tsp. celery, dill, or caraway seeds
   Pepper, paprika

Cook, peel, and mash 3 medium potatoes to make 2 cups. Add 1 tablespoon butter. Beat in 2 egg yolks, ¼ cup milk, and 1 teaspoon salt. Add a generous ½ teaspoon seeds—your choice of celery, dill, or caraway. Season with pepper and paprika. Spoon mounds onto a greased baking sheet and bake at 450°F. for about 10 minutes, until the puffs are piping hot and gilded.

NUTTED PUFFS

Follow preceding recipe for Seedy Puffs, but instead of herb seeds, add 2 tablespoons chopped pistachios, pine nuts, almonds, or pecans. Bake as directed.

CHEESE BALLS

2 cups mashed potatoes
2 ozs. sharp Cheddar cheese
   Salt, pepper
1 egg
2 Tbsp. milk
   Cracker crumbs

Blend 2 cups leftover mashed potatoes with ½ cup grated sharp Cheddar cheese (2 ounces). Taste and adjust seasoning with salt and pepper. Shape into balls. Beat 1 egg with 2 tablespoons milk. Roll the cheese balls in the beaten egg and then in finely crushed cracker crumbs. Bake on a greased baking sheet at 450°F. until browned, about 10 minutes.

MOCK FILLETS

1½ lbs. potatoes
1 Tbsp. butter
1 egg
½ cup milk
   Salt, pepper
6 slices bacon

Boil, peel, and mash 4 medium-large potatoes (1½ pounds).
Gradually add 1 tablespoon butter, 1 egg, and ½ cup milk, beat-
ing well after each addition. Season with salt and pepper to taste.
Shape by ½-cup portions into 6 rounds less than 1-inch thick.
Wrap each mock fillet with a slice of bacon. Bake on a greased
baking sheet at 350°F. about 25 minutes, until bacon is crisp.

MAINE CRACKNELS

2 cups mashed potatoes
1 onion
2 eggs
2 cups soda cracker crumbs
¼ tsp. sage
   Salt, pepper

Mix 2 cups mashed potatoes with a finely chopped onion and 2
eggs. Beat well. Crush salted soda crackers, the thin or puffy type,
to make 2 cups fine crumbs. Add to the potato mixture with ¼
teaspoon sage, and salt and pepper to taste. Flatten spoonfuls of
mixture into thin cakes in a pan generously coated with melted
beef or bacon fat. Bake about 20 minutes at 400°F., until brown.

Tit for Tat If raw potatoes in their skins darken your
hands, use a piece of cut potato to clean them. Alkaline
action again!

POTATO CROQUETTES

Leftover mashed potatoes can be used in many ways, but croquettes are one of their most elegant reincarnations. If you begin with freshly mashed potatoes, on a day when you must start from scratch, be sure to let the mixture cool before attempting to shape and fry it. The ideal frying temperature for croquettes is 380°F.— see the chapter on kettle-frying for more information on this subject.

NOTE: Because croquettes are fried, and because they are rather rich mixtures to begin with, servings can be smaller than usual. Experience shows that mixtures made with one pound of potatoes (two cups of mashed potatoes) will make adequate servings for four or five persons. Increase the amounts in accordance with your own needs, and in accordance with the amount of leftover potatoes you have on hand.

POTATO CROQUETTES, HOME STYLE

1 *lb. potatoes*
2 *Tbsp. butter*
1 *egg yolk*
   Onion salt, white pepper
1 *tsp. double-acting baking powder*
1 *egg*
   Dry bread crumbs

Boil, peel, and mash or rice 3 potatoes (1 pound), or use 2 cups hot freshly mashed potatoes. Work in 2 tablespoons butter and 1 egg yolk. Season to taste with onion salt and white pepper. Sprinkle with 1 teaspoon double-acting baking powder and blend. Spread on a plate to cool. Shape into cones or any desired form. Dip into 1 egg beaten with a little water, coat with dry bread crumbs or crushed shredded wheat cereal, and fry in deep hot fat (380°F.).

48

FOR VARIETY: Add to the croquette mixture ½ cup grated cheese (2 ounces) or ¼ cup chopped cooked ham, or mushrooms or onions sautéed in the butter.

POTATO CROQUETTES AMANDINE

2 *cups mashed potatoes*
3 *egg yolks*
  Salt, pepper
  Flour
1 *egg*
½ *cup chopped almonds*

Use 2 cups cooled freshly mashed or leftover potatoes for these croquettes, but they should be rather dry. Beat in 3 egg yolks and season well with salt and pepper. Shape the mixture into small cones or balls. Spread flour on a shallow soup plate; beat an egg lightly in a second soup plate; spread ½ cup finely chopped or minced or slivered almonds, blanched but not toasted, on a third plate. Roll each croquette in flour, dip it into the beaten egg, and finally roll it in the nuts. Fry in deep hot fat (380°F.) or in an inch of fat in a skillet, until brown on all sides.

FOR VARIETY: Flavor the croquette mixture with a dash of nutmeg or about ¼ teaspoon thyme; or add a little sherry with the egg yolks. Use bread crumbs instead of flour and nuts to coat the egg-dipped croquettes.

Appeal for Peels Most of the valuable potato nutrients are found near the skin. If you peel potatoes before cooking them, make the peelings as thin as possible. A floating-knife peeler is the potato cook's best friend.

POTATO FRITTERS

1 *lb. potatoes*
3 *Tbsp. flour*
1 *tsp. double-acting baking powder*
1 *egg*
¼ *cup milk*
½ *tsp. salt*
  Dash pepper

Cook 3 medium potatoes (1 pound) in boiling salted water to cover. Cool. Peel and grate the potatoes. Mix 3 tablespoons flour with ½ teaspoon double-acting baking powder and add to potatoes. Beat 1 egg well with ¼ cup milk and stir in. Add ½ teaspoon salt and a dash of pepper, to taste. The mixture should be thick enough to hold its shape on a spoon; if necessary, add a little more flour. Drop by spoonfuls into hot deep fat (380°F.) and fry until puffed and brown. Serve hot.

HOT POTATO BALLS

2 *cups mashed potatoes*
2 *eggs*
2 *tsp. milk*
2 *tsp. grated onion*
2 *ozs. Cheddar cheese*
½ *cup dry bread crumbs*
¼ *tsp. chili powder*
⅛ *tsp. dry mustard*
  Salt, pepper

Blend 2 cups hot, freshly mashed potatoes with 2 beaten eggs, 2 teaspoons milk, and 2 teaspoons grated onion. Mix ½ cup grated Cheddar cheese (2 ounces) with ½ cup dry bread crumbs. Add half this mixture to the potatoes, reserving the rest for coating the potato balls. Season the potato mixture well with ¼ teaspoon chili powder, ⅛ teaspoon dry mustard, and salt and pepper to taste. Cool. Shape into small balls, roll in reserved crumb-and-cheese mixture, and fry in deep hot fat (380°F.) until golden brown.

CRUNCH BALLS

3 *slices day-old white bread*
2 *Tbsp. butter*
2 *cups mashed potatoes*
1 *egg, separated*
  Salt, pepper

Crumble 3 slices not-too-soft white bread (if you have no day-old bread, leave fresh bread open to the air for a few hours so that it dries out a little). Melt 2 tablespoons butter in a small skillet, add the crumbs, and stir over moderate heat until the crumbs are lightly browned. Add 2 cups leftover mashed potatoes and 1 egg yolk. Beat well and season to taste with salt and pepper. Beat the egg white stiff and fold it carefully into the potato mixture. Drop by small spoonfuls into deep hot fat (380°F.) and fry until brown.

POTATO PUFFS

2 *cups mashed potatoes*
1 *cup flour*
2 *tsp. double-acting baking powder*
½ *tsp. salt*
2 *eggs*
2 *tsp. minced parsley*
  Pepper

Use 2 cups leftover or cooled freshly mashed potatoes, adjusting the seasoning accordingly. Toss 1 cup flour with 2 teaspoons double-acting baking powder and ½ teaspoon salt. Add the mashed potatoes and blend well. Beat in 2 eggs, 2 teaspoons chopped parsley, and a dash of pepper. Fry by small spoonfuls in deep hot fat (380°F.).

> *Second Time Around* If you want to serve leftover mashed potatoes as plain mashed potatoes again, put them in the top of a double boiler, over boiling water, to heat. Whisk in hot milk to make a light, fluffy mixture.

5

Saucepan Potatoes, Creamed and Stewed

To combine potatoes with a creamy sauce (which may or may not contain milk or cream) is apparently doing what comes naturally. Otherwise there is no accounting for the number and variety of creamy potato dishes people enjoy all over the world. Some of these dishes are made with cooked potatoes, some with raw; some can be prepared in a few minutes and some take hours.

The accommodating compatibility of the potato's own unobtrusive flavor makes it possible to achieve great variety through seasonings. Parsley, bay, savory, thyme—any herb or combination of herbs—can be added to creamed potatoes. Lemon juice and onion are often used to add sharpness. Paprika and green pepper lend color and zest. Herb mixtures and seasoned salts of many kinds are a good addition. Recipes in the classic repertory usually include a dash of nutmeg along with salt and pepper. Grated cheese, ham slivers, or crisp bacon dice add considerable interest. The possibilities are endless.

And, of course, creamed and stewed potatoes can serve as a main dish when they are supplemented with substantial amounts of a protein food—eggs, meat, poultry, and fish can be added to the seasoned potatoes or cooked with them.

CLASSIC CREAMED POTATOES

2 lbs. potatoes
4 Tbsp. butter
2 Tbsp. flour
2 cups milk
  Salt, pepper
  Chopped parsley, paprika

Peel and dice 6 medium potatoes (2 pounds). Cook in boiling salted water to cover until tender. While the potatoes are cooking, melt 4 tablespoons butter (¼ cup or ½ stick) in a sauce pan. Stir in 2 tablespoons flour and cook a few minutes, stirring constantly, without allowing the roux to take on color. Heat 2 cups milk and gradually stir into the saucepan. Cook, stirring, until the sauce is thick and smooth. Drain the cooked potato dice and add to the sauce, with salt and pepper to taste. Serve sprinkled with chopped parsley and paprika. These potatoes can be kept hot in the top of a double boiler or over a table warmer, or they can be reheated in the broiler or in the oven.

TIP: To vary any creamed potatoes, add grated cheese or onion to the sauce, or a spoonful of caraway seeds. Or season ad lib with your favorite mixed seasoning salt or herb preparation. Or add a cup of cooked green peas, carrots, or other vegetables (the sauce can be extended and thinned a little with the vegetable liquid). Garnish with colorful strips of green pepper or pimiento, or chopped chives, paprika, or sliced stuffed olives.

DELMONICO POTATOES

Next to plain mashed, French Fries, and baked potatoes, Delmonico potatoes probably appear more frequently on restaurant menus than any other potato preparation—and it is very often safer to order them than the other choices. To make them at home, simply spread creamed potatoes, made by any method you prefer, on a buttered shallow dish that can be put under the broiler. Sprinkle with grated cheese or not, as you like. Broil until brown and hot. If you are using leftover creamed potatoes, put the dish a little farther from the flame, so that the potatoes have a chance to heat through before they brown.

CREAMED POTATOES MAITRE D'HOTEL

2 lbs. potatoes
¾ cup milk
  Salt, pepper
3 Tbsp. butter
  Chopped chives, paprika for garnish

Cook 6 medium potatoes (2 pounds). Cool and peel. Or use leftover boiled or baked potatoes. Dice or slice thinly into the top of a double boiler. Add ¾ cup milk and salt and pepper to taste. Cover and cook over boiling water until almost all the milk is absorbed and the potatoes are piping hot. Stir in 3 tablespoons butter. Taste, and add more salt and pepper as needed. Serve garnished with chopped chives or paprika, or both.

PAN-CREAMED POTATOES

2 lbs. potatoes
½ onion
2 cups milk
1 tsp. salt
  Pepper
2 Tbsp. butter
  Chopped parsley for garnish

Peel and dice 6 medium potatoes (2 pounds). Put the dice in a heavy skillet on an asbestos pad. Add half a small onion, finely chopped, 2 cups milk, and about 1 teaspoon salt or more, to taste. Cover the pan and cook slowly for about 30 minutes, stirring often. If all the milk is absorbed before the potatoes are soft, add a little more, to make a creamy mixture. Adjust the seasoning with more salt and a little pepper and swirl in 2 tablespoons butter. Sprinkle with chopped parsley.

GRATED PAN-CREAMED POTATOES

Peel 6 medium potatoes (2 pounds) and grate them directly into a bowl of cold water. Drain well. Proceed as for Pan-Creamed Potatoes, above. Grating the potatoes cuts the cooking time in half.

OLD-FASHIONED CREAMED POTATOES

Peel and dice potatoes very finely. Put the potatoes into the top of a double boiler over boiling water. Cover with half-and-half or light cream and season to taste with butter, salt, and pepper. Cover and cook over boiling water for 5 hours. Check occasionally to replenish the boiling water and to add a little more cream, as needed, to keep the mixture moist.

This dish of creamed potatoes was very practical when the economical heat of a wood or coal stove was always available. As a finishing touch, the potatoes were sometimes spooned into a casserole, sprinkled with bread crumbs and melted butter, and quickly browned under direct heat.

55

QUICK CREAMED POTATOES

2 *lbs. potatoes*
1 *cup boiling water*
1 *cup half-and-half or light cream*
3 *Tbsp. butter*
  Salt, pepper
  Chopped parsley for garnish

Peel 6 medium potatoes (2 pounds), cut into small uniform dice, and put into a saucepan with 1 cup boiling water and a little salt. Cover and cook rapidly 5 minutes. Add 1 cup half-and-half or light cream. Cover, lower the heat, and cook gently about 10 minutes longer, just until the potatoes are tender. If the sauce seems thin, boil it rapidly for a minute to reduce it. Add more salt and pepper to taste, and 3 tablespoons butter. Serve sprinkled with chopped parsley; or spread on heat-proof serving dish and brown the top quickly under the broiler.

FOR VARIETY: Sprinkle the potatoes before broiling with 2 ounces (½ cup) very finely crumbled blue cheese or Roquefort.

POTATOES WITH SOUR CREAM

2 *lbs. potatoes*
1 *cup dairy sour cream*
1 *tsp. sugar*
  Salt, pepper, paprika, dry mustard
2 *Tbsp. chopped chives*

Cook 6 medium potatoes (2 pounds) in boiling salted water. Peel and cut into cubes. Gently heat 1 cup sour cream (an 8-ounce container) and season it with 1 teaspoon sugar, plus salt, pepper, and paprika to taste. A little dry mustard may be added if you like. Stir the potatoes into the cream and heat gently together. Do not boil. Sprinkle with 2 tablespoons chopped chives.

POTATOES SCHNEIDER

Cut freshly cooked or leftover potatoes into dice. Put the dice into a heavy saucepan and add just enough boiling consommé to cover. The broth may be made with bouillon cubes or with canned consommé, diluted as directed. Simmer, covered, until the consommé is almost all absorbed. Taste and add a speck of pepper if desired—more salt will probably not be needed. Finish with a little butter and a sprinkling of parsley.

> Mark Twain (*Samuel Clemens*) Katy Leary, who for twenty-five years was housekeeper for the Clemens family, went with them to England to mind the children and interfere in the kitchen. She complained bitterly that there was no one in the British Isles who could be taught how to make creamed potatoes fit for the Clemenses' regular Sunday night treat. A slander, obviously.

STEWED POTATOES AU JUS

1 onion
2 Tbsp. butter
1 can condensed chicken consommé
2 lbs. potatoes
  Salt, cayenne pepper
  Parsley for garnish

Chop a large onion and cook in 2 tablespoons melted butter until just golden. Add 1 can condensed chicken consommé, undiluted, and bring to a boil. Peel and finely dice 6 medium potatoes (2 pounds). Cook the potatoes, covered, in the consommé mixture about 10 minutes, until tender. If the sauce seems scant, add a little water. Taste and adjust the seasoning with more salt, if desired, and a dash of cayenne pepper. Serve sprinkled with chopped parsley.

SAUERKRAUT STEW

1½ cups sauerkraut
3 cups tomato juice
1 tsp. caraway seeds
2 lbs. potatoes
Pepper
Croutons for garnish

Drain 1½ cups sauerkraut very well and mix with 3 cups tomato juice in a stew pan. Bring to a boil. Add 1 teaspoon caraway seeds. Peel 6 medium potatoes (2 pounds) and cut into quarters. Cook with the sauerkraut, covered, about 25 minutes, until tender. Taste and adjust the seasoning with pepper and perhaps a little salt. Top with small croutons. Especially good with smoked pork chops, frankfurters, or ham.

PAPRIKASCH POTATO STEW

2 Tbsp. butter
1 onion, chopped
2 lbs. potatoes
2 tsp. paprika
Salt
2 Tbsp. flour
2 cups sour cream

Melt 2 tablespoons butter in a shallow saucepan. Add a finely chopped medium onion, and cook slowly until the onion is golden. Peel and slice 6 medium potatoes (2 pounds) with a slicer, if possible, to make very thin slices. Add to the pan. Season with 2 teaspoons paprika, and salt to taste. Add water until it shows through the potatoes. Cover the pan and simmer gently about 10 minutes, until the potatoes are just tender. Make a paste of 2 tablespoons flour and a little water and dilute it with some of the hot pan liquid. Stir the paste into the pan and simmer 5 minutes longer to cook the flour. Slowly stir in about 2 cups sour cream (or less if the sauce is plentiful) and heat. Do not boil. More paprika may be necessary, depending on your taste and on the quality of the paprika you use.

VEGETABLE STEW

3 *Tbsp. butter*
2 *onions*
2 *carrots*
1 *cup slivered celery*
2 *cups water*
2 *chicken bouillon cubes*
¼ *tsp. thyme*
1 *bay leaf*
  Sprig parsley
  Sprig leafy celery top
1½ *lbs. potatoes*
1 *tsp. monosodium glutamate*
  Salt, pepper

Melt 3 tablespoons butter in a stew pan. Thinly slice 2 onions and 2 carrots, add 1 cup slivered celery, and cook in the butter for 5 minutes, stirring often to prevent browning. Add 2 cups boiling water, 2 chicken bouillon cubes and ¼ teaspoon dried thyme. Add a bay leaf, a sprig of parsley, and a leafy celery top, tied together with string. Peel and cut 4 medium large potatoes (1½ pounds) into small, thickish slices, and cook with the other vegetables, covered, about 20 minutes, until the potatoes are tender. Add 1 teaspoon monosodium glutamate, more salt if necessary, and pepper to taste. Discard the herb bouquet before serving.

TOMATO STEW

2 lbs. potatoes
2 Tbsp. salad oil
1 onion, sliced
1 can (1 lb. 4 ozs.) tomatoes
½ tsp. Worcestershire sauce
½ tsp. sugar
Salt, pepper

Peel 6 medium potatoes (2 pounds) and cut into small cubes. Heat 2 tablespoons salad oil or bacon fat in a saucepan and cook the potato cubes until golden, stirring and turning often with a spatula to color them evenly. Slice a medium onion thinly and cook with the potatoes until just translucent. Add 1 can (2½ cups) solid-pack or Italian-style plum tomatoes, ½ teaspoon each Worcestershire sauce and sugar, and salt and pepper to taste. Bring to a boil, lower the heat, and simmer, covered, about 20 minutes, until the potatoes are tender. If the sauce seems thin, boil it rapidly for a minute or two to reduce it. Taste and add more salt and pepper.

GREEN POTATO STEW

3 slices bacon
1 onion
1 clove garlic
1 cup water
1 bouillon cube
1 lb. green beans
1 lb. potatoes
Salt, pepper

Cook 3 slices bacon in a saucepan until crisp. Pour off all but 3 tablespoons fat. Crumble the bacon and reserve it. Chop a large onion coarsely and a garlic clove very finely. Cook both in the bacon fat for a minute or two, without letting them brown. Add 1 cup hot water and a bouillon cube, any flavor, and bring to a boil. Meanwhile, trim and cut 1 pound green beans into 2-inch lengths (or use 1 package, about 10 ounces, frozen beans). Peel 3 medium potatoes (1 pound) and cut the potatoes into thick slices. Add both vegetables to the hot bouillon, cover, and simmer about 15 minutes, until the vegetables are just tender. Adjust the seasoning with salt and pepper. Sprinkle with the reserved crumbled bacon.

STEWED POTATOES, FAMILY STYLE

3 Tbsp. butter
1 onion
3 Tbsp. flour
2½ cups water
   Salt, pepper
   Pinch thyme, bay leaf
2 lbs. potatoes
   Chopped parsley or chives for garnish

Melt 3 tablespoons butter in a saucepan. Coarsely chop a medium onion and cook in the butter until golden. Sprinkle with 3 tablespoons flour and cook, stirring constantly, until the roux is a rich golden brown. Gradually add 2½ cups boiling water and cook, stirring, until the sauce is thickened and smooth. Add salt and pepper to taste, and a pinch of thyme or a bit of bay leaf. Peel 6 medium potatoes (2 pounds) and cut each into 8 or 10 wedges. Cook the potatoes gently in the sauce until they are tender but not so soft that they fall apart. Test after 20 minutes. Adjust the seasoning with more salt and pepper. Serve sprinkled with chopped fresh parsley or chives.

6

Oven
Casseroles

While the cook relaxes, potatoes can be baked in a casserole—or
a baking dish or muffin pans or pie plate—in any of several de-
lightful ways. They can be scalloped, the raw slices baked in milk
or broth until they absorb the liquid and are flavorfully tender.
They can be grated raw and made into the puddings so popular
in hearty-eating Mittel Europa. They can be cooked, then baked
in a creamy sauce—a quick version of scalloped potatoes, and a
good and appetizing use for leftovers. Or they can be mashed and
beaten light with eggs to make ethereal soufflés—the kind that
work every time, even if, like all soufflés, they begin to lose some
of their majesty as they cool. They can also be made into puffs,
which rise less but sink hardly at all.

> *Time Cut* Use the quick direct heat of the range to
> shorten baking time for any potato dish you put into the
> oven. Heat the milk or sauce for a potato casserole before
> combining it with the potatoes. Or use a flameproof oven
> casserole, and heat casserole and contents together over
> direct heat before baking.

PIONEER SCALLOPED POTATOES

2 *lbs. potatoes*
1 *onion*
4 *Tbsp. butter*
3 *Tbsp. flour*
 Salt, pepper
2 *cups milk*
 Chopped parsley and paprika for garnish

Peel and thinly slice 6 medium potatoes (2 pounds). Fill a greased baking dish with alternate layers of potato slices, thin slices of 1 onion, bits of 3 tablespoons butter and 3 tablespoons flour, and salt and pepper to taste. Make the final layer potatoes, and dot it with 1 tablespoon more butter. Add 2 cups hot milk, or enough to show through the layers. Bake at 350°F. about 1 hour, covered. Uncover and bake until the potatoes are tender and the topping browned. Garnish with paprika and chopped parsley, if desired. Serve in the baking dish.

FOR VARIETY: Layer the potatoes with drained canned corn, sautéed mushrooms or other vegetables, diced ham or crumbled bacon, chopped cooked meat, hard-cooked eggs, or grated cheese. Instead of milk, butter, and flour, use canned condensed creamed soups—asparagus, celery, mushroom, or chicken—plus milk or water to make about 2 cups liquid in all.

MAINE SCALLOP

2 lbs. potatoes
3 onions
6 Tbsp. flour
    Salt, pepper
6 Tbsp. butter
2 cups milk

Peel 6 medium potatoes (2 pounds) and cut into ⅛-inch slices. Cut 3 onions into similar slices. Put ⅓ the potatoes in a buttered 6-cup casserole and cover with ⅓ the onions. Sprinkle with 2 tablespoons flour, salt, and a little pepper. Dot with 2 tablespoons butter. Repeat twice more, using 6 tablespoons each butter and flour. Add about 2 cups milk, or enough to come just to the top of the potatoes. Bake, covered, at 300°F. for about 2 hours, until the potatoes are tender. After 1½ hours, remove the cover so that the top can brown. If the mixture seems too dry, add a little more milk. Baking the scallop in a moderately slow oven keeps the milk from boiling and curdling.

POTATOES DAUPHINOISE

3 cups milk
½ small onion
1 clove garlic
2 lbs. potatoes
1 egg
    Salt, pepper
2 ozs. Swiss cheese

Bring 3 cups milk to a boil with half a small onion, sliced, and a garlic clove. Discard garlic and onion. Peel 6 medium potatoes (2 pounds) and slice thinly directly into the milk. Simmer 5 minutes. Beat an egg and add it to the mixture. Season with salt and pepper to taste. Fill a buttered casserole, sprinkle with ½ cup grated Swiss cheese (2 ounces) and bake at 350°F. about 50 minutes, until the potatoes are tender and the topping browned.

POTATOES BOULANGERE

2 *lbs. potatoes*
2 *onions*
   Salt, pepper
6 *Tbsp. butter*
1½ *cups water*
   Parsley for garnish

Peel 6 medium potatoes (2 pounds) and slice very thin. Slice 2 large onions thin. Toss together with salt and pepper. Butter a large oven-to-table platter and spread the potato mixture on it in a layer less than an inch thick. Soften 6 tablespoons butter (¾ stick) and spread it over the potatoes. Add 1½ cups boiling water (or bouillon, in which case use less salt). Bake at 350°F. about 45 minutes, until the potatoes are tender and the top browned. Serve sprinkled with parsley.

POTATOES SAVOYARD

Prepare Potatoes Boulangère, above, with bouillon instead of water. Sprinkle ¼ cup grated Swiss cheese between the layers of potato and onion, and a second ¼ cup (2 ounces in all) on top of the potatoes. Bake as directed.

BREAD CRUMB SCALLOP

2 *lbs. potatoes*
   Onion salt, pepper
1 *cup soft bread crumbs*
3 *Tbsp. butter*
1¾ *cups milk*

Peel and thinly slice 6 medium potatoes (2 pounds). Put ⅓ the potato slices in a buttered 6-cup casserole. Season with onion salt and pepper to taste, sprinkle with ⅓ cup soft, fresh bread crumbs, and dot with 1 tablespoon butter. Repeat, using 1 cup crumbs (3 slices bread) and 3 tablespoons butter in all. Very carefully pour into the casserole 1¾ cups hot milk. Cover the casserole and bake at 350°F. about 30 minutes; then remove the cover and continue to bake about 30 minutes longer, until the potatoes are tender and the top browned.

QUICK DELMONICO SCALLOP

1½ *cups milk*
1 *tsp. salt*
Pepper
2 *lbs. potatoes*
¼ *cup fine bread crumbs*
¼ *cup grated cheese*
Paprika
2 *Tbsp. butter*

Bring 1½ cups milk to a boil in a flameproof serving casserole. Add about 1 teaspoon salt, and pepper to taste. Peel and slice 6 medium potatoes (2 pounds) directly into the casserole. Cook, covered, about 15 minutes, until the potatoes are tender and the milk almost absorbed. Sprinkle with ¼ cup fine bread crumbs mixed with ¼ cup grated cheese, any kind, and a little paprika. Dot with 2 tablespoons butter and put under the broiler to brown quickly.

MUSHROOM SCALLOP

1 *can cream of mushroom soup*
1 *can (4 ozs.) sliced mushrooms*
2 *lbs. potatoes*
1 *small onion*
2 *Tbsp. butter*
Paprika

Blend 1 can condensed cream of mushroom soup with a small can of sliced mushrooms, or mushroom bits and pieces, including the liquid. Peel and thinly slice 6 medium potatoes (2 pounds). Slice a small onion and separate the rings. Fill a buttered 6-cup baking dish with alternate layers of potatoes, mushrooms, and onions, making the final layers potatoes and mushrooms. Dot with 2 tablespoons butter and sprinkle with paprika. Bake covered at 375°F. about 1 hour; uncover and bake until the top browns a little. Or when the potatoes are tender, put the dish under the broiler to brown the top quickly.

LEEK SCALLOP

4 *leeks*
2 *lbs. potatoes*
¼ *cup chopped parsley*
  Salt, pepper
2 *cups chicken broth*
¼ *cup butter*

Wash 4 leeks very carefully and chop the white parts finely. Peel and thinly slice 6 medium potatoes (2 pounds). Fill a well-buttered, flameproof baking dish with alternate layers of potatoes, leeks, and ¼ cup chopped parsley. Sprinkle the layers with salt and pepper. Add sufficient chicken broth (about 2 cups, home-made, diluted canned, or made with bouillon cubes) to come to the top of the potatoes. Dot with ¼ cup (½ stick) butter. Bring to a boil over direct heat. Bake, covered, at 375°F. about 45 minutes, until the potatoes are tender.

CHEESE SCALLOP

2 *lbs. potatoes*
2 *Tbsp. flour*
½ *tsp. dry mustard*
  Salt, pepper, paprika
6 *ozs. cheese slices*
1½ *cups milk*

Peel 6 medium potatoes (2 pounds) and slice very thin. Toss in a bowl with 2 tablespoons flour, ½ teaspoon dry mustard, and salt and pepper to taste. Sliver 6 ounces any sliced cheese and add (or use 1½ cups grated cheese). Toss well with the potatoes. Thickly butter a deep pie plate and spread the potato mixture in it, patting down firmly. Add about 1½ cups milk, or enough to reach the top. Sprinkle with paprika and bake, covered, at 350°F. about 45 minutes. Remove cover and bake until potatoes are tender.

CARROT CHARLOTTE

4 *medium carrots*
¾ *cup water*
5 *medium potatoes*
3 *eggs, separated*
¼ *cup matzo meal or cracker meal*
3 *Tbsp. melted fat*
1 *tsp. sugar*
½ *tsp. ginger*
  Salt, pepper

Peel and grate 4 medium carrots to make 1 cup. Add ¾ cup water, cover, and simmer for 15 minutes. Cool. Peel and grate 5 medium potatoes (1⅔ pounds) into the carrots. Add 3 egg yolks, ¼ cup matzo meal or cracker meal, and 3 tablespoons melted butter, bacon drippings, or chicken fat. Season with 1 teaspoon sugar, ½ teaspoon ginger, a dash of pepper, and salt to taste. Beat the 3 egg whites stiff and fold in. Bake in a greased 2-quart straight-sided baking dish or soufflé mold at 375°F. for about 40 minutes, until puffed and browned. Good with chicken.

POTATO CHARLOTTE

2 *slices bread*
1 *onion*
¼ *cup rendered chicken fat*
  Salt, pepper
1½ *lbs. potatoes*
2 *eggs*

Tear 2 slices bread into pieces and soak in cold water for a few minutes. Squeeze out as much water as possible and crumble. Chop an onion and cook it for a few minutes in 3 tablespoons rendered chicken fat, until just golden. Mix with the bread and add a generous teaspoon salt and a dash of pepper. Peel and grate 4 medium-large potatoes (3 cups grated potato) directly into the bread mixture. Beat in 2 eggs and adjust the seasoning with more salt and pepper, to taste. Grease a shallow baking dish with 1 tablespoon more chicken fat (¼ cup in all). Bake the pudding at 400°F. until browned and crisp-crusted, about 40 minutes.

POTATO SQUARES

1½ *lbs. potatoes*
1 *cup milk*
1 *onion*
3 *Tbsp. chopped green pepper*
4 *ozs. Cheddar cheese*
  Salt, pepper
3 *eggs*
2 *Tbsp. butter*

Peel 4 medium-large potatoes (1½ pounds) and grate directly into 1 cup milk in a well-buttered 8-inch square baking pan. Grate a small onion into the milk and add 3 tablespoons chopped green pepper, 1 cup (4 ounces) grated Cheddar cheese, and salt and pepper to taste. Beat 3 eggs well and combine. Dot with 2 tablespoons butter. Bake at 350°F. about 50 minutes to 1 hour, until the pudding is richly browned. Cut into squares to serve.

New World   The white potato is native to South America. Sixteenth-century Spanish explorers brought it back to Spain from Peru, where they had found a variety of white-fleshed potatoes and evidence that pre-historic Indian tribes had cultivated this "ground nut which when boiled becomes as soft as a cooked chestnut." Irish, did you say?

EGG AND OLIVE CASSEROLE

2 *lbs. potatoes*
  Salt, pepper
3 *hard-cooked eggs*
1 *small can sliced black olives*
2 *Tbsp. butter*
2 *Tbsp. flour*
2 *cups milk*
2 *ozs. grated cheese*

Cook 6 medium potatoes (2 pounds) in boiling salted water to cover. Peel and slice. Put ⅓ the potatoes in a buttered baking dish and sprinkle with salt and pepper to taste. Chop 3 hard-cooked eggs and mix with 1 small can (4 or 6 ounces) sliced or chopped black olives, drained. Sprinkle half this mixture on the potatoes. Add a second layer of ⅓ the potatoes, season, and add the remaining egg mixture. Cover with the remaining potatoes. Melt 2 tablespoons butter in a saucepan, stir in 2 tablespoons flour, and cook for a few minutes, stirring, without allowing the roux to color. Gradually stir in 2 cups milk and cook, stirring, until the sauce is smooth and thickened. Add ¼ cup grated cheese to the sauce and stir until the cheese melts. Add salt and pepper to taste. Pour the cheese sauce into the baking dish. Sprinkle with ¼ cup grated cheese (using ½ cup in all). Bake at 350°F. until the casserole is bubbling hot and browned, about 25 minutes.

CUSTARD POTATO CASSEROLE

2 *lbs. potatoes*
  Salt, pepper
6 *ozs. Swiss cheese*
4 *eggs*
1 *cup milk*
  Cayenne or tabasco
2 *Tbsp. butter*
  Chopped parsley for garnish

Cook 6 medium potatoes (2 pounds) in boiling salted water to cover. Peel and cut into thin slices. Fill a buttered casserole with alternate layers of potato slices seasoned with salt and pepper and 6 ounces thinly sliced Swiss cheese (Monterey Jack or Muenster cheese can also be used as a pleasant change). Beat 4 eggs with 1 cup milk and salt, pepper, and a dash of cayenne or tabasco to taste. Pour over the potatoes. Dot with 2 tablespoons butter. Bake at 350°F. until the custard is set and the top browned, about 30 minutes. Sprinkle with chopped parsley.

TOMATO-POTATO CASSEROLE

    2 lbs. potatoes
 1½ Tbsp. potato starch
 1½ cups half-and-half or light cream
      Salt, pepper
    2 Tbsp. fine dry bread crumbs
    2 tomatoes
      Pinch dry basil
    2 Tbsp. butter

Cook 6 medium potatoes, peel, and cut into large dice directly into a greased 6-cup casserole. Mix 1½ tablespoons potato starch to a paste with a little water and combine it with 1½ cups half-and-half or light cream. Season with salt and pepper to taste and pour over the potatoes. Sprinkle with 2 tablespoons or more fine dry bread crumbs, to cover. Peel 2 tomatoes by dipping them into boiling water for a minute to loosen the skins. Cut into thick slices and arrange on top of the crumbs in an orderly pattern. Crush a generous pinch of dried basil leaves between the fingers to release the flavor and sprinkle it on the tomatoes. Dot with 2 tablespoons butter and add salt and pepper. Bake at 350°F. until the casserole is bubbling hot and browned, about 30 minutes. You can shorten the baking time by bringing the potato starch and cream mixture just to the boiling point, stirring constantly, before pouring it over the potatoes.

SOUR CREAM CASSEROLE

2 lbs. potatoes
2 Tbsp. butter
½ onion
1 cup dairy sour cream
   Salt, pepper
2 ozs. cheese

Cook 6 medium potatoes (2 pounds) in boiling salted water to cover. Peel and slice. Pack in layers in a buttered 6-cup baking dish. Melt 2 tablespoons butter in a small pan, add half an onion, chopped, and cook until golden. Off the heat stir in 1 cup (an 8-ounce container) thick sour cream, with salt and pepper to taste. Pour the cream mixture over the potatoes and sprinkle with ½ cup grated Cheddar or Swiss cheese (2 ounces). Bake at 375°F. about 30 minutes, until the scallop is bubbling hot and the topping browned.

FOR VARIETY: Top the creamy potatoes with thick slices of peeled tomato and sprinkle thickly with seasoned bread crumbs. Dot with butter and bake as directed.

ONION-POTATO SOUFFLE

2 Tbsp. butter
¼ cup chopped onion
2 Tbsp. flour
1 cup chicken broth
½ cup half-and-half or light cream
   Salt, pepper
4 eggs, separated
1½ cups mashed potatoes

Melt 2 tablespoons butter and cook 4 tablespoons chopped onion until just translucent. Sprinkle with 2 tablespoons flour and cook, stirring, for a few minutes. Do not let the mixture brown. Gradually stir in 1 cup chicken broth (can be made with a bouillon cube) and cook, stirring, until the sauce is thick and smooth. Stir in ½ cup half-and-half or light cream. Season well with salt and pepper to taste and cool slightly. Add 4 egg yolks, stirring with a whisk to blend thoroughly. Add 1½ cups rather dry mashed potatoes, freshly made or leftover, and blend again until the mixture is smooth. Beat 4 egg whites stiff and fold in. Bake in an unbuttered 6-cup straight-sided baking dish, at 375°F., for about 40 minutes or until the soufflé is well puffed and richly browned. Serve at once.

CHEESE SOUFFLE

    2 cups mashed potatoes
    1 cup milk
    2 Tbsp. butter
    ½ tsp. prepared mustard
      Salt, pepper, cayenne pepper
    ¼ lb. Cheddar or Swiss cheese
    3 eggs, separated

Blend 2 cups mashed potatoes with 1 cup milk. Add 2 tablespoons butter and ½ teaspoon prepared mustard. Taste and adjust the seasoning with salt, pepper, and a dash of cayenne. Grate or cut finely 4 ounces Cheddar (or Swiss) cheese and stir into the potato mixture. Or use 1 cup ready-grated cheese, any kind you prefer. Cook over low heat, stirring constantly, just until the cheese melts. Cool slightly. Beat 3 egg whites until very stiff but not dry. With the same beater (no need to wash it) beat the 3 egg yolks. Add the egg yolks to the cheese mixture and blend well. Fold ⅔ of the beaten egg white into the mixture very thoroughly, then fold in the rest lightly. Bake in a 2-quart straight-sided casserole, ungreased, at 375°F., about 40 minutes or until the soufflé is well puffed and browned. Serve at once.

SPINACH AND POTATO SOUFFLE

2 Tbsp. butter
1 pkg. frozen chopped spinach
1½ cups mashed potatoes
   Salt, pepper
4 eggs, separated

Melt 2 tablespoons butter in a small pan. Add 1 package frozen chopped spinach (about 10 ozs.). Cover and cook, without allowing the butter to brown, until the spinach is thawed. Hasten the thawing by breaking up the frozen block. Combine with 1½ cups mashed potatoes, leftover or freshly made with 2 medium-large potatoes. Add salt and pepper to taste. Cool slightly. Beat in 4 egg yolks, one at a time. Beat 4 egg whites until stiff but not dry and fold in. Bake in a buttered 6-cup straight-sided baking dish, about 40 minutes at 375°F. until the soufflé is puffed and richly browned. Serve at once.

POTATO PUFF PIE

2 lbs. potatoes
½ cup hot milk
1 bouillon cube
3 Tbsp. butter
   Celery salt, white pepper
2 eggs
   Paprika

Cook 6 medium potatoes (2 pounds) in boiling salted water to cover. Peel and mash. Dissolve a bouillon cube in ½ cup hot milk and add with 3 tablespoons butter and celery salt and white pepper to taste. Beat 2 eggs well with a fork. Reserve 2 tablespoons of egg to brush on the pudding, and beat the rest into the potatoes. Pile on a buttered glass pie plate, swirling the top decoratively, and brush with the reserved egg. Sprinkle with paprika. Bake at 400°F. until the top browns slightly. Serve piping hot, in wedges.

TAPIOCA SOUFFLES

3 Tbsp. quick-cooking tapioca
1¼ cups milk
1 Tbsp. butter
⅓ cup grated Swiss cheese
Salt, paprika
3 eggs, separated
¾ cup mashed potatoes
Pepper

Cook 3 tablespoons quick-cooking tapioca in 1¼ cups milk until clear. Stir in 1 tablespoon butter and ⅓ cup grated Swiss cheese, stirring until the cheese melts. Add salt and paprika to taste. Beat 3 egg yolks with ¾ cup mashed potatoes, freshly cooked or leftover. Season as necessary with salt and pepper. Combine the two mixtures and again taste for seasoning. Beat 3 egg whites stiff and fold them in gently but thoroughly. Fill 6 ungreased custard cups half full, set in a pan of hot water, and bake at 350°F. about 20 minutes or until the soufflés are puffed and well browned.

CREAM CHEESE PUFF

2 lbs. potatoes
½ lb. cream cheese
½ cup chopped onion
2 canned pimientos, slivered
Salt, pepper
1 egg

Cook 6 medium potatoes (2 pounds) in boiling salted water to cover. Peel, mash, and combine with a half-pound package of Philadelphia-type cream cheese. Add ½ cup finely chopped onion and 2 canned pimientos, drained and slivered. Season with salt and pepper to taste. Add a whole egg and beat well. Bake in a buttered 6-cup casserole at 350°F. about 45 minutes, until well browned.

POTATO PUFF PARMIGIANA

1 lb. potatoes
1 Tbsp. butter
  Salt, pepper
1 egg
1 Tbsp. chopped chives
¼ cup grated Parmesan cheese
4 ozs. Mozzarella cheese
3 Tbsp. soft bread crumbs
  Tomato sauce for garnish

Cook 3 medium potatoes (1 pound) in boiling salted water to cover. Peel and mash. Season with 1 tablespoon butter and salt and pepper to taste. Beat 1 egg well and combine with the potatoes. Beat in 1 tablespoon chopped chives or parsley. Put ⅓ the potatoes into a buttered baking dish. Sprinkle with 1 tablespoon grated Parmesan. Sliver ¼ pound Mozzarella cheese (the kind used for pizza) and sprinkle ⅓ the slivers on the potatoes. Repeat. Sprinkle the top layer of potatoes and Mozzarella with 3 tablespoons bread crumbs and 2 tablespoons grated Parmesan, using ¼ cup grated cheese in all. Bake at 350°F. about 45 minutes, until the mixture is puffed and browned. Serve with tomato sauce, as a savory accompaniment for crusty fried chicken, veal scallopini, or fish. Or serve with meatballs in tomato sauce.

Herb Talk Potatoes gain interesting what-is-it flavor if you put a sprig of fresh herbs into the boiling pot—mint, tarragon, dill, savory, or any other herb that grows in your garden.

7

New
Potatoes

New potatoes—each no bigger than a golf ball—have a chapter to
themselves in this book because their quality deserves special
treatment. Of course, the dishes in this chapter can be made with
large new potatoes, and even with old potatoes. And other recipes in the book can be made with new potatoes, as well as with
old. But new potatoes remain something special. Food-freezing
technology has elevated (or maybe degraded) new green peas
and the first strawberries, once harbingers of spring, into year-
round commodities that we take for granted. But it is still true
that we can enjoy new potatoes only during the few late spring
and early summer months. Frozen potato balls, attractive and
useful as they are, are not new potatoes, and they do not taste
like new potatoes. Discover the difference for yourself this year,
when tiny new potatoes, clean and fresh in their papery skins,
come to market. They are worth waiting for, and worth fixing in
one of the ways particularly designed for them.

HOW TO COOK NEW POTATOES

Buy 1½ pounds new potatoes, of uniform size if possible, for four to six servings. Wash the potatoes, and, if you like, peel an extremely thin strip around the middle of each with a floating knife peeler. (This is an optional refinement that looks attractive and makes it even easier to peel the potatoes when they are cooked.) If you scrub the raw potatoes with a stiff brush, or shake them in a bag with coarse salt, à la Colette's *Gigi*, you will remove most of the peel.

Cover the prepared potatoes with boiling salted water and cook until tender, about 25 minutes, with the pan lid on. Test with a skewer after 20 minutes or so. Drain off the water and shake the pan over the heat to dry the potatoes thoroughly. Hold on a fork and strip off the peel quickly. Keep the pan covered with a napkin, which will absorb the steam and help to keep the potatoes hot and dry.

You can also steam the potatoes *over* boiling water, not in it. This takes about 35 to 40 minutes. Use a steamer or a colander in a kettle with a tightly fitted lid. Or you can use a pressure cooker, following the manufacturer's directions for correct pressure and timing.

The simplest and possibly the best way to serve cooked new potatoes—the very first of the season surely ought to be served this way—is to present them unpeeled in a napkin on a hot serving dish. Pass the pepper grinder, the salt shaker or a dish of coarse salt, and a small pitcher of clarified butter—clear golden butter poured off the milky sediment that settles to the bottom when butter is melted.

NEW POTATOES MAITRE D'HOTEL

1½ *lbs. new potatoes*
¼ *cup butter*
Salt, pepper, paprika
1 *Tbsp. lemon juice*
¼ *cup minced parsley*

Cook 1½ pounds uniform new potatoes. Peel. Melt ½ stick butter
(¼ cup) and season with salt, pepper, and paprika to taste. Add
1 tablespoon lemon juice and ¼ cup minced parsley. Roll the
hot potatoes in this mixture to coat.

> *Bouquet*   Add a leafy stalk of celery, a bay leaf, or a slice
> of onion—or all three tied together with string—to the water
> in which potatoes are boiling.

NEW POTATOES A LA MENTHE

Cook 1½ pounds new potatoes as usual, but add a few sprigs of
fresh mint to the water in which they are boiled. Roll in ¼ cup
melted butter and ¼ cup chopped fresh mint leaves.

NEW POTATOES AU CITRON

1½ lbs. new potatoes
¼ cup butter
1 Tbsp. olive oil
1 Tbsp. minced green onion
1 Tbsp. chopped parsley
1 tsp. thyme
Salt, pepper
Juice and grated rind of ½ lemon

Cook 1½ pounds new potatoes and peel. While the potatoes are
cooking, melt ½ stick butter (¼ cup) with 1 tablespoon olive oil,
1 tablespoon each minced green onion and chopped parsley, and
1 teaspoon dried thyme. Add the juice and grated zest of half a
lemon and pour the hot sauce over the hot potatoes.

NEW POTATOES AUX HERBES

1½ lbs. new potatoes
3 bouillon cubes
¼ cup butter
¼ cup chopped parsley or 2 Tbsp. chopped chives,
    mint, or tarragon

Wash and cook 1½ pounds new potatoes until tender, adding 3 bouillon cubes to the cooking water. Meanwhile, melt half a stick of butter (¼ cup) and add any of the following chopped fresh herbs: ¼ cup parsley, or 2 tablespoons chopped chives, mint, or tarragon. Or use half parsley and half chives or tarragon. Peel the potatoes, pile in a serving dish, pour the herb butter over them, and serve hot.

DILLED NEW POTATOES

1½ lbs. new potatoes
1 cup sour cream
  Salt
2 Tbsp. chopped fresh dill

Cook 1½ pounds tiny new potatoes in salted boiling water to cover. Peel. Cover with 1 cup dairy sour cream (an 8-ounce container) and sprinkle with salt to taste. Heat gently without boiling, turning the potatoes to coat them with the sauce. Sprinkle with chopped dill. Serve hot.

FOR VARIETY: Use chopped parsley or chives instead of dill, or a mixture of both. Sprinkle with a scant teaspoon of caraway seeds before heating in the sour cream. For extra color, add a dash of paprika.

DILLED POTATOES AND BEANS

Use only 1 pound new potatoes in the preceding recipe for
Dilled New Potatoes. Cook separately 1 package (10 ounces)
green beans (or 1 pound fresh green beans, tipped and cut into
1-inch lengths) until just tender. Combine with the potatoes and
heat with the sour cream and dill.

NEW POTATOES AND PEAS

1½ lbs. new potatoes
1 pkg. tiny frozen peas
½ tsp. basil
2 Tbsp. butter
¼ cup cream
Salt, white pepper

Cook 1½ pounds new potatoes in boiling salted water to cover
for 20 minutes or less. Peel the potatoes (they should not be completely cooked) and return them to the pan with ½ cup boiling
water. Add 1 package (about 10 ounces) frozen green peas, the
tiny variety if possible, and ½ teaspoon leaf basil. Crush the leaves
to help release the flavor, or use ground basil. Continue to cook
slowly about 5 minutes longer, until potatoes and peas are just
tender. Drain off any remaining liquid. Add 2 tablespoons butter,
¼ cup cream, and salt and white pepper to taste. Heat gently and
serve.

TIP: Instead of dried basil, use a couple of fresh leaves. Or substitute dill, marjoram, or mint, dried or fresh.

NEW POTATOES WITH ANCHOVIES

1½ lbs. new potatoes
 1 onion
 2 Tbsp. butter
½ cup sour cream
   Small can (about 2 ozs.) anchovies

Cook 1½ pounds new potatoes and peel. Meanwhile, chop an onion and cook gently in 2 tablespoons butter until translucent. Stir in ½ cup sour cream and heat without boiling. Wash, dry, and mince finely 4 or 5 anchovies (use the flat fillets). Taste the sauce and add the anchovies gradually to get the amount of anchovy flavor you prefer. Add a dash of pepper, but no salt, naturally! Pour the anchovy dressing over the hot potatoes. Good pickup with bland cold roast veal or pork.

SAVORY BROWNED NEW POTATOES

1½ lbs. new potatoes
¼ cup rendered poultry fat
   Garlic salt, pepper, paprika

Cook 1½ pounds new potatoes as directed. Drain and peel. Heat ¼ cup rendered poultry fat (or use bacon drippings or butter, but not a tasteless neutral fat) and brown the potatoes lightly on all sides, shaking them often. Season generously with garlic salt, pepper, and paprika. For variety, use celery salt, onion salt, or any of the mixed-seasoning salts instead of garlic salt.

CHEESED NEW POTATOES

1½ lbs. new potatoes
¼ cup melted butter
   Salt, pepper, paprika
   Grated dry cheese

Cook 1½ pounds new potatoes in boiling salted water to cover.
Peel. Roll at once in ¼ cup melted butter seasoned to taste with
salt, pepper, and paprika. Dust lightly with grated Parmesan or
Romano cheese. Bake on a greased baking sheet at 400°F. about
15 minutes, until the cheese melts and browns.

NEW POTATOES A LA FRANCAISE

1½ lbs. new potatoes
 3 Tbsp. butter
 2 Tbsp. water
   Salt, white pepper
   Herb for garnish

Peel 1½ pounds new potatoes, or peel a thin band around the
centers to make peeling easier at eating time. Put in a heavy
saucepan fitted with a tight lid. Add 3 tablespoons butter, 2 tablespoons water, and salt and white pepper to taste. Place the pan
over moderate heat until the liquid comes to a boil. Then reduce
the heat to very low and cook the potatoes, covered, until they
are tender, 35 minutes or longer. Shake the pan occasionally to
roll the potatoes and help them cook evenly. Check very frequently to make sure the liquid has not boiled away—add a very
little water, as needed. Serve sprinkled with fresh chopped parsley, chives, or other herbs.

PITTSBURGH POTATOES

1½ lbs. new potatoes
2 Tbsp. butter
1 onion
2 Tbsp. flour
2 cups milk
4 ozs. Cheddar cheese, grated
2 canned pimientos
   Salt, pepper

Cook 1½ pounds new potatoes in boiling salted water to cover. Peel and cut in half. While the potatoes are boiling, melt 2 tablespoons butter. Chop a small onion and cook in the butter until just translucent. Stir in 2 tablespoons flour and cook, stirring, for a minute or two. Gradually add 2 cups milk and continue to cook, stirring constantly, until the sauce is smooth and thickened. Add ½ cup grated cheese (2 ounces) and 1 pimiento, finely diced. Season well with salt and pepper to taste. Pile the potatoes in a buttered baking dish. Cover them with the sauce and sprinkle with the remaining ½ cup grated cheese. Bake at 350°F. until the cheese topping melts and begins to brown. Garnish with another pimiento, cut into strips or fancy shapes, and serve hot.

NEW POTATOES PRINTEMPS

1½ lbs. new potatoes
1 pkg. frozen peas and carrots
2 Tbsp. butter
¼ cup chopped scallions
1 cup half-and-half or light cream
   Pinch salad herb mixture
   Salt, pepper, sugar
   Parsley and paprika for garnish

Cook 1½ pounds new potatoes in boiling salted water to cover for 10 minutes. Peel. Meanwhile, thaw slightly 1 package (about 10 ounces) frozen peas and carrots. Melt 2 tablespoons butter in a range-to-table casserole fitted with a lid. Add the carrots and peas and toss, breaking the frozen block with a fork. Chop a few scallions, with the greens, to make ¼ cup. Scald and add 1 cup half-and-half. Add a pinch of mixed herbs and salt, pepper, and a little sugar, to taste. Stir well. Add the peeled potatoes and stir carefully to coat. Cover the casserole tightly and bake at 350°F. about 20 minutes, or until the potatoes are tender. Taste the sauce, adding more salt, pepper, and sugar, as desired. Sprinkle with chopped parsley and a little paprika, and serve in the casserole.

NEW POTATO SCRAMBLE

1½ lbs. new potatoes
10 slices bacon
1 onion
 Salt, pepper
3 eggs
3 Tbsp. milk

Cook 1½ pounds new potatoes in boiling salted water to cover. Peel. While the potatoes are cooking, cook 10 or 12 slices bacon until crisp, in a range-to-table skillet or an electric fry pan that you can use as a serving dish. Drain the bacon and reserve ¼ cup fat. Dice an onion, add to the fat, and cook until just translucent. Add the peeled potatoes and cook them for a few minutes, until they are coated with fat and beginning to brown. Add salt and pepper to taste. Beat 3 eggs with 3 tablespoons milk or water. Season with salt and pepper. Pour the eggs into the pan and cook, stirring gently, just until the eggs are thick and creamy. Garnish with the crisp bacon and serve at once.

NEW POTATO SALAD

  2 *lbs. small new potatoes*
  2 *Tbsp. grated onion*
  ½ *cup white wine*
  ½ *cup vinegar*
     Salt, pepper
     Salad oil
  1 *cucumber*
  ¼ *cup mayonnaise*
  1 *hard-cooked egg*
     Anchovies (optional)

If you can find them, use 2 pounds (about 2 heaping cups) of
very tiny, new potatoes. If the potatoes are larger, cut them into
bite-size quarters or halves after they are cooked. Cook as usual,
in boiling salted water to cover. Cool slightly and peel. Sprinkle
with 2 tablespoons grated onion. Heat ½ cup white wine with ½
cup vinegar and season with dashes of salt and pepper. Pour the
hot wine mixture over the potatoes and let them stand in a cool
place for an hour or so, turning them occasionally. Most of the
wine will be absorbed (pour off any excess). Add a spoonful of
good salad oil—enough to coat the potatoes. Score a medium cucumber with a fork, slice it paper thin, and toss with the potatoes.
Mound on lettuce in a salad bowl and spoon ¼ cup mayonnaise
over the top. Rice the white and yellow of a hard-cooked egg
separately and use as garnish. A few anchovy fillets may be scattered over all, if desired.

Cleaner Potatoes Wash potatoes under running water
with a rust-proof metal or plastic pot-scrubber that you
keep especially for this purpose. It will easily remove dirt,
scales, and excess skin from old potatoes, and most of the
skin from new potatoes.

NEW POTATOES HUNGARIAN

1½ lbs. new potatoes
   Flour for dredging
6 tablespoons butter or bacon drippings
1 can (1 lb.) stewed tomatoes
   Salt, paprika

Cook 1½ pounds new potatoes for 10 minutes in boiling salted water to cover. Peel, roll in flour, and brown lightly on all sides in 6 tablespoons melted butter or bacon drippings. Add a 1-pound can of stewed tomatoes—the kind prepared with green pepper, onion, and seasonings—and simmer, stirring occasionally, until the sauce is thickened and smooth. Add salt and paprika to taste and simmer, covered, until the potatoes are tender, about 10 minutes longer.

NEW POTATOES AU GRATIN

1 qt. milk
1 egg
¼ lb. Swiss cheese
   Salt, pepper, nutmeg
2 lbs. new potatoes

Heat 1 quart milk without letting it boil. Beat an egg lightly with a fork, warm it with a little milk, and stir it into the pan. Grate 4 ounces Swiss cheese (1 cup) and add half of it to the milk, with salt, pepper, and nutmeg to taste. Peel and slice 2 pounds small new potatoes. Spread the potatoes in a thin layer on a buttered, shallow baking dish, and cover them with the sauce. Sprinkle with the remaining Swiss cheese and bake at 400°F. about 1 hour, until the potatoes are tender.

NEW POTATOES BASQUAISE

 2 *Tbsp. butter*
 1 *onion*
 1 *large carrot*
 3 *stalks celery*
 1 *clove garlic*
1½ *lbs. new potatoes*
 1 *can condensed consommé*
 ¾ *cup water*
   Salt, pepper
   Parsley for garnish

Melt 2 tablespoons butter in a saucepan and add 1 onion and 1 large carrot, both finely grated, 3 stalks celery, finely slivered, and 1 clove garlic, thinly sliced. Cook gently, covered, about 10 minutes. Meanwhile, scrub 1½ pounds new potatoes under running water with a stiff brush to remove most of the papery peel. Add 1 can condensed beef consommé and ¾ cup water to the vegetables, heat, and season with salt and pepper to taste. Add the prepared potatoes and simmer, covered, about 25 minutes, until the potatoes are tender. If necessary, boil the sauce rapidly to reduce it a little at the end. Serve sprinkled with chopped parsley.

8

Stuffings
and
Dumplings

Potato stuffings and dumplings are often used and highly valued when money is scarce and food expensive. They are delicious, hearty, and satisfying, and make a little meat go a long way. In more prosperous times, they seem to do a strange turnabout and become luxuries to enjoy only infrequently on special occasions. It is not easy to say why this happens, although they do take a little more time and effort to make than mashed potatoes or scalloped potatoes. But they are well worth the trouble. Make fruit dumplings for dessert some evening when you're planning a light or cold supper. And next year, roast a goose for Christmas with potato stuffing, and discover how to make Christmas dinner even more like Christmas! However, you do not need to stuff a bird, a crown roast of pork, or even a flank steak or boned ham to have stuffing on the menu. Any stuffing mixture can be baked in a casserole. Add a little bouillon or gravy if you like, to moisten it and give it a meaty flavor.

BASIC POTATO STUFFING

2 *lbs. potatoes*
8 *slices white bread*
¾ *cup rendered poultry fat*
3 *onions, chopped*
¼ *cup chopped parsley*
2 *eggs*
1 *tsp. sage*
1 *tsp. poultry seasoning*
   Salt, pepper

Cook 6 medium potatoes (2 pounds) in boiling salted water to cover. Peel and rice. Trim the crusts from 8 slices of day-old white bread and crumble. Toss potatoes and bread crumbs together. In a skillet, heat ¾ cup fat—rendered poultry fat gives best flavor, but 1½ sticks butter will do. Cook 3 large onions, coarsely chopped, in the fat until they are translucent. Add to the potato mixture. Add ¼ cup chopped parsley. Beat 2 eggs lightly and add, tossing lightly. Add 1 teaspoon each sage and poultry seasoning. Adjust the seasoning with salt and pepper. This makes about 2 quarts of stuffing mixture, enough for an 8-pound bird.

FOR VARIETY: The taste may be varied by adding about 1 cup cooked, diced poultry giblets (gizzard, heart, and liver), sliced, browned pork sausage, celery, diced apple, chestnuts or pecans. Caraway seeds, 1 teaspoon or more to taste, may be added to the basic mixture.

Parmentier Antoine-Auguste Parmentier has a monument more enduring than bronze—whenever his name appears on a menu, it means a superb potato dish. Parmentier, a prisoner of war in Prussia during the Seven Years War, brought potatoes—his prison diet—back to France, and spent the rest of his life teaching the French to enjoy them.

POTATO-CELERY STUFFING

½ *lb. pork sausage*
2 *onions, chopped*
3 *large celery stalks*
2 *lbs. potatoes*
1 *tsp. celery salt*
  Pepper, paprika

Cook ½ pound pork sausage meat, preferably the bulk type, until the meat is no longer pink, stirring with a fork to break it up. Add 2 onions, coarsely chopped, and cook over low heat until translucent. Chop the leafy tops of 3 celery stalks, add, and cook a minute longer. Sliver the celery stalks and add. Peel and grate 2 pounds potatoes into the mixture and season highly with 1 teaspoon celery salt, and pepper and paprika to taste. Cook about 10 minutes, stirring often. Cool before using to stuff the bird. Makes enough stuffing for a 5-pound roasting chicken.

APPLE STUFFING

4 *large tart apples*
2 *cups mashed potatoes*
1 *onion, chopped*
1 *cup raisins*
6 *slices bread*
½ *cup butter or rendered poultry fat*
1 *tsp. poultry seasoning, sage, or thyme*
  Salt, pepper

Peel and coarsely chop 4 large tart apples. Blend with 2 cups mashed potatoes, 1 chopped onion and 1 cup raisins. Trim the crusts from 6 slices fresh bread and crumble bread to make 2 cups crumbs. Add to the potatoes with ½ cup melted butter or rendered poultry fat. Season well with 1 teaspoon poultry seasoning, sage, or thyme, and salt and pepper. Makes about 2 quarts. This is a classic stuffing for goose and duck.

GOOSE LIVER STUFFING

2 lbs. potatoes
2 Tbsp. butter
2 onions
  Goose liver
1 tsp. poultry seasoning
  Salt, pepper

Cook 6 medium potatoes (2 pounds) in boiling salted water to cover. Peel and mash. Meanwhile, melt 2 tablespoons butter in a skillet. Add 2 coarsely chopped onions, and the liver of the goose, cut finely. Cook until the onion is translucent. Combine liver, onions, and potatoes and season highly with 1 teaspoon poultry seasoning, salt, and a generous amount of pepper. Stuff a goose and roast as usual. Or bake the stuffing separately in a casserole, alongside the bird, until it is hot and lightly browned.

TURKEY OR CHICKEN LIVER STUFFING

Instead of the goose liver, use a turkey liver plus a couple of chicken livers, or use about ½ pound chicken livers.

SAUERKRAUT STUFFING FOR GOOSE

3 onions, chopped
2 Tbsp. rendered poultry fat
2 cans (1 pound each) sauerkraut
1 lb. potatoes
1 tsp. caraway seeds
  Salt, pepper

Cook 3 onions, coarsely chopped, in 2 tablespoons rendered poultry fat until translucent. Drain 2 pounds sauerkraut and add. Peel and grate 3 medium potatoes (1 pound) and add to the pan with 1 teaspoon caraway seeds, and salt and pepper to taste. Cook over low heat about 15 minutes, stirring often, until the mixture is thickened and the potatoes cooked. Add a little water, if necessary, but keep the stuffing dry. Cool before using to fill a goose.

> *Vitamins* A medium potato supplies as much Vitamin C as a glass of tomato juice and as much iron as an egg—for less than 100 calories.

PRUNE STUFFING

    2 *lbs. potatoes*
  ½ *cup milk*
    1 *onion*
  ½ *cup butter or rendered poultry fat*
    1 *cup prunes*
    1 *cup dry bread crumbs*
    1 *tsp. oregano*
    1 *tsp. poultry seasoning*
       Salt, pepper

Cook 6 medium potatoes (2 pounds) in a small amount of salted water, peel, and mash with ½ cup milk. Chop 1 small onion and cook until translucent in ½ cup butter or poultry fat. Combine with the potatoes. Slice 1 cup pitted prunes. The new soft prunes require no soaking, but others may need to soak half an hour or so in hot water. Add the fruit to the potatoes with 1 cup dry bread crumbs. Add 1 teaspoon each oregano and poultry seasoning, or more, and salt and pepper to taste. Blend lightly. Makes enough stuffing for a medium goose or small turkey.

OLD-FASHIONED PORK STUFFING

½ *lb. ground fresh pork*
2 *cups water*
½ *lb. ground salt pork*
2 *cups mashed potatoes*
1 *onion, chopped*
6 *slices dry bread*
1 *egg*
1 *tsp. sage*
½ *tsp. thyme*
   Salt, pepper

Cook ½ pound ground fresh pork with a little salt in 2 cups water, until tender. Reserve 1 cup of the cooking broth. Combine the pork with ½ pound ground salt pork, 2 cups mashed potatoes, and 1 onion, chopped. Trim the crusts from 6 slices stale bread. Crush the bread to make 2 cups coarse crumbs. Add to the potato mixture with 1 egg and blend well. Season with 1 teaspoon sage and ½ teaspoon thyme, plus salt and pepper to taste. Moisten with about 1 cup of the reserved pork liquid. Enough for a 6-pound bird.

NEW BRUNSWICK PORK STUFFING

1 *lb. lean fresh pork*
¼ *lb. pork fat*
2 *lbs. potatoes*
2 *onions, chopped*
4 *slices toasted bread*
2 *tsp. poultry seasoning*
   Salt, pepper

Have the butcher put 1 pound very lean fresh pork through a grinder with ¼ pound pork fat (or use 1¼ pounds streaky pork). Peel and dice 6 potatoes (2 pounds) and cook in a small amount of boiling salted water. Drain and mash, reserving the potato water. Cook the pork in a heavy skillet, stirring with a fork to separate the bits, until the meat loses its pink color. Add 2 onions, chopped, and continue to cook until the onion is translucent. Stir often. Crumble 4 slices toast and add. Combine the pork mixture with the mashed potatoes and season to taste with 2 teaspoons or more poultry seasoning, and salt and pepper. If the stuffing seems dry, moisten it with a little of the potato water. Cool before using. Makes about 6 cups of stuffing for a crown roast of pork, or for chicken or turkey.

CUSTARD STUFFING CASSEROLE

1½ *cups mashed potatoes*
 2 *eggs*
 2 *cups milk*
 4 *cups soft bread crumbs*
¼ *cup butter*
½ *cup finely chopped onion*
½ *cup finely chopped celery*
    Salt, pepper, sage

Use hot mashed potatoes for this dressing—the dehydrated potato flakes are a fine shortcut. Prepare 3 servings according to package directions, to make 1½ cups. Or cook 2 medium large potatoes, peel and mash. Beat 2 eggs with 2 cups milk. Add 4 cups soft bread crumbs (about 12 slices bread, trimmed of crusts) and let soften. Combine with the potatoes. Melt ¼ cup butter (½ stick) and cook ½ cup each finely chopped onion and celery in the butter until the onion is translucent. Add to the dressing. Add salt and pepper to taste, and sage (or poultry seasoning) if you like. Bake in a greased casserole, at 325°F., 45 minutes to 1 hour, and serve with roast pork.

STUFFING CASSEROLE

>   1 *lb. potatoes*
>   6 *slices bread*
>   1 *onion, chopped*
>   ¼ *cup melted butter*
>   1 *egg*
>   ½ *tsp. sage*
>   ½ *tsp. thyme*
>   ½ *tsp. poultry seasoning*
>   2 *chicken bouillon cubes*
>   2 *cups boiling water*
>   *Salt, pepper*

Cook 1 pound potatoes in a small amount of boiling salted water. Cool, peel, and grate. Trim the crusts from 6 slices bread, crumble bread, and add. Cook a small onion, chopped, in ¼ cup butter until translucent. Add to the potato mixture. Beat 1 egg lightly and add. Season with ½ teaspoon each sage, thyme, and poultry seasoning (or use all poultry seasoning). Dissolve 2 chicken bouillon cubes in 2 cups boiling water and stir in to make a moist but not runny mixture. Add more water if necessary. Taste and add salt and pepper to suit. Bake uncovered in a buttered casserole, along with a roast, until hot and browned. The baking time will vary with the oven temperature required for the roast—from 35 minutes to nearly an hour.

POTATO DUMPLINGS

Here are examples of the various kinds of potato dumplings you can cook with a stew, or boil and add to a hearty soup to make it into a meal, or serve with pot roast or another main dish. The fruit-stuffed dumplings—what a wonderful dessert they make after a light meal!—are among the desserts, and more examples will be found in Chapter 20.

Making good dumplings requires good judgment on the part of the cook. The basic principle is that the less binder (flour, starch, bread crumbs) you use, the lighter the finished product. But too little binder produces a dumpling that will disintegrate as it cooks. Many experienced cooks still take the precaution of following the recipe precisely, then making a test dumpling and adjusting proportions accordingly. This is good advice for the beginner, too.

BREAD DUMPLINGS

1 *lb. potatoes*
½ *onion*
  Chopped parsley (optional)
1 *egg*
4 *slices white bread*
  Salt, pepper
  Flour for dredging

Cook 3 medium potatoes (1 pound) in boiling salted water to cover until tender. Cool, peel, and grate. Finely chop half a small onion and add, along with a little chopped parsley, if desired. Beat 1 egg well and combine with potatoes. Tear 4 average slices bread into small pieces, soak in cold water, and press to remove as much water as possible. Crumble the bread and combine it with the potato mixture. Add salt and pepper to taste. Shape small balls and roll in flour. Cook in gently boiling salted water, covered, for about 15 minutes. Or drop the balls on top of a bubbling stew, cover, and cook 15 minutes. Test for doneness by breaking open one dumpling.

> *Sailor's Delight*   In the old days at sea, scurvy was no threat to sailing men on a long voyage when there were potatoes aboard—preserved in molasses or vinegar—to supply the preventive Vitamin C.

QUICK DUMPLINGS

2 cups mashed potatoes
½ small onion
2 Tbsp. fat
1 egg
   Salt, pepper, nutmeg
1 cup flour

Mix 2 cups cold mashed potatoes with half a small onion, grated or finely chopped. Beat in 2 tablespoons soft or melted butter, bacon drippings, or chicken fat, depending on which flavor you prefer. Add 1 egg and mix well. Taste for seasoning, adding salt, pepper, and a very little nutmeg to taste. Work in 1 cup flour or more, to make a dough that can be handled. Shape into about a dozen balls and drop into boiling salted water. Cook, covered, about 15 minutes. Test the dumplings for doneness by breaking one with a fork.

SURPRISE DUMPLINGS

1 lb. potatoes
1 cup potato starch
1 egg
   Onion salt, pepper
1 slice white bread
   Butter

Cook 3 medium potatoes (1 pound) in boiling salted water to cover. Peel and mash. Combine with 1 cup potato starch and 1 egg. Add onion salt and pepper to taste. Cut 1 slice of white bread into small cubes and brown the cubes in melted butter. Shape small balls of potato mixture around a browned bread cube. If the dough seems too soft, add more potato starch. Drop into boiling salted water. When the dumplings rise to the top, cook for a few minutes longer. Test by breaking one in half. Serve with bread crumbs browned in butter, or with meat gravy.

PUFFED DUMPLINGS

1 *lb. potatoes*
  Salt
½ *cup water*
¼ *cup butter*
  Dash pepper
½ *cup flour*
2 *eggs*

Cook 3 medium potatoes (1 pound) in salted boiling water to cover. Peel and mash. Add salt to taste. Or use 2 cups leftover, very dry mashed potatoes. Make a *pâte à choux:* Bring ½ cup water to a boil in a small saucepan, with ¼ cup butter (½ stick), ½ teaspoon salt, and a dash of pepper. Add ½ cup flour, all at once, and beat with a wooden spoon over low heat until the mixture forms a ball and leaves the sides of the pan. Off the heat, beat in 2 large eggs, one at a time. Beat well. (This *pâte à choux*, or cream puff paste, is the same mixture used to make fritters and eclair shells. It combines with potatoes in a classic recipe for potato fritters.) Blend the paste with the mashed potato. Shape into 2-inch fingers and cook in boiling salted water, uncovered, at a very gentle simmer, about 15 to 20 minutes. Test by breaking one open. Serve with melted butter or meat gravy.

PUFFED GNOCCHI

Drain the cooked dumplings and spread them in a buttered, shallow baking dish. Sprinkle with ½ cup grated Parmesan cheese and dot generously with 3 tablespoons butter. At serving time, brown the topping under the broiler. Serve hot, plain or with tomato sauce or another spaghetti sauce, or with a rich cheese sauce.

EASY GNOCCHI

  1½ *lbs. potatoes*
   1 *egg yolk*
      Salt, pepper
  ½ *cup flour*
   2 *Tbsp. melted butter*
   3 *Tbsp. grated Parmesan cheese*

Cook 4 medium large potatoes (1½ pounds) in boiling salted water to cover. Peel and mash. (You can use 3 cups leftover mashed potatoes, but they should be very dry.) Beat in an egg yolk and salt and pepper to taste. Gradually add about ½ cup flour, using just enough to make a dough that can be kneaded. Knead until smooth, roll out ¾-inch thick, and cut into 2-inch fingers. Drop the gnocchi into a shallow pan of boiling salted water, a single layer at a time, and cook until they bob up to the surface. Drain and transfer to a buttered baking dish. When all are cooked, sprinkle with 2 tablespoons melted butter and 3 table-spoons grated Parmesan cheese. Brown the topping under the broiler.

STEAMED RAW POTATO DUMPLINGS

   1 *lb. potatoes*
  1½ *cups flour*
  1½ *tsp. baking soda*
   1 *tsp. salt*
   1 *tsp. chopped basil leaves*
   2 *Tbsp. milk*

Peel and grate 3 medium potatoes (1 pound) into cold water in a mixing bowl. Toss 1½ cups flour with 1½ teaspoons baking soda and a scant teaspoon salt. Drain and dry the potatoes, add the flour, and blend well. Add 1 teaspoon chopped fresh basil, or ⅓ teaspoon dry leaves, well crushed. (Rosemary or oregano may be used if you prefer.) Add about 2 tablespoons milk, to make a mixture the consistency of firm bread dough. Shape Ping-Pong size balls and lay them carefully on top of the meat and vegetables in a stew, not in the liquid. Cover and cook 30 to 40 minutes. Test by breaking open a dumpling.

STEAMED DUMPLINGS

1 *cooked potato*
1 *Tbsp. bacon drippings*
½ *tsp. salt*
  Pepper
1 *cup flour*
2 *tsp. double-acting baking powder*
½ *cup milk*

Grate or rice a cold, leftover boiled or baked potato to make ⅔ cup potato. Blend with 1 tablespoon bacon drippings and season well with ½ teaspoon salt and pepper to taste. Toss 1 cup flour with 2 teaspoons double-acting baking powder and work this into the potato mixture. Add gradually about ½ cup milk, or just enough to make a dough that can be handled. On a floured board, roll or pat the dough ½-inch thick and cut into small shapes with a knife or cutter. Arrange the dumplings side by side in a greased steamer, or in a greased colander. Cook over boiling water, tightly covered, for 12 to 15 minutes. Test for doneness by breaking one dumpling. Serve with meat gravy, or with melted butter and browned bread crumbs.

CARAWAY DUMPLINGS

2 lbs. potatoes
1 Tbsp. fat
¼ onion, chopped
  Salt, pepper
1 tsp. caraway seeds
2 eggs
¾ cup flour

Reserve a smallish potato, which you will later grate to make ½ cup gratings. Cook 5 potatoes (the remainder of 2 pounds) in boiling salted water. Peel and mash. Heat 1 tablespoon fat and cook a quarter of a small onion, chopped, until the onion is translucent. Peel and grate the reserved potato and press the gratings to extract as much liquid as possible. Cook the potato with the onion until the mixture thickens, stirring often. Cool and combine with the mashed potatoes. Add salt and pepper to taste, and 1 teaspoon (or more) caraway seeds. Beat in 2 eggs and add about ¾ cup flour, to make a dough that can be shaped into balls. Cook in boiling salted water about 15 minutes. Test by breaking open one dumpling. Serve with butter or meat gravy. Serves 6 or more.

Potato Perfection, Boiled Cook potatoes as if you were going to make mashed potatoes, but this time do not peel and do not mash them. Just serve, right away, in a heated dish covered with a napkin. Pass a pitcher of melted butter, salt, and the pepper grinder.

9

Potato
Pancakes

Potato pancakes are often served as a main course at breakfast, luncheon, or supper, accompanied by fruit (usually applesauce) and sometimes bacon or ham. They probably are at their best with meat at dinner, especially when the meat is a succulent pot roast.

Choose a frying fat that suits the way you plan to serve the pancakes. Hydrogenated shortenings and salad oils are more satisfactory than butter, which tends to burn at the necessary high temperatures, and bacon drippings and rendered poultry fat are best of all because of the good flavor they add. Use plenty of fat, unless otherwise directed.

Grated raw potatoes discolor rapidly on exposure to air. Grating them directly into cold water retards the darkening process, but there is some loss of valuable nutrients thrown away with the soaking water. The batter will begin to darken as soon as the potatoes are added, so the recipes that follow are for amounts that can be quickly prepared, to serve 2 as a main dish, 3 or 4 as a side dish. For more servings, mix successive batches in turn while the pancakes are frying.

A potato-pancake batter made with 1 pound potatoes, 1 egg, and a little thickening will make about a dozen 3-inch pancakes. Additional ingredients such as large amounts of flour and milk will increase the yield accordingly.

Potato pancakes made with grated raw potatoes are crisply distinctive; made with mashed potatoes they are light, tender, and meltingly soft. Some of both kinds are described here, and there are more examples in the chapters on national specialties (Latkes, for instance) and among the desserts (Crêpes).

TIP: Next time you make breakfast pancakes with a mix, enrich the batter with leftover mashed potatoes. Wonderful things happen when you add potatoes to cakes, whether they are baked in the oven or on a griddle.

VARIETY PANCAKES

Begin with your favorite potato pancake recipe and add any of the following: half a small jar of shredded chipped beef and 1 tablespoon chopped parsley (cut down on salt accordingly); or 2 strips bacon, diced and cooked until crisp (use the bacon fat to fry the pancakes); or ¼ cup diced ham.

CRISP CAKES

1 lb. potatoes
1 onion
Juice of ½ lemon
Salt, pepper
Fat

Peel and grate 3 medium potatoes (1 pound). Use the coarse grater for the potatoes. Peel and grate an onion, this time using the finest grater. Add the juice of half a lemon, and salt and pepper to taste. Drop by tablespoonfuls into ¼ inch of hot fat—bacon drippings or rendered poultry fat are particularly good—and flatten with the back of the spoon. Brown on both sides, turning only once.

MAINE POTATO PANCAKES

  2 *eggs, separated*
1½ *cups milk*
1½ *tsp. salt*
  1 *lb. potatoes*
1½ *cups sifted flour*
¼ *tsp. double-acting baking powder*
  1 *Tbsp. butter or bacon drippings*

Beat 2 egg yolks with 1½ cups milk and 1½ teaspoons salt. Peel 3 medium potatoes (1 pound) and grate them directly into the liquid. Gradually stir in 1½ cups sifted flour and ¼ teaspoon double-acting baking powder. Melt 1 tablespoon butter or bacon drippings and add. Beat the 2 egg whites until stiff but not dry and fold them carefully into the batter. Drop by ¼ cupfuls onto a hot, generously greased griddle and bake slowly, turning once to brown both sides. Serve with butter and syrup.

SWEET CREAM PANCAKES

½ *cup bread crumbs*
½ *cup heavy cream*
 1 *egg*
 1 *tsp. onion salt*
  Pepper
 1 *lb. potatoes*

Soak ½ cup fine, dry bread crumbs (not the seasoned commercial type) in ½ cup heavy cream for 10 minutes. Beat 1 egg with 1 teaspoon onion salt and a dash of pepper. Combine with the cream. Peel 3 medium potatoes (1 pound) and grate directly into the egg mixture. Brown by spoonfuls on both sides on a hot, generously greased griddle.

BUTTERMILK BREAKFAST PANCAKES

2 cups flour
2 tsp. double-acting baking powder
1 tsp. baking soda
1 tsp. salt
1 Tbsp. sugar
2 eggs
2 cups buttermilk
½ lb. potatoes
2 Tbsp. butter
1 to 2 tsp. vanilla

Toss or sift 2 cups flour, 2 teaspoons double-acting baking powder, and 1 teaspoon each baking soda and salt. Add 2 tablespoons sugar. Beat 2 eggs, add 2 cups buttermilk, and beat well. Add all at once to the flour mixture and stir just until flour is moistened. Peel and finely grate 1 large potato or 2 smallish ones (about 1 cup grated) directly over the batter and stir it in. Melt 2 tablespoons butter and add. Stir in 1 to 2 teaspoons vanilla, if you like the flavor. Bake on a hot greased griddle, turning once when the bottom is brown and the top bubbly. Serve with butter and syrup.

MASHED POTATO PANCAKES

2 cups mashed potatoes
1 Tbsp. sugar
Salt
½ cup flour
1½ tsp. double-acting baking powder
3 eggs

Season 2 cups mashed potatoes, leftover or freshly mashed without milk, with 1 tablespoon sugar and salt to taste. Combine ½ cup flour with 1½ teaspoons double-acting baking powder, and stir into potatoes. Beat 3 eggs and combine, stirring well to make a smooth batter. If necessary, add a little milk. Bake on a hot greased griddle, turning once to brown both sides. Sprinkle with cinnamon sugar, and serve with a lemon wedge.

SOUR CREAM DIAMONDS

1 lb. potatoes
Salt, pepper
1 cup flour
1 cup sour cream
Fat

Cook 3 medium potatoes (1 pound) in boiling salted water to cover. Cool, peel, and grate. Add salt and pepper to taste. Add 1 cup flour and enough sour cream to make a soft dough that can be rolled out, about 1 cup. On a floured board, pat the dough (or roll it) less than ¼ inch thick. Cut into diamond shapes. Heat a thin layer of fat in a skillet. Brown the diamonds on both sides and serve hot, with frizzled ham or bacon strips and applesauce, as a luncheon or supper specialty.

Percentage Potatoes are about 80 percent water, so when you add potatoes to the batter for pancakes, breads, and cakes, you need less liquid.

SOUR CREAM PANCAKES

2 *eggs, separated*
¼ *cup sour cream*
2 *Tbsp. flour*
½ *tsp. salt*
¾ *lb. potatoes*

Beat 2 egg yolks with ¼ cup sour cream. Beat in 2 tablespoons flour and ½ teaspoon salt. Peel and grate 2 medium-large potatoes (there should be about 1½ cups gratings) directly into the batter. Beat egg whites stiff and fold in. Brown by spoonfuls on both sides on a generously greased skillet or griddle. Serve at once, with more sour cream as a sauce.

LUNCHEON PANCAKES

1 *egg*
2 *Tbsp. flour*
¼ *tsp. double-acting baking powder*
1 *Tbsp. grated onion*
1 *lb. potatoes*
  Salt, pepper
  Fat

Beat 1 egg and add 2 tablespoons flour and ¼ teaspoon double-acting baking powder. Add 1 tablespoon finely grated onion. Peel and grate 3 medium potatoes (1 pound) into a bowl of cold water. Drain and dry the gratings and add to the egg mixture. Blend well. Season with salt, a scant teaspoon or more to taste, and a dash of pepper. Heat bacon drippings or hydrogenated shortening ¼ inch thick in a skillet. Drop pancake batter by spoonfuls into hot fat. Cook over moderate heat until brown and crisp. Turn and brown the other side. Serve with applesauce and ham or bacon, as a main dish at luncheon or supper.

❧ 10
❧

Appetizers

Two kinds of appetizers are on the American menu these days—the kind eaten as a formal first course at the table, with a knife and fork, and the finger snacks that go with cocktail parties or a before-dinner drink. There are potato specialties for all these occasions, ranging from an elegant Quiche and the Scandinavian-inspired Anchovy Casserole to "pigs" in potato pastry blankets, Potato Knishes, and the instant ease of frozen French Fries, zestfully seasoned for the occasion, and potato chips to escort bowls of savory dips. Remember that the purpose of a before-dinner appetizer is to whet the appetite, not satiate it, and regulate servings accordingly. But also remember that successful cocktail parties have a way of stretching into and beyond the dinner hour —and it is sometimes the better part of hospitality to provide a hearty and ample cocktail buffet that will take the place of dinner!

❧

FROZEN POTATO SNACKS

Use frozen French Fries (and the other bite-size deep-fried potato specialties you will find in the freezer case at your grocers) as cocktail snacks. The frozen puffs, nibbles, bites, or whatever they may be called are all essentially mixtures of potatoes and seasonings, usually bound with flour and egg. They probably will not need extra seasoning—taste and see—but you might want to add a dash of chili powder or paprika at serving time. To whet a guest's appetite, French Fries need the lift of salt and pepper, or seasoned salt (garlic, onion, or herb) or grated cheese. Serve any of these crisp nibbles with a dip—ketchup, seafood cocktail sauce, Russian dressing (half mayonnaise, half chili sauce), or with mayonnaise flavored with curry or mustard. Cook them in relays so that you can serve them hot, on hot canapé trays or over a candle-warmer on the table.

NEW POTATO SNACKS

Choose uniformly small new potatoes, allowing 3 or 4 for each guest. Wash and dry well. Stand each potato on its flat side—if necessary, slice off a bit to make the potato stand without rolling. Use a curved knife point, or the point of the floating-knife peeler, to hollow out the opposite side of the potato, making a tiny cup. Dip the potato cups into salad oil and sprinkle with salt and pepper. Fill the hollows with blue cheese or a bit of semicooked pork sausage or frankfurter. Bake at 400°F. until the potatoes are tender and browned, about 20 minutes. Serve hot.

ROLL-UP SNACKS

Spread thin slices of ham, bologna, dried beef, or salami with well-seasoned leftover mashed potatoes. Fasten the rolls with wooden picks. Broil until hot and sizzling. Serve with a mustard or ketchup dip, as hot hors d'oeuvre.

STUFFED PIGS

Slit cocktail frankfurters without separating the halves. Fill with well-seasoned mashed potatoes and fasten with a skewer. Put two franks on each skewer. Broil or bake until the potatoes are browned and hot. Serve with mayonnaise flavored with mustard to taste.

PIGS IN BLANKETS

2 *cups flour*
½ *tsp. salt*
  Dash cayenne or dry mustard
½ *cup hydrogenated shortening or lard*
½ *cup mashed potatoes*
  Cold water
1 *lb. cocktail frankfurters*

Season 2 cups flour with ½ teaspoon salt and a dash of cayenne or powdered mustard. Cut in ½ cup hydrogenated shortening or lard until the mixture looks like fine meal. Cut in ½ cup mashed potatoes—leftover potatoes will do very well for this. Add a very little ice-cold water, if necessary, to make it possible to press the crumbs into a dough. Roll out on a lightly floured board as thin as possible. Cut into strips as wide as the cocktail franks are long, and as long as necessary to cover them with a small overlap. Roll up a cooked cocktail sausage in each pastry blanket, press to seal the seam, and place on a baking sheet, seam-side down. Bake at 400°F. about 15 minutes, until the pastry is brown. Serve hot with a mustard dip.

Frozen History   Before 1945 no one had ever heard of commercially frozen French Fries. In 1968 they were number one, by a mile, among all frozen foods.

CORNISH PASTIES

Tender Pastry (see below)
2 *potatoes*
1 *cup finely chopped onion*
1 *lb. ground beef*
1 *Tbsp. chopped parsley*
Salt, pepper, Worcestershire sauce

Make Tender Pastry, below. Roll out, half at a time, on a lightly floured board and cut into 3-inch circles to make two-bite-size pasties. Peel and dice very small 2 medium-large raw potatoes (there should be about 1½ cups dice). Combine with 1 cup finely chopped onion and 1 pound ground beef (chuck has the best flavor). Add parsley and seasonings. The mixture should be well salted and highly spiced—add black or red pepper and Worcestershire sauce, or hot pepper sauce, or curry or chili powder, tasting as you go. Put a spoonful of this mixture on half of each pastry round. Fold and crimp the edges to seal the pasties. Bake at 375°F. about 45 minutes, until the crust is nicely browned. Good hot or cold, or reheated. Makes about 50 cocktail snacks. For lunch or supper, make 5-inch pasties. Better than sandwiches for a picnic!

TENDER PASTRY

2 *cups flour*
1 *tsp. salt*
1 *tsp. sugar*
1 *cup mashed potatoes*
¾ *cup shortening*

Toss 2 cups flour with 1 teaspoon each salt and sugar. Cut in 1 cup dry, cold mashed potatoes with a pastry blender or two knives until the mixture looks like coarse meal. Cut in ¾ cup shortening, in the same way. Press the crumbs together to make a ball of dough. If the mixture is too dry to form a ball—not very likely —add a very little ice water, drop by drop, to moisten it slightly. Makes an easy-to-roll pastry for any purpose.

CREAM CHEESE TURNOVERS

1 lb. potatoes
1 onion
1 Tbsp. chopped parsley
½ lb. cream cheese (Philadelphia-type)
½ cup milk
    Salt, pepper
    Pastry dough for 2-crust pie
    Melted butter

Cook 3 medium potatoes (1 pound) in boiling salted water to cover. Peel and mash. Chop or grate a small onion and add with 1 tablespoon chopped parsley. Soften ½ pound cream cheese at room temperature. Cream the cheese well and blend it with the potatoes. Gradually add ½ cup milk. The filling should be moist, but stiff enough to hold its shape. Season with salt and pepper to taste. Roll out pastry dough—any kind—and cut into small rounds. Put a spoonful of filling on half of each round, fold over, and crimp the edges to seal. Brush with melted butter and bake at 450°F. until richly browned. Top with a few red salmon roe, or with black caviar. Serves 8 or more as hors d'oeuvre. Good as a main dish at luncheon or supper, with sour cream and a salad.

ANCHOVY TURNOVERS

1½ *cups mashed potatoes*
1 *tsp. anchovy paste*
1 *tsp. lemon juice*
White pepper
Pastry dough for 2-crust pie

Season 1½ cups leftover mashed potatoes with 1 teaspoon or more anchovy paste, to taste. Add 1 teaspoon lemon juice and a little white pepper, but no additional salt. Roll out pie pastry, any kind, on a lightly floured board. Cut 2-inch rounds and put a spoonful of anchovy filling on each. Fold the rounds in half and pinch them closed. If necessary, moisten the edges of the rounds with water. Bake at 450°F. about 15 minutes, until well browned. Serve hot. Makes about 20 cocktail turnovers.

CHEESE CRACKERS

1 *cup mashed potatoes*
1 *cup flour*
½ *cup butter*
1 *egg*
1 *cup grated cheese*
Pepper, cayenne pepper
½ *tsp. salt*

Use freshly mashed or leftover potatoes—in either case they should be very dry. Blend with 1 cup flour. Soften ½ cup butter (1 stick) at room temperature and work it into the mixture with a fork or pastry blender. Add 1 egg, blend well, and add 1 cup grated Swiss or Cheddar cheese, or a combination. Season with pepper, cayenne pepper, and ½ teaspoon or more salt. Drop by small spoonfuls on a greased baking sheet and flatten lightly with a fork. Or force through a cooky press to make fancy shapes or fluted strips. Bake at 450°F. about 12 minutes, until the crackers begin to brown.

POTATO KNISHES

Pastry dough for 2-crust pie
1   *onion*
¼   *cup rendered chicken fat*
2   *cups mashed potatoes*
    Salt, black pepper

Use your favorite pie pastry recipe for a two-crust pie; or use strudel dough, puff pastry, philo, or thousand-leaf pastry, obtainable in Greek and near-Eastern groceries, or even biscuit dough. Roll the dough as thinly as possible on a floured board and cut it into 3-inch squares or rounds. To make the filling, chop 1 onion finely and sauté it until golden in ¼ cup rendered chicken fat. You can use butter or bacon fat, and the result will taste very good—but it will not be a knish. Add 2 cups hot or reheated mashed potatoes and blend well. Season generously with salt and black pepper (the mixture should be very spicy). Put a spoonful of potato on each round or square of dough, fold the dough over to enclose the filling, and press the edges to seal them. If necessary, moisten the edges and press them together with the tines of a fork. Bake at 450°F. about 15 minutes, to a rich brown. Serve hot.

LIVER KNISHES

Cook ¼ pound chicken livers with the onion, and chop or mash finely. Blend with the potatoes and proceed as directed.

Seasoning   Pinches of dried herbs—poultry seasoning, sage, thyme, oregano, basil—add a little something extra to mashed or baked stuffed potatoes.

SEEDY STICKS

  1 *cup mashed potatoes*
  1 *cup flour*
    Salt
½ *cup butter*
  1 *egg yolk*
  2 *Tbsp. milk*
  1 *Tbsp. caraway seeds*

Blend 1 cup rather dry mashed potatoes with 1 cup flour. Add salt if necessary. Soften 1 stick butter (¼ pound) at room temperature and work it into the potato mixture, to make a soft dough. Chill the dough until firm. Roll into a thin rectangle and transfer to a greased baking sheet. Beat an egg yolk with 2 tablespoons milk. Brush the dough with this, and sprinkle with salt and 1 tablespoon or more caraway seeds. Cut the dough with a sharp knife into sticks of the desired size. Bake at 400°F. about 12 minutes, until the fragile sticks are crisp and lightly browned.

FOR VARIETY: Use sesame or celery seeds instead of caraway, or make some of each kind.

QUICHE

1⅓ *cups dry mashed potatoes*
    Salt
  2 *Tbsp. flour*
¼ *cup butter*
  4 *ozs. Swiss or Cheddar cheese*
  3 *strips bacon*
½ *onion*
  2 *eggs*
½ *cup half-and-half, light cream, or milk*

Use about 1⅓ cups rather dry mashed potatoes; or cook 2 medium potatoes, cool, and grate or mash. Season with salt to taste. Work in 2 tablespoons flour and ¼ cup softened butter (½ stick), to make a firm but light dough. Grease and flour a shallow 9-inch pie plate. Press the dough evenly into the pie plate, building up the sides and fluting the rim. Chill. Toss 1 cup (4 ounces) grated Swiss or Cheddar cheese, or a combination, with 3 strips bacon, cooked until crisp and crumbled, and half a small onion, very finely slivered. Beat 2 eggs with ½ cup half-and-half, light cream, or milk. Combine with the cheese mixture and blend well. Pour into the chilled crust. Bake at 375°F. about 30 minutes, until the filling is set and the potato crust golden. Good warm or cold. Serves 6 to 8 as hors d'oeuvre, 4 to 6 at luncheon or supper, with a fruit or vegetable salad.

CODFISH CAKES

1 cup salt codfish
2 lbs. potatoes
1 egg
1 Tbsp. butter
1 Tbsp. chopped parsley
  Pepper
2 Tbsp. milk or cream

Shred 1 cup salt codfish and soak it for several hours in cold water. Peel and cut 6 medium potatoes (2 pounds) into small cubes. Drain the fish and add it to a generous amount of boiling water, along with the potatoes. Cook until the potatoes are tender. Drain well and mash. Beat in 1 egg, 1 tablespoon butter, 1 tablespoon finely minced parsley, and a little pepper to taste. Add up to 2 tablespoons milk or cream, a little at a time, to keep the mixture stiff enough to hold its shape. Form into small cakes and brown on both sides in hot butter or bacon fat. Serve with ketchup or tomato sauce, or with tartar sauce.

CODFISH BALLS: Shape the mixture into small balls and fry until brown in deep hot fat. Tiny codfish balls make fine hot hors d'oeuvre, with a chili-sauce dip.

117

COCKTAIL MEAT BALLS

1 lb. beef
½ lb. pork sausage meat
1 small potato
¼ onion
  Salt, pepper, sage

Have the butcher put 1 pound lean round steak through the grinder twice. Blend this with ½ pound bulk sausage meat. Peel 1 small raw potato and grate directly over the meat. Blend at once. Grate ¼ onion and add. Adjust seasoning to taste with salt, pepper, and sage. Shape bite-size balls and arrange on a foil-lined baking sheet. Bake 15 minutes at 375°F., until thoroughly cooked. Serve hot, on picks, with Chinese sweet-and-sour sauce or ketchup as a dip. Makes 40 or more meat balls.

HERRING HORS D'OEUVRE

2 or 3 pickled herring fillets
2 waxy potatoes
1 large apple
2 pickles
1 can (8 ozs.) diced pickled beets
½ onion
3 Tbsp. white wine vinegar
1 Tbsp. sugar
  Pepper
1 hard-cooked egg for garnish

(You can vary the proportions of ingredients in this recipe to suit your own taste—the quantities given are useful merely as a guide.)

Cut 2 pickled herring fillets into small pieces (or use a 12-ounce or 1-pound jar of fillets). Boil 2 potatoes in well-salted water, peel, and cut into small cubes. Core and dice a large, tart apple, but do not peel it. Dice 2 medium pickles, dilled or sweet. Drain and discard the liquid from a buffet-size can (1 cup) pickled beets. Grate half a small onion. Toss all together with 3 tablespoons white wine vinegar and 1 tablespoon sugar. If you used jar herring, the liquid can be used as dressing for the salad. Adjust the seasoning to taste with pepper. Shape the salad into a mound. Separately force the white and yellow of a hard-cooked egg through a sieve, and sprinkle on the salad. Makes 5 or more knife-and-fork hors d'oeuvre servings.

ANTIPASTO

    1 lb. potatoes
    1 Tbsp. lemon juice
    1 can tuna fish
    1 can tiny shrimp
    2 Tbsp. black olives
    ¼ cup mayonnaise
    ½ tsp. dried oregano
      Salt, pepper
    2 Tbsp. capers
    2 tomatoes
    8 radishes
    3 hard-cooked eggs
      Italian dressing

Cook 3 medium waxy potatoes (1 pound) in a small amount of boiling salted water. Peel and dice. Sprinkle with 1 tablespoon lemon juice. Drain and flake 1 can (about 7 ounces) solid-pack white tuna. Keep the flakes large. Drain a small can of shrimp— or use 1 cup or less cut up or small, freshly cooked shrimp. Drain 2 tablespoons sliced black olives. Toss fish, shrimp, and olives with the potatoes and add ¼ cup mayonnaise and ½ teaspoon oregano. Season to taste with salt, pepper, and more lemon juice, if desired. Pile the salad in the center of a serving platter. Sprinkle with 2 tablespoons capers. Peel and slice 2 large tomatoes and cut the slices in half. Trim 8 radishes and cut 3 hard-cooked eggs into slices or quarters. Use these to garnish the platter. Pass a bowl of salad dressing—the garlic-seasoned oil-and-vinegar Italian type is best—for guests to add to taste. Makes 6 to 8 antipasto servings. Serves 4 as a main dish at luncheon or supper.

ANCHOVY SAVORY

¼ cup fine bread crumbs
6 potatoes
2 cans (about 2 ozs. each) anchovy fillets
2 Tbsp. minced onion
3 Tbsp. melted butter

Butter a shallow 1-quart bake-and-serve casserole. Sprinkle with bread crumbs—tip and tap the bowl to retrieve extra crumbs. Peel and slice thinly 6 potatoes. Rinse and dry 2 cans anchovy fillets (the flat type). Put a layer of ⅓ the potatoes into the prepared baking dish, cover with half the anchovy fillets, 1 tablespoon minced onion, and ⅓ the remaining crumbs. Repeat, ending with potato slices and crumbs. Sprinkle with 3 tablespoons melted butter. Bake at 400°F., covered, until potatoes are tender, about 30 to 45 minutes. Serve in the baking dish. Makes 6 or more knife-and-fork servings, with before-dinner drinks; or serve as a first course at the table.

TIP: For a milder version of this savory, use only 1 can of anchovy fillets. Pour 2 cups milk over the layered potatoes, anchovy, and onion in a 6-cup casserole. Bake at 400°F., covered, for 30 minutes. Remove cover and bake until potatoes are tender, 15 to 30 minutes longer.

❧ 11
❧

Soups

There is a potato soup for every menu, every budget, and every occasion from an elegant formal dinner (see Vichyssoise) to a quick and hearty luncheon for hungry children home from school (Monday Lunch). There are potato soups that call for cream and eggs and expensive vegetables that put them in the luxury class (Asparagus Soup). And some soups, just as delicious, can be made with whatever is left in the vegetable bin at the end of the week (Old-fashioned Vegetable Chowder). There are thin, light potato soups to serve as appetizers, hearty potato soups to introduce a light meal, and substantial potato soups that are a meal in themselves. Sometimes potatoes are the main ingredient of the soup, sometimes they are an essential ingredient, and sometimes they are merely a thickener that adds a bonus in flavor and texture not supplied by other thickening agents.

It is hard to make a bad potato soup, and you may find it very easy to invent new, good potato soups if you use the recipes in this chapter as a rough guide to methods and ingredients.

TIP: Your pressure cooker will never be more useful than in the soup department!

VICHYSSOISE

2 Tbsp. butter
1 onion
3 leeks
4 potatoes
1 cup boiling water
1 can condensed chicken consommé
1 cup heavy cream
  Salt, white pepper
  Chives

Melt 2 tablespoons butter in a saucepan. Chop 1 onion and slice thinly the white parts only of 3 well-washed leeks. Cook both in butter until translucent. Peel and dice 4 potatoes and add with 1 cup salted boiling water. Simmer over low heat until the potatoes are very soft. Add 1 can consommé, undiluted, and heat to the boiling point. (You can use chicken bouillon cubes to make this broth—2 cubes to 1½ cups water.) Strain the soup, forcing the vegetables through the strainer; or whirl in a blender to make a smooth puree. Cool and chill. Add 1 cup heavy cream and adjust the seasoning, adding salt and white pepper to taste. Serve cold. Garnish with chopped chives, or, for a change, with a few paper-thin slices of young cucumber, with the peel.

FREEZER VICHYSSOISE

1 can frozen potato soup
  Milk
2 chicken bouillon cubes
  Chopped chives for garnish

Prepare 1 can frozen potato soup as directed on the can, adding with the milk, 2 chicken bouillon cubes or 2 teaspoons powdered chicken soup base. Serve chilled, sprinkled with chopped chives. A little finely grated young cucumber makes a good addition to any vichyssoise.

ASPARAGUS SOUP

1 *lb. asparagus*
3 *potatoes*
1 *qt. water*
  Salt
2 *Tbsp. butter*
2 *egg yolks*
½ *cup cream*

Wash 1 pound asparagus carefully and scrape the stalks if they seem tough (young, thin, all-green spears make the best soup and the best eating). Cut off and reserve about 1 inch of the tip ends to use as garnish for the finished soup. Cut the stalks into small pieces. Peel and dice 3 potatoes. Combine the vegetables in a saucepan with 1 quart water and a little salt. Bring to a boil and simmer until both are very tender. Add 2 tablespoons butter. Force the soup through a sieve or food mill, or whirl it in the blender. Cook the reserved asparagus tips separately, in a very little salted water, until they are just crackling tender. Just before serving, beat 2 eggs with ½ cup cream, warm with a little hot soup, and stir into the saucepan. Adjust the seasoning with salt and pepper to taste. Divide the asparagus tips among 6 soup cups, and serve piping hot. If you like a thinner soup, add milk.

MUSHROOM SOUP

    3 *potatoes*
    1 *onion*
    1 *stalk celery*
    2 *Tbsp. butter*
    2 *Tbsp. flour*
    4 *cups chicken broth*
    ½ *lb. small mushrooms*
       Salt, pepper
       Chopped parsley for garnish

Peel and dice 3 potatoes. Sliver 1 onion and 1 stalk celery. Add boiling water to cover and cook until tender. Meanwhile, melt 2 tablespoons butter, add 2 tablespoons flour, and cook, stirring, until the flour is lightly browned. Gradually stir in the liquid in which the potatoes were cooked and stir until smooth. Add the cooked vegetables, 4 cups hot chicken broth (canned or made with bouillon cubes), and ½ pound mushrooms. Cut the mushroom stems finely, but leave the little caps whole. Or use a small package of dried mushrooms, for a special touch. Simmer about 30 minutes. Taste and adjust the seasoning with salt and pepper. Serve sprinkled with parsley.

CABBAGE SOUP

    2 *Tbsp. butter*
    ½ *medium onion*
    1 *small cabbage*
    3 *potatoes*
    1 *cup boiling water*
    3 *cups light cream*
       Salt, pepper
       Croutons for garnish
       Paprika

Melt 2 tablespoons butter in a saucepan. Mince half a medium onion and cook in butter until translucent. Finely slice a small head of cabbage to make about 2 cups shreds. Peel and dice 3 potatoes. Add cabbage and potatoes to the saucepan with 1 cup boiling water and a little salt. Simmer over low heat until the potatoes are soft. Add 3 cups light cream and heat slowly. Adjust the seasoning with salt and pepper to taste. Float a few crisp croutons on each serving and garnish with a dash of paprika.

> *Borscht* The famous Slavic beet soup is always served with a freshly boiled potato in the plate. And it does not matter whether the Borscht is hot or cold, so long as the potato is hot.

CURRIED POTATO BISQUE

2 *Tbsp. butter*
2 *Tbsp. flour*
1 *tsp. curry powder*
3 *cups milk*
1½ *cups mashed potatoes*
2 *tsp. onion juice or grated onion*
Salt, pepper

Melt 2 tablespoons butter in a saucepan, stir in 2 tablespoons flour and 1 teaspoon curry powder, and cook for a minute, stirring constantly. Scald 3 cups milk and combine well with 1½ cups mashed potatoes. Stir this mixture into the roux, and cook slowly, stirring, until hot and smooth. Season with 2 teaspoons onion juice or grated onion, and salt and pepper to taste.

TIP: This bisque is very good without the curry, if curry is not a favorite at your house. If you like, finish it with a sprinkle of paprika, for color and extra flavor. Or use a seasoned salt instead of ordinary salt. Or add one or two chicken bouillon cubes or monosodium glutamate (a teaspoon or more).

POTAGE PRINTANIERE

3 *potatoes*
5 *cups water*
Salt, pepper, nutmeg
1 *pkg. frozen peas and carrots*
½ *cup hot milk*
2 *Tbsp. butter*
Chopped chives or parsley for garnish

Peel and dice 3 potatoes and cook until very tender, about 30 minutes, in 5 cups lightly salted water. Force the mixture through a sieve or food mill, or whirl it in a blender to make a smooth puree. Season to taste with more salt, pepper, and a grating of fresh nutmeg. Add 1 package (about 10 ounces) frozen peas and carrots or cut green beans and cook until the vegetables are tender. Add ½ cup milk and 2 tablespoons butter. Serve garnished with chopped chives or parsley. Other vegetables, fresh or frozen, may be substituted for the peas and carrots (tiny new peas are especially good).

CREAM OF VEGETABLE SOUP

¼ *cup butter*
2 *potatoes*
2 *carrots*
2 *onions*
2 *stalks celery*
1 *thin slice cooked ham*
4 *cups chicken broth*
2 *egg yolks*
1 *cup light cream*
Salt, white pepper
Parsley for garnish

Melt ¼ cup butter. Peel and dice 2 potatoes and 2 carrots. Slice 2 onions. Cut 2 stalks celery into diagonal slivers. Cut 1 slice ham (about 1 ounce) into thin slivers. Toss all in melted butter over low heat for a few minutes. Add 4 cups chicken broth (home-made, diluted canned, or made with bouillon cubes) and bring to a boil. Simmer ½ hour. Beat 2 egg yolks with 1 cup light cream or milk, add a little hot soup to the mixture to warm it, and stir into the soup. Heat without boiling. Taste and adjust seasoning with salt and white pepper. Serve sprinkled with chopped parsley.

CREAM OF ONION SOUP

2 *potatoes*
1 *leek*
2 *large onions*
  Parsley sprigs
4 *cups water*
  Salt, pepper
2 *Tbsp. butter*
½ *cup cream*
  Chopped parsley for garnish

Peel and dice 2 potatoes. Wash the white part of 1 leek thoroughly and cut it into thin slices. Cut 1 large onion into dice. Combine the vegetables in a saucepan with a few sprigs of parsley, 4 cups water, and a little salt and pepper. Bring to a boil and simmer 30 minutes, until the vegetables are soft. Force through a sieve or food mill, or whirl in an electric blender. Meanwhile, cut a second large onion into thin slices. Melt 2 tablespoons butter and cook the onion gently until it is translucent and beginning to turn golden. Add onion and butter to the puree and simmer all together 5 minutes. Heat ½ cup cream and stir into the soup. Adjust the seasoning with salt and pepper to taste. Sprinkle with chopped parsley.

TIP: Thicken this soup (or any soup) with a tablespoon or more potato starch mixed to a paste with a little cold liquid.

TURNIP SOUP

1½ *lbs. turnips*
1½ *lbs. potatoes*
6 *cups water*
1 *tsp. salt*
2 *cups milk*
3 *Tbsp. butter*
 Salt, pepper
 Chopped parsley for garnish

Peel and dice 1½ pounds each young turnips and potatoes (4 medium-large). Cover with 6 cups boiling water and add 1 teaspoon salt. Boil for 35 minutes, or until the potatoes have fallen apart. Beat with a rotary beater to make a smooth mixture. If the turnips are not young, it may be necessary to force the soup through a sieve, and discard the stringy hard bits. Add 2 cups milk, or more if the soup seems thick, and 3 tablespoons butter. Heat gently and adjust the seasoning with salt and pepper to taste. Sprinkle with finely chopped parsley.

CHEDDAR CHEESE SOUP

4 *potatoes*
2 *slices bacon*
1 *small onion*
2 *tsp. flour*
3 *cups milk*
¼ *lb. Cheddar cheese*
2 *tsp. celery salt*
 Pepper, Worcestershire sauce
 Parsley for garnish

Peel, dice, and cook 4 potatoes in a very small amount of salted water until very tender. Put through a sieve with the liquid, or whirl in a blender, or force through a ricer. Dice 2 slices bacon and brown in a saucepan. Remove bacon with a slotted spoon and drain it. In the fat in the skillet cook 1 onion, finely chopped, until translucent. Stir in 2 teaspoons flour and cook a minute, stirring. Bring 3 cups milk to the boiling point and gradually stir it into the roux. Grate or shred 4 ounces Cheddar cheese (there will be 1 cup shredded cheese) and add. Stir until the cheese melts. Add 2 teaspoons celery salt and the potatoes with their liquid and heat to the boiling point. Adjust the seasoning with pepper and Worcestershire sauce to taste. Sprinkle with bacon bits and chopped parsley.

GOLDEN VEGETABLE SOUP

3 Tbsp. butter
1 onion
5 carrots
2 potatoes
4 cups water
1 Tbsp. monosodium glutamate
    Salt, pepper
    Chopped parsley for garnish

Melt 3 tablespoons butter in a saucepan. Finely chop 1 onion and cook in the butter for a few minutes, until translucent but not brown. Peel and thinly slice 5 carrots. Add to the saucepan and cook in the butter a few minutes, stirring occasionally to prevent browning. Peel and dice 2 potatoes and add with 4 cups water. Bring to a boil, reduce the heat, and simmer for 1 hour. Add 1 tablespoon monosodium glutamate and salt and pepper to taste. This soup may be forced through a sieve, or whirled in a blender to make a puree. Serve garnished with a little chopped parsley or a pinch of oregano.

OLD-FASHIONED VEGETABLE CHOWDER

2 ozs. salt pork
3 potatoes
3 carrots
½ medium turnip
1 onion
1 stalk celery
1 green pepper
   Salt, pepper
2 Tbsp. butter
2 Tbsp. flour
2 cups milk
   Chopped parsley for garnish

Cut 2 ounces fat salt pork into uniform small dice; or use 3 strips of bacon, diced. Brown until crisp in a saucepan. Peel and uniformly dice 3 potatoes, 3 carrots, and half a medium turnip. Chop 1 onion and cut 1 stalk celery into diagonal slivers. Clean pith and seeds from a green pepper and cut into strips. Add all the vegetables to the saucepan, sprinkle with salt and pepper, and brown lightly, stirring often to prevent scorching. Add 2 cups or more boiling water to cover, bring to a boil, and simmer until the vegetables are tender, about 30 minutes. Meanwhile, melt 2 tablespoons butter in a small pan, stir in 2 tablespoons flour, and cook until golden, stirring constantly. Gradually add 2 cups milk and continue to cook and stir until the sauce is smooth and slightly thickened. Stir this sauce into the finished chowder. Taste and adjust the seasoning with salt, pepper, and monosodium glutamate (optional). Float a pat of butter on each serving and sprinkle with chopped parsley.

The Famine Ireland was the first European country to recognize the potential of the potato, and for a century and a half it was the country's most important food crop. In 1847, after a succession of potato crop failures, the Irish faced famine and the great mass immigration to America began. That ill wind blew a million and a half Irishmen to our shores.

MONDAY LUNCH

3 *potatoes*
½ *onion*
1 *stalk celery*
1 *cup boiling water*
1 *tsp. salt*
4 *frankfurters*
2 *cups milk*
2 *Tbsp. butter*
  Cayenne, black pepper
  Paprika

Peel and cut 3 medium potatoes into small dice. Grate or dice ½ onion. Sliver 1 stalk celery, with the green. Combine in a saucepan with 1 cup boiling water and 1 teaspoon salt. Cover and simmer about 20 to 25 minutes, until potatoes are so tender that they fall apart. Mash slightly. Slice 4 frankfurters and add. Stir in 2 cups milk and 2 tablespoons butter and heat slowly to the boiling point. Adjust the seasoning, adding cayenne and black pepper to taste. Sprinkle each serving with a little paprika or with chopped parsley or chives. Makes 4 main-dish servings.

CORN CHOWDER

4 *strips bacon*
1 *onion*
3 *large potatoes*
2 *cups water*
1 *can (about 12 ozs.) kernel corn*
3 *cups milk*
  Salt, pepper

Dice 4 strips bacon and fry in a saucepan until crisp. Drain and set aside. Chop 1 onion and cook in the bacon fat until translucent. Meanwhile, peel and dice 3 large potatoes and cook in 2 cups water, lightly salted, until tender. Add the onion and the contents of a 12-ounce can of vacuum-packed whole-kernel corn (the type packed with bits of green and red pepper makes a very colorful chowder). Add 3 cups milk and heat slowly, stirring occasionally, until soup is piping hot. Adjust seasoning to taste with salt and pepper. Sprinkle with bacon bits as a garnish.

BOSTON CLAM CHOWDER

2 *Tbsp. bacon fat*
1 *large onion*
4 *potatoes*
1 *cup water*
2 *cans minced clams (10 ozs. each)*
1 *qt. milk*
  Salt, celery salt, pepper

Heat 2 tablespoons bacon fat in a saucepan and add 1 large onion, chopped fine. Cook only until the onion is translucent, not browned. Peel and cut into small dice 4 medium-large potatoes— there should be about 3 cups dice. Add to saucepan with a little salt and about 1 cup water, enough to cover. Simmer until potatoes are tender. Add 2 cans clams and their liquid (or approximately the same amount of canned crabmeat or lobster) and 1 quart milk. Heat very slowly to the boiling point and simmer 5 minutes. Adjust the seasoning with salt, celery salt, and pepper. Makes 10 servings. If you wish, thicken the chowder with a paste made by rubbing 1 tablespoon each butter and flour together. Add this paste bit by bit to the chowder, until the desired thickness is reached. The French, who invented this thickening method, call the paste *beurre manié*, or kneaded butter.

MANHATTAN CLAM CHOWDER

3 *potatoes*
1 *cup water*
  Salt
2 *strips bacon*
1 *onion*
½ *green pepper*
2 *stalks celery*
1 *cup tomato puree*
1 *can minced clams*
  Thyme, pepper, sugar

Peel 3 medium potatoes and cut into cubes. Add boiling water to cover, about 1 cup, and a little salt, and cook until just tender. Meanwhile, dice 2 strips bacon and cook in a saucepan until the fat begins to melt. Chop 1 onion, half a green pepper, and 2 stalks celery and cook until the onion is translucent but not brown. Add 1 can (8 ounces) tomato puree (the lightly seasoned puree, not tomato sauce), the liquid drained from 1 can (10½ ounces) chopped minced clams, and the potatoes and their liquid. Simmer for a few minutes to blend. Season with a generous pinch of thyme, and salt, pepper, and a very little sugar, to taste. Add the clams and heat quickly.

FRIDAY CHOWDER

1 *large potato*
2 *medium carrots*
2 *cups water*
1 *tsp. salt*
½ *tsp. monosodium glutamate*
½ *lb. fish fillets*
2 *strips bacon*
½ *onion*
1½ *Tbsp. flour*
1 *cup milk*
   Hot pepper sauce

Peel and dice small 1 large potato and 2 medium carrots. Cover with 2 cups water. Add 1 teaspoon salt and ½ teaspoon monosodium glutamate, bring to a boil, and simmer, covered, for 10 minutes. Cut ½ pound fresh or frozen fish—use cod, flounder, or similar fish—into smallish pieces and add. Cook 5 minutes longer. Meanwhile, cut 2 strips bacon into small pieces and cook in a small skillet until crisp and brown. Remove the bacon from the pan with a slotted spoon and set it aside to use as a garnish for the chowder. Cook ½ onion, chopped, in the bacon fat, until translucent. Stir in 1½ tablespoons flour and cook a minute or two, stirring constantly, without letting the roux brown. Gradually stir in 1 cup milk. Continue to cook, stirring, until the mixture is smooth and thickened. Add this sauce to the potato mixture. Simmer all together for 10 minutes, over very low heat. Stir often to prevent scorching. Serve in deep bowls, with crisp bacon bits. Makes 4 servings.

❦ 12
❦

Potato
Salads

There are as many good recipes for potato salad as there are good cooks—or maybe more. And there are also many good recipes for salads that have potatoes as an important ingredient, if not as the principal ingredient. The potato's pleasant texture and accommodating mildness make it go well with almost everything. You can safely give your imagination free rein in composing a potato salad that is uniquely your own. As a beginning, you might want to note the following facts:

1. Two pounds of potatoes make about 4 cups of cubes or slices; in a simple salad this will serve 5 or 6 people. Added ingredients mean additional servings, of course.
2. You will need ½ to 1 cup mayonnaise or other dressing for 2 pounds potatoes, or more when you add sizable quantities of other ingredients—hard-cooked egg, celery, etc.—to the mixture.
3. Since potatoes vary greatly in their absorptive power, be prepared to adjust the amount of dressing.

4. Potatoes do not thrive on chilling, in the raw state or in a salad. If you must refrigerate a potato salad, remove it from the refrigerator half an hour before dinner so that you can serve it at room temperature. The best potato salads are mixed and dressed while the potatoes are still warm, and served cooled but not chilled. Leftover potatoes can make very satisfactory hot potato salad, with a hot dressing. They are not suitable for cold potato salad, since cold potatoes will not properly absorb cold salad dressing.

A WORD OF WARNING: Some potatoes simply will not hold up in a potato salad—if the potatoes begin to fall apart as you cook them, they will definitely not cut neatly and will crumble when you try to toss them with the dressing. For firm slices choose waxy potatoes rather than mealy types.

CLASSIC POTATO SALAD

2 lbs. potatoes
1 small onion
½ cup vinegar-and-oil salad dressing
Salt, pepper
1 cup mayonnaise
2 Tbsp. chopped parsley

Boil 6 waxy potatoes (2 pounds) in boiling salted water to cover. Peel and cut into uniform pieces, cubes, dice, or small slices. Grate or mince a small onion and add. Toss with ½ cup salad dressing, your own or any of the bottled dressings made with a vinegar-and-oil base—that is, French style or Italian style. Season with salt and pepper and let stand in a cool but not cold place for half an hour or more. Toss once or twice more to distribute the dressing. If any dressing is not absorbed, pour it off. Add about 1 cup mayonnaise, or just enough to coat the potatoes. Sprinkle with 2 tablespoons chopped parsley and serve at room temperature.

FOR VARIETY: To the salad mixture add small amounts of chopped cucumber; red or green pepper; tomato; celery; black, green, or pimiento-stuffed green olives; dill or sweet pickle (or pickle relish); watercress, or capers. Vary seasonings with mustard or mustard seed; celery salt or celery seed; chopped green onion tops or chives. Mix the mayonnaise with chili sauce or ketchup to taste; or mix it half and half with sour cream and a dash of lemon juice. Hard-cooked eggs have a natural affinity for potato salad, whether they are chopped and mixed with the potatoes, or sliced or cut into wedges and used as a garnish. Or grate the whites and yolks of the eggs separately, mix the whites with chopped parsley, and sprinkle both on the salad in an attractive pattern.

HERBAL POTATO SALAD

2 lbs. potatoes
2 Tbsp. chopped chives or green onions
⅔ cup mayonnaise
Milk
Salt, white pepper
2 Tbsp. chopped parsley
2 Tbsp. chopped mint

Cook 6 medium, waxy potatoes (2 pounds) in boiling salted water to cover. Cool slightly, peel, and cut into cubes. Sprinkle with 2 tablespoons chopped chives or green onion tops. Thin ⅔ cup mayonnaise with enough milk to make a pourable mixture, and pour it over the potatoes. Toss gently and add salt and white pepper to taste. Mix 2 tablespoons each chopped fresh parsley and chopped fresh mint leaves and sprinkle over salad. The first time you make this salad, you might want to reduce the amount of fresh mint you use—once you have tasted this exotic combination, you will probably want to increase it!

PICNIC POTATO SALAD

2 lbs. potatoes
2 hard-cooked eggs
½ sweet onion
1 cucumber
3 Tbsp. vinegar
⅔ cup evaporated milk
2 tsp. prepared mustard
1 Tbsp. celery seed
  Salt, pepper
  Cherry tomatoes, gherkins for garnish

Cook 6 waxy potatoes (2 pounds) until tender in boiling salted water to cover. Peel and cut into cubes. Coarsely chop 2 hard-cooked eggs. Cut half a small red onion into thin rings. Dice a cucumber. Combine lightly.

DRESSING: Stir 3 tablespoons vinegar into ⅔ cup evaporated milk. Season with 2 teaspoons prepared mustard, 1 tablespoon celery seed, and salt and pepper to taste. Gently toss the salad mixture with the dressing. Chill. Pack in plastic refrigerator containers and carry to a picnic in an insulated iced bag, if possible, although this kind of dressing is safe for a picnic even without refrigeration. Pack cherry tomatoes and gherkins separately to serve as a garnish.

POTATO SALAD ROLL

4 hard-cooked eggs
1 Tbsp. mayonnaise
2 Tbsp. chopped green pepper
  Salt, pepper, cayenne
  Mashed potato salad

Mash 4 hard-cooked eggs, moisten with 1 tablespoon mayonnaise, or enough to make a paste, and add 2 tablespoons finely chopped green pepper and salt, pepper, and cayenne to taste. Prepare Mashed Potato Salad (next page), reserving the chives. Spread 1-inch thick on a rectangle of waxed paper. Cover with the egg mixture and roll as you would a jelly roll, lifting the waxed paper. Sprinkle with the chopped chives, chill thoroughly, and slice to serve.

VINTNER'S POTATO SALAD

2 *lbs. potatoes*
1 *cucumber*
2 *green onions*
1 *cup thinly sliced celery*
1½ *cups dry white wine*
4 *hard-cooked eggs*
½ *cup mayonnaise*
2 *Tbsp. prepared mustard*
1 *Tbsp. lemon juice*
Salt, pepper

Cook 6 medium, waxy potatoes (2 pounds) in a small amount of boiling salted water until tender. Cool slightly, peel, and cut into cubes. Thinly slice 1 cucumber, with the green peel if possible (this is *not* possible if the cucumber is old and tough-skinned, or if the skin is protected with wax). Chop 2 large scallions, including the green parts. Add both to the potatoes with 1 cup thinly sliced celery. Cover with 1½ cups dry white wine. Let stand in a cool place for about an hour, or until serving time. If any wine is not absorbed, drain it off and reserve it for another cooking use. Add 4 hard-cooked eggs, coarsely chopped. Make a dressing by mixing ½ cup mayonnaise with 2 teaspoons prepared mustard and 1 tablespoon lemon juice. Gently combine the dressing with the salad and add salt and pepper to taste. Yields generous servings for 6 or more.

MASHED POTATO SALAD

2 cups mashed potatoes
½ cup mayonnaise
1 cup slivered celery
¼ cup chopped black olives
1 Tbsp. mustard
   Salt, pepper
   Chopped chives

Moisten 2 cups mashed potatoes with ½ cup mayonnaise or more. Add 1 cup finely slivered celery and ¼ cup chopped black olives. Season with prepared mustard to taste—from 1 teaspoon to 1 tablespoon. Adjust the seasoning with salt and pepper. Serve sprinkled with chopped chives.

OLD-FASHIONED MASHED POTATO SALAD

2 lbs. all-purpose potatoes
1 egg
3 Tbsp. wine vinegar
1 tsp. sugar
1 tsp. salt
2 Tbsp. cream
1 green pepper
½ small onion
   Salt, pepper, prepared mustard

Cook 6 potatoes (2 pounds) in boiling salted water to cover. Peel and mash. While the potatoes are cooking, combine 1 egg, 3 tablespoons vinegar, and 1 teaspoon each sugar and salt in the top of a double boiler over hot water. Cook, stirring frequently, until thickened. Add 2 tablespoons cream. Chop together a small green pepper and half a small onion. Combine with the potatoes. Add the hot dressing and blend well. Adjust the seasoning with salt and pepper. Serve hot.

POTATO SALAD MOLD

1 *lb. potatoes*
  Juice of ½ lemon
2 *Tbsp. grated onion*
  Salt, pepper
1 *envelope gelatin*
¼ *cup water*
1 *Tbsp. sugar*
¾ *cup mayonnaise*
1 *cup sour cream*
¼ *cup stuffed olives*
2 *Tbsp. chopped parsley*
2 *stalks celery, slivered*

Cook 3 medium, waxy potatoes (1 pound) in a small amount of boiling salted water. Peel, cut into dice, and sprinkle with the juice of ½ lemon, 2 tablespoons grated onion, and a little salt and pepper. Soak 1 envelope plain, unflavored gelatin in ¼ cup water in a small saucepan until it swells, about 5 minutes. Add 1 tablespoon sugar and stir over hot water about 3 minutes, until the gelatin dissolves and the mixture is clear. Stir the gelatin into ¾ cup mayonnaise and 1 cup dairy sour cream (an 8-ounce container). Combine well. Stir in ¼ cup sliced pimiento-stuffed green olives and 2 tablespoons chopped parsley. Sliver 2 stalks celery and add. Carefully fold in the prepared potatoes. Taste and add salt and pepper. Oil a 1-quart ring mold and fill it with the salad mixture. Chill until firm. To serve, unmold on salad greens and garnish with tomato wedges and green-pepper rings. The center of the ring may be filled with cole slaw or another salad.

Boon for Dieters Low-calorie salad dressings, now on the market in many flavors, are the best thing that ever happened to a diet. Use them as sauce for baked or boiled potatoes, as dressing for potato salad, as a seasoning for mashed or baked stuffed potatoes, and as a dip for potato meat balls.

BLUE-CHEESE POTATO SALAD

2 *lbs. potatoes*
2 *scallions*
2 *stalks celery*
2 *Tbsp. chopped parsley*
2 *ozs. blue cheese*
1 *cup dairy sour cream*
2 *Tbsp. lemon juice*
  Pepper, salt

Cook 6 medium, waxy potatoes (2 pounds) in their skins in boiling salted water to cover. Cool, peel, and dice coarsely. Chop 2 scallions with the green parts, and sliver 2 stalks celery. Sprinkle on potatoes with 2 tablespoons chopped fresh parsley.

DRESSING: Crumble 2 ounces blue cheese to make ½ cup. Add 1 cup sour cream (½ pint container) and 2 tablespoons lemon juice. Taste and add a dash of pepper and a little salt if desired, but be careful—the blue cheese may be very spicy. Toss the dressing with the salad and let all mellow in the refrigerator for several hours. Remove from the refrigerator half an hour before serving.

GERMAN POTATO SALAD

2 *lbs. potatoes*
1 *stalk celery*
1 *small dill pickle*
1 *scallion*
¼ *cup vinegar*
3 *Tbsp. salad oil*
  Salt, pepper, paprika
  Chopped parsley

Cook 2 pounds waxy potatoes (6 medium) in boiling salted water to cover. A stalk of celery, with the leaves, added to the water to improve the flavor, is particularly appropriate for this salad. Cool slightly, peel, and cut into small, thickish slices. Finely chop a small dill pickle. Mince 1 scallion, or substitute 2 tablespoons minced sweet red onion or 1 tablespoon chopped chives. Mix ¼ cup vinegar with 3 tablespoons salad oil, add the chopped pickle and onion, and season to taste with salt and pepper. Pour this mixture over the warm potatoes, cover the bowl, and let stand in a warm place to absorb the dressing. Sprinkle with paprika and a little chopped parsley. Serve at room temperature or warm—not chilled.

SPANISH POTATO SALAD

2 lbs. potatoes
3 Tbsp. olive oil
¼ cup lemon juice
1 small clove garlic
   Salt, pepper
2 tomatoes
1 green pepper

Cook 2 pounds waxy potatoes (6 medium) in their skins in salted boiling water to cover. Cool slightly, peel, and cut into slices. Combine 3 tablespoons olive oil with ¼ cup lemon juice. Other oils can be used, but olive oil will give the salad a typically Spanish taste. Mince finely a small clove of garlic, or force it through a garlic press. Add to the dressing, along with salt and pepper to taste. Pour over the still-warm potato slices and toss very gently. Spread on a shallow platter and cool. Peel 2 well-chilled tomatoes by dipping them for a moment into boiling water to loosen the skins. Slice thin. Scoop out the pith and seeds of a large green pepper and cut thin rings. Use tomato slices and green pepper rings to garnish the salad.

PENNSYLVANIA DUTCH HOT POTATO SALAD

2 *lbs. potatoes*
4 *strips bacon*
1 *onion*
1 *green pepper*
¼ *cup vinegar*
1 *tsp. salt*
1 *tsp. sugar*
  Pepper
1 *egg*
3 *hard-cooked eggs*
½ *carrot*

Cook 6 medium, waxy potatoes (2 pounds) in boiling salted water to cover. Peel and cut into uniform cubes. Meanwhile, dice 4 strips bacon and brown in a skillet. Remove and reserve bacon bits. Chop 1 medium onion and 1 medium green pepper and cook in bacon fat until onion is translucent. Add ¼ cup vinegar, 1 teaspoon each salt and sugar, and a dash of pepper. Beat 1 egg lightly, warm with a little of the vinegar, and stir into the pan. Cook for a minute, stirring constantly, until the dressing is smooth. Add 3 hard-cooked eggs, coarsely chopped, and half a carrot, grated. Pour the dressing over the warm potatoes. Sprinkle with crisp bacon and serve hot.

WALDORF SALAD

1 *lb. potatoes*
1 *cup dairy sour cream*
¼ *cup lemon juice*
1 *tsp. salt*
  Pepper
1 *large tart red apple*
2 *stalks celery*
½ *cup walnut meats*

Boil 3 medium, waxy potatoes (1 pound) in boiling salted water to cover. Cool slightly, peel, and cut into dice. Combine 1 cup sour cream (½ pint container) with ¼ cup lemon juice, 1 teaspoon salt, and a dash of pepper. Pour over potatoes and toss lightly. Chop a large tart red apple without peeling it, but discard core and seeds. Cut 2 stalks of celery into thin slivers. Add apple and celery to the potatoes with ½ cup broken walnut or pecan meats, and toss again. Serve cool, but not ice cold. Serve on lettuce leaves, with a dab of mayonnaise if desired.

COTTAGE CHEESE SALAD

1½ *lbs. potatoes*
2 *Tbsp. salad dressing*
2 *hard-cooked eggs*
1½ *cups cottage cheese*
2 *Tbsp. sour cream*
1 *green pepper*
3 *scallions*
1 *carrot*
Salt, pepper, cayenne
Parsley, pimiento

Cook 4 medium-large, waxy potatoes (1½ pounds) in boiling salted water to cover. Peel, cut into small slices, and season with 2 tablespoons Italian-style salad dressing, or with 1 tablespoon each oil and lemon juice and salt and pepper to taste. Set aside in a cool place. Remove the yolks from 2 hard-cooked eggs, cutting the whites neatly so that they can be used later to make a decorative garnish. Mash the yolks and combine them with 1½ cups cottage cheese (a 12-ounce container) and 2 tablespoons or more sour cream, to make a moist but not runny mixture. Add a small, finely slivered green pepper, 3 scallions chopped with the green, and 1 small carrot, grated. Adjust the seasoning with salt, pepper, and cayenne to taste. Chill until serving time. Spoon the cheese over the potatoes and garnish with strips or fancy shapes cut from the egg white, chopped parsley, and strips of pimiento, if desired.

CHEESE SALAD

1 lb. potatoes
2 Tbsp. chopped onion
½ cup slivered celery
   Small jar sweet pickles
¼ lb. Cheddar cheese
2 hard-cooked eggs
½ cup mayonnaise
   Salt, pepper

Cook 3 medium, waxy potatoes (1 pound) in boiling salted water to cover. Peel and cut into cubes. Sprinkle with 2 tablespoons chopped onion and ½ cup slivered celery. Drain ¼ cup liquid from a jar of sweet pickles—gherkins or "bread-and-butter" pickles are best. Moisten the potatoes with this liquid and set aside to cool. At serving time, cut ¼ pound Cheddar cheese into 1 cup very tiny cubes (you can use another cheese, if you prefer, so long as it is not the processed type). Grate or chop 2 hard-cooked eggs. Add cheese and egg to the potato mixture, and toss with ½ cup or more mayonnaise. Taste and add more salt and pepper, as desired. Garnish with sliced gherkins or pickle slices. This is a particularly good potato salad to serve in small portions with sliced ham or other cold meats.

ZUCCHINI SALAD

4 Tbsp. olive oil
   Garlic clove
4 zucchini squash
   Salt, pepper
½ tsp. dried basil
2 lbs. potatoes
1 cup Italian-style salad dressing
1 can (8 ozs.) pitted black olives

Heat 4 tablespoons olive oil in a skillet with a garlic clove. Discard the garlic. Scrub and slice 4 young zucchini—the green-striped summer squash. Do not peel them. Sprinkle with salt and pepper and cook gently in the hot oil until they begin to look translucent. Sprinkle with ½ teaspoon dried basil, or 2 teaspoons fresh minced basil leaves. Cool slightly. Meanwhile, cook 6 medium, waxy potatoes (2 pounds) in boiling salted water to cover. Cool slightly, peel, and cut into small, chunky slices. Cover the warm potatoes with about 1 cup Italian-style salad dressing. Combine with the squash and whatever oil remains in the skillet and toss gently. Taste and add salt and pepper. Drain a small can of pitted ripe olives—the smallest, least expensive olives do nicely—and sprinkle over the salad.

HARLEQUIN SALAD

2 *lbs. potatoes*
1 *cup Italian-style salad dressing*
1 *can (8 ozs.) cubed beets*
2 *Tbsp. piccalilli*
12 *green or black olives*
2 *canned pimientos*
3 *hard-cooked eggs*

Cook 6 medium, waxy potatoes (2 pounds) in salted boiling water to cover. Peel and cut into uniform cubes. While the potatoes are still warm, pour over them 1 cup Italian-style salad dressing, or your favorite oil-and-vinegar dressing, well-seasoned with salt, pepper, and mustard, if desired. Keep in a cool place—not the refrigerator—until just before serving. Drain and add 1 cup cubed beets, plain or pickled as you like, along with about 2 tablespoons well-drained piccalilli or sweet pickle relish or corn relish. Chop or slice a dozen green or black olives and 2 canned pimientos. Combine with potatoes and toss gently to mix. Mound salad in a lettuce-lined bowl. Grate 3 hard-cooked eggs, whites and yolks separately, and sprinkle on salad as garnish.

RUSSIAN SALAD

1 *pkg. frozen cut green beans*
1 *pkg. frozen peas and carrots*
1 *lb. potatoes*
  Bottled salad dressing
2 *cups diced cooked meat*
1 *can (8 ozs.) diced beets*
  Salt, pepper

Cook separately 1 package (about 10 ounces) each frozen cut green beans (not the "Frenched" style) and frozen peas and carrots until just tender and still crisp. Drain. Cook 3 potatoes (1 pound) in boiling salted water to cover. Peel and dice. Combine the warm vegetables and pour over them enough bottled French dressing, or the clear Italian type, to moisten well. Add 2 cups diced cooked meat—leftover roast beef, veal or lamb, ham, or tongue are all good, as are turkey and chicken—and let stand in a cool place for an hour or longer. Pour off any excess dressing before serving, or add more dressing, if necessary. Drain a small can of diced beets (1 cup) and toss with the salad at serving time. Adjust the seasoning with salt and pepper. Top with mayonnaise, if desired.

HAM SALAD

1½ *lbs. potatoes*
  1 *Tbsp. grated onion*
  ¾ *cup French dressing*
  1 *tsp. prepared mustard*
  1 *lb. cooked ham*
  1 *cucumber*
  1 *tomato*
    Salt, pepper, paprika

Cook 4 medium-large potatoes (1½ pounds) in boiling salted water to cover. Peel and dice. Sprinkle with 1 tablespoon grated onion. Blend ¾ cup French dressing with 1 teaspoon prepared mustard and pour it over the potatoes. Cut 1 pound cooked ham into bite-size cubes. This is a fine use for leftover ham, or for bologna, frankfurters, or similar meats. Toss the meat with the potatoes. Let cool. At serving time, add a chilled cucumber, diced, and a chilled tomato, peeled and diced. Toss gently and adjust the seasoning with salt, pepper, and paprika. Makes 6 or more hearty main-dish servings.

FOR VARIETY: Substitute dill pickle—preferably the half-sour new-dill type—for the fresh cucumber. Add a little chopped green or red pepper, or a few chopped pimiento-stuffed olives. Garnish with chopped hard-cooked egg. Just before serving, top the salad with mayonnaise.

CRABMEAT SALAD

2 *lbs. potatoes*
1 *lb. crabmeat*
1 *large cucumber*
¾ *cup mayonnaise*
¼ *cup chili sauce*
  Lettuce
2 *hard-cooked eggs*
2 *tomatoes*

Cook 6 medium, waxy potatoes (2 pounds) in boiling salted water to cover. Peel and cut into uniform cubes. Pick over about 1 pound crabmeat (canned, frozen, or fresh) and discard any bits of shell or membrane. (You can use less crabmeat for an economical salad.) Cut a large cucumber into dice, peeling it only if the shell has been waxed. Combine potatoes, crabmeat, and cucumber. Blend ¾ cup mayonnaise with ¼ cup chili sauce, add to the salad mixture, and toss. Mound on lettuce leaves and garnish with 2 hard-cooked eggs, cut into quarters, and 2 tomatoes, peeled and cut into eighths. Makes 6 hearty main-dish servings.

SALMON SALAD

 1 *lb. potatoes*
 1 *can (1 lb.) salmon*
 ½ *cup French dressing*
   Salt, pepper
 1 *cucumber*
 1 *stalk celery*

Cook 3 medium, waxy potatoes (1 pound) in boiling salted water to cover. Peel and dice. Drain and flake 1 can salmon (1 pound), discarding any bones and skin. Combine potatoes and salmon, and add ½ cup French dressing, plus salt and pepper to taste. Let the salad stand at least half an hour in a cool place. At serving time, thinly slice 1 cucumber and 1 stalk celery, add, and toss gently. Or use 1 cup cooked, cold green peas instead of the cucumber and celery. Add a little mayonnaise, if desired.

GOLDEN SALMON SALAD

 2 *lbs. potatoes*
 1 *small onion*
 2 *Tbsp. chopped parsley*
 1 *cup diced celery*
 2 *Tbsp. light cream*
 2 *Tbsp. prepared mustard*
 2 *Tbsp. sugar*
 2 *Tbsp. vinegar*
   Salt, pepper
 1 *can (1 lb.) salmon*

Cook 6 medium, waxy potatoes (2 pounds) until tender in boiling salted water to cover. Peel and dice. Sprinkle with 1 small onion, chopped, 2 tablespoons finely chopped parsley, and 1 cup diced celery. Make a dressing by whisking together 2 tablespoons each light cream, prepared mustard, sugar, and vinegar; season with salt and a little pepper. Pour the dressing over the potatoes and toss gently to coat. Flake a 1-pound can of salmon, discarding bones and skin. Gently fold the salmon into the potatoes. Let stand in a cool place for an hour. Makes 6 or more main-dish servings.

SARDINE SALAD

1½ *lbs. potatoes*
   2 *cans sardines*
   2 *or 3 stalks celery*
   2 *hard-cooked eggs*
 ¼ *cup sliced radishes*
 ¾ *cup sour cream*
   1 *tsp. grated onion*
   1 *tsp. prepared mustard*
      Salt, pepper
      Lettuce

Cook 4 medium-large, waxy potatoes (1½ pounds) in boiling salted water to cover. Peel and cut into small, thick slices. Drain 2 cans (about 3 ounces each) sardines. If they are large, break them into bite-size pieces and discard the bones. Reserve three for garnish. Sliver 2 or 3 large stalks of celery. Grate 2 hard-cooked eggs. Add ¼ cup sliced radishes and toss all together very gently to mix. Season ¾ cup dairy sour cream with 1 teaspoon each grated onion and prepared mustard, and salt and pepper to taste. Pour over potato mixture and toss gently. Mound in a salad bowl lined with greens and garnish with the reserved whole sardines. Additional garnishes of green-pepper rings, tomato slices, and quartered hard-cooked eggs are optional.

HERRING SALAD

1 *lb. potatoes*
1 *jar (12 ozs.) herring fillets in wine*
1 *heart celery*
⅓ *cup sour cream*
   Salt, pepper, paprika
   Lemon juice

Cook 3 medium, waxy potatoes (1 pound) in boiling salted water to cover. Peel and dice. Drain a jar of herring fillets—the kind packed in wine with sliced onion, if possible. Reserve the wine. Dice the herring and the onion. (If there is no onion, add half a small onion, finely chopped.) Combine the herring and onion with the still-warm potatoes and the reserved herring liquid. Dice a small heart of celery, leaves and all, and add. Then add ⅓ cup sour cream, or enough to moisten well, and toss. Season to taste with salt, pepper, and paprika. You may want to add a little lemon juice, depending on the kind of herring you use.

SALADE NICOISE

1 *lb. potatoes*
1 *pkg. frozen cut green beans*
½ *cup olive oil*
¼ *cup lemon juice*
   Garlic salt
   Pepper
   Romaine lettuce
1 *can anchovy fillets*
2 *tomatoes*
12 *pitted black olives*
1 *Tbsp. capers*

Cook 3 medium, waxy potatoes (1 pound) in salted boiling water to cover. Peel and dice. Cook 1 box (about 10 ounces) frozen cut green beans as directed on the package, until tender but still crisp, and drain. Mix ½ cup olive oil with ¼ cup lemon juice and garlic salt and pepper to taste. Toss potatoes and beans with half this dressing, reserving the rest. Cool until serving time. Line a salad platter with Romaine, or use another leaf lettuce. Mound the beans and potatoes in the center of the platter. Drain and dry 1 can (3 ounces) anchovy fillets and scatter them on the potato mixture. Peel and slice 2 large tomatoes and arrange them around the border. Garnish with a dozen or so large, pitted black olives. Add 1 tablespoon capers to the remaining dressing and pour over all. A can of tuna, broken into large flakes, can be added to the platter.

TUNA CRUNCH SALAD

1 can (7 ozs.) tuna fish
¼ cup coarsely grated carrot
¼ cup chopped green pepper
1 Tbsp. finely chopped onion
2 cups finely shredded cabbage
½ cup mayonnaise
2 Tbsp. vinegar
2 cups potato chips

Drain and flake 1 can (about 7 ounces) tuna fish. Combine fish with ¼ cup each grated carrot and green pepper. Add 1 tablespoon chopped onion and 2 cups shredded cabbage and toss lightly. Mix together ½ cup mayonnaise and 2 tablespoons vinegar. Combine with salad. Just before serving, add 2 cups potato chips and toss lightly.

CREAMY FRENCH DRESSING

1 medium potato
⅔ cup salad oil
¼ cup vinegar
½ tsp. sugar
Salt, pepper, paprika
Garlic clove (optional)

Boil a medium potato in its jacket until very soft, in salted boiling water to cover. Peel and mash smooth. Stir together ⅔ cup good salad oil—olive, corn, or peanut—and ¼ cup vinegar. (Wine vinegars make the best dressing, and you can choose from wine vinegars flavored with a variety of herbs.) Add ½ teaspoon sugar and salt, pepper, and paprika to taste. Stir in the mashed potato, blending well. If you like garlic, crush a medium clove and add it to the dressing, but remove it before using. Stir or shake the dressing again before using.

TARTAR MAYONNAISE

½ lb. cooked potatoes
1 hard-cooked egg
1 slice onion
1 Tbsp. chopped parsley
¾ cup light cream or half-and-half
Juice of 1 lemon
2 Tbsp. pickle relish
Dry mustard, salt, pepper

Peel and grate 1 large cooked potato (about ½ pound). Grate the yolk only of a hard-cooked egg and 1 thick slice onion. Add 1 tablespoon finely chopped parsley. Add ¾ cup light cream or half-and-half. Beat with a rotary beater until the mixture is smooth and creamy. Beat in the juice of a large lemon (about 4 tablespoons). Add 2 tablespoons chopped sweet-pickle relish, drained, and a pinch of dry mustard, salt, and pepper to taste. This makes about 2 cups thick, mayonnaise-like sauce you can use as tartar sauce or mayonnaise with fish and salads.

❧ 13
❧

Potato Breads, Cakes, Cookies, Pies

Probably no one has ever done any serious research into the question of why our ancestors, on both sides of the ocean, used potatoes in baking breads and cakes. It is a fact that they did, however, as attested by old recipes that have come down to us. There were probably two very good reasons.

First, using potatoes was economical on several counts. Wheat was often scarce and wheat flour expensive, so that it was important to supplement or at times replace it completely with the more readily available potatoes. Then, too, there was the problem of how to make use of potatoes left over from one meal and not enough to make another meal, but far too much to throw away wantonly. There is also a possibility that those wise ladies (after all, legend says that they knew about penicillin centuries before modern science "discovered" it) knew that the water in which potatoes were cooked contained nutrients that were worth using in soups, stews, or as the liquid in baking.

The second reason for baking with potatoes is possibly more important for modern cooks. The economical housewife shortly discovered that breads, biscuits, cakes—whatever she baked with potatoes or potato water—had special qualities lacking in cakes made with flour alone. They were more tender, more moist, richer, heartier. And they stayed fresh and delectable far longer.

For people accustomed to commercial bakery breads and packaged-mix cakes, there is a highly descriptive word for this phenomenon—old-fashioned. Whatever you bake with potatoes tastes deliciously, nostalgically old-fashioned. You can make these recipes, unless specifically stated otherwise, with freshly mashed, leftover, or instant mashed potatoes. If you use leftover potatoes with large amounts of seasoning and milk in them, adjust the recipes accordingly—judgment is an important asset of the canny user of leftovers in any area of cooking.

WHITE BREAD

1 potato
Milk
1 envelope granulated yeast
2 Tbsp. sugar
2 tsp. salt
2 Tbsp. butter
5 cups flour

Peel 1 medium potato, dice it, and cook in boiling water to cover until tender. Drain off water, measure, and add milk to make 1½ cups liquid in all. Scald. Cool just until very warm. Sprinkle with 1 envelope granulated yeast. Mash the potato and add 2 tablespoons sugar, 2 teaspoons salt, and 2 tablespoons butter. Stir yeast to dissolve it, combine with potatoes, and blend well. Measure 5 cups flour and add gradually to yeast mixture, beating with a spoon or electric mixer until the dough is too stiff to beat. Turn the dough out onto a floured board and knead in the remaining flour. Knead until smooth. Grease the mixing bowl and roll dough in it. Cover with towel and set in a warm place to double in bulk, about 1½ hours. To test the dough, poke it with a finger—if the depression remains, the dough is light. Punch the dough down and knead it for a minute. Let rise again. Punch down again and shape into two loaves. Let rise in greased pans until light. Bake at 400°F. for 20 minutes, then reduce heat to 375°F. and bake 20 to 30 minutes longer, until the bread shrinks from the sides of the pan and sounds hollow when tapped.

COUNTRY WHEAT BREAD

  ¾ *pound potatoes*
  2 *cups water*
  1 *envelope granulated yeast*
  2 *tsp. salt*
  3 *cups whole wheat flour*
  3 *cups white flour*

Peel and dice 2 medium-large potatoes (¾ pound) and boil them in 2 cups water until soft. Drain off the potato water and set aside to cool. Rice the potatoes, or mash them thoroughly. Sprinkle the still very warm potato water with 1 envelope granulated yeast (if you use cake yeast, the water should not be as hot as for granulated yeast). Stir to dissolve the yeast, and add to the cooled, riced potatoes. Add 2 teaspoons salt. Gradually beat in about 3 cups each white and whole wheat flour, to make a firm dough. Turn out on a floured board and knead until smooth. Cover with a towel and set in a warm place to rise until double, about 1½ hours. Poke the dough to test it—if the impression of your finger remains, the dough is light. Punch down, knead briefly again, and shape into two or three loaves. Let rise again until nearly double in bulk, about 45 minutes. Bake at 350°F. an hour or longer, until the loaves are well browned and sound hollow when tapped.

FOR VARIETY: Follow the recipe as given, but use all wheat or all white flour; add 1 tablespoon caraway or cumin seed for flavor.

REFRIGERATOR ROLLS

　　1　*envelope granulated yeast*
　　¼　*cup warm water*
　　¾　*cup milk*
　1½　*cups mashed potatoes*
　　⅓　*cup sugar*
　　⅓　*cup butter*
　　2　*tsp. salt*
　　2　*eggs*
　　5　*cups flour*

Sprinkle 1 envelope granulated dry yeast on ¼ cup very warm water—if you use cake yeast, the water should be just lukewarm. Bring ¾ cup milk to a boil and set it aside to cool. Put 1½ cups mashed potatoes (2 medium-large potatoes), freshly cooked or reheated, into a large mixing bowl. Add ⅓ cup sugar and blend well. Add ⅓ cup butter (⅔ stick) cut into bits, and stir until butter melts. Add 2 teaspoons salt and the milk. Beat in 2 eggs, one at a time. Add the yeast and blend well. Beat in about 5 cups flour, a cup at a time. Beat with an electric mixer, if you like, until the mixture becomes too stiff; then use a wooden spoon. Add just enough flour to make a dough that cleans the sides of the bowl. Continue to beat with the spoon, or with floured hands, until the dough is smooth. Cover with a towel and set in a warm place to rise until double in bulk, about 1½ hours. Test by poking the dough with a finger—if the impression remains, the dough is light. Punch down and shape. Pat or roll out on a floured board and cut into desired shapes. Or pinch off pieces to shape 3 small balls, dip in butter, and bake in muffin tins for clover-leaf rolls. Let rise on a greased baking sheet or in muffin tins until double, about 1 hour. Bake at 400°F. about 20 minutes, until well browned. This dough keeps well in the refrigerator. Store the dough in the refrigerator after the first rising and let it return to room temperature before proceeding with shaping, rising, and baking as directed. Makes 2 dozen small rolls.

CRESCENTS

    1 *envelope granulated yeast*
    1 *cup potato water*
    1 *cup milk*
    6 *Tbsp. butter*
    6 *Tbsp. sugar*
1½ *tsp. salt*
    1 *egg*
    6 *cups flour*
       Softened butter

Sprinkle 1 envelope yeast on 1 cup very warm potato water. If
you use cake yeast, the potato water should be only lukewarm.
(The water that remains in the pot after potatoes are boiled contains some valuable nutrients, and also gives rolls extra keeping
quality and tenderness.) Bring 1 cup milk to a boil with 6 tablespoons each butter and sugar, and 1½ teaspoons salt. Cool to
lukewarm. Combine the milk with yeast mixture and stir until
yeast is dissolved. Beat in 1 egg and gradually add about 6 cups
flour, 1 cup at a time, to make a soft dough that can be handled.
Turn the dough out on a lightly floured board and knead it until
it is smooth and satiny, and will not stick to the fingers. Roll it in
a greased bowl, cover with a towel, and let stand in a warm place
until double in bulk. To test the dough, plunge a fingertip into it.
If the depression remains, the dough is fully risen. Punch the
dough down, divide it in half, and let rest on the floured board,
covered, for 10 minutes. (The rest makes it easier to handle.)
Roll out each portion into a round about ½-inch thick. Spread
with soft butter. Cut each round into pie-shaped wedges. Roll
from the wide side to the point and curve the ends slightly to
form half moons. Let rise on a greased baking sheet until again
double in bulk. Bake at 400°F. about 20 minutes, until well
browned. Serve hot.

FOR VARIETY: This dough can be used to make quick "Danish
pastry." Roll very thin, butter, sprinkle with chopped nuts and
raisins or with cinnamon and sugar, and bake as directed.

SWEET ROLL DOUGH

1 envelope granulated yeast
1½ cups warm water
⅔ cup sugar
1½ tsp. salt
⅔ cup butter
1 cup mashed potatoes
2 eggs
7 cups flour

Sprinkle 1 envelope dry yeast on 1½ cups warm water—if you use cake yeast, the water should be just lukewarm. If you have potato water, use it. Stir to dissolve the yeast. Stir in ⅔ cup sugar, 1½ teaspoons salt, and ⅔ cup butter (1⅓ sticks), cut into bits. Add 1 cup mashed potatoes, still warm or reheated to lukewarm, and blend well. Beat in 2 eggs. Add about 7 cups flour, cup by cup, beating it in with an electric mixer until the dough is too heavy for the mixer; then use a wooden spoon. Turn the dough out on a floured board and knead it until it is smooth and satiny and will not stick to your hands. Grease a bowl, roll the dough in it to coat all sides, and leave the dough in the bowl in the refrigerator, lightly covered with a damp towel, until wanted. About 2 hours before baking, shape as desired and let rise until double in bulk, about 1½ hours in a warm place. Follow general cookbook directions for shaping rolls, sweet rolls, or coffee cakes. Rolls take about 15 minutes at 400°F., coffee cakes about 25 to 35 minutes at 350°F. to 375°F., depending on their size and shape.

Low-Calorie Tip   Season mashed or riced potatoes with salt, pepper, and a dash of lemon juice. Beat stiff an egg white or two and fold in. Makes light, fluffy potatoes without adding excessive calories. Less than 100 calories for a ⅔-cup serving!

PIONEER CINNAMON ROLL

1 *envelope granulated yeast*
¼ *cup very warm water*
¾ *cup potato water*
1 *cup milk*
¼ *cup butter*
2 *tsp. salt*
¾ *cup sugar*
6 *cups flour*
2 *tsp. cinnamon*

Sprinkle 1 envelope yeast on ¼ cup warm water. (If you use cake yeast, the water must be just lukewarm.) Scald ¾ cup potato water (water drained from cooked potatoes and reserved) with 1 cup milk, ¼ cup butter (½ stick), 2 teaspoons salt, and ¼ cup sugar. Cool to lukewarm and add to the yeast. Gradually beat in about 6 cups flour to make a fairly soft but not sticky dough. Turn out on a floured board and knead for a few minutes. Grease a bowl, turn the dough in it, and cover. Set in a warm place to rise until doubled, 1½ hours or longer. Punch the dough down, divide it in half, and let it rest 10 minutes. Roll each half into a rectangle and sprinkle with a spicy mixture of ½ cup sugar (¾ cup sugar in all) plus 2 teaspoons or more cinnamon. Roll up like a jelly roll and fit into 2 greased loaf pans. Cover and let rise again until doubled in bulk, about 1 hour. Bake at 400°F. about 40 minutes, until the crust is browned and the bread sounds hollow when tapped. Except for the substitution of commercially made yeast for the homemade variety, this is truly an old-fashioned dessert bread with the characteristic potato tenderness and moistness.

TIP: Water drained from potatoes can be used instead of plain water in any of your favorite bread recipes—particularly for rye breads.

RICH RAISIN BREAD

    1 envelope granulated yeast
    ¼ cup very warm water
    ¼ cup sugar
    6 cups flour
    2 tsp. salt
    1½ cups warm mashed potatoes
    ½ cup butter
    1 egg
    1 cup cream
    1 cup raisins

Sprinkle 1 envelope granulated dry yeast on ¼ cup warm water. (If you use cake yeast, crumble it into lukewarm water.) Add ¼ cup sugar. Toss 6 cups flour in a large mixing bowl with 2 teaspoons salt. Add 1½ cups warm mashed potatoes and ½ cup (1 stick) butter, cut into small pieces. Blend. Beat 1 egg with 1 cup cream. Stir the yeast mixture to dissolve it. Pour liquids all at once into the mixing bowl and blend well. If necessary, add more warm water to make a firm dough. Plump 1 cup raisins in boiling water for a minute, drain, and work into the dough. Turn the dough out on a floured board and knead until smooth. Cover with a towel and set in a warm place to rise until double in bulk, about 1½ hours. Punch down, shape into 2 loaves, and let rise again until double, about 45 minutes. Bake at 400°F. for 10 minutes, then reduce heat to 350°F. and bake 45 to 55 minutes longer, until the loaves are richly browned and sound hollow when you tap them.

POTATO YEAST STARTER

    1½ lbs. potatoes
    4 cups boiling water
    ½ cup salt
    ½ cup sugar
    1 cake or envelope yeast
    ¼ cup warm water

Peel and grate 4 medium-large potatoes (1½ pounds) and cook with 4 cups boiling water and ½ cup each salt and sugar until the mixture is clear. Cool to lukewarm. Meanwhile, soften a cake or envelope of yeast in ¼ cup warm water. Dissolve the softened yeast in the potato mixture. Pour into a jug and let stand open, in a warmish place, until the yeast begins to rise and bubble. Stir down, cork tightly, and store in a cool place. Half a cup of this yeast is the equivalent of 1 cake or envelope of yeast in baking. It can also be used instead of purchased yeast to start a new batch.

However, like sour-dough starter (which also served our pioneer women very well indeed), this yeast does not seem practical under ordinary circumstances. For one thing, the mixture tends to have a strong odor, and few of us have suitable storage conditions for the jug. Also, any homemade yeast seems to need the extra help contributed by the natural yeast spores that live in fresh, unpolluted country air, an ingredient that is rare and becoming rarer. Still, the recipe is a piece of culinary history, and a demonstration of another side of the versatility and usefulness of the multipurpose potato.

BUTTERMILK SCONES

  1 lb. potatoes
  ½ cup buttermilk
  2 cups flour
  ½ tsp. baking soda
  1 tsp. salt
  2 eggs

Cook 3 medium potatoes (1 pound) in boiling salted water to cover. Peel. While the potatoes are still hot, mash them, adding ½ cup buttermilk. Toss or sift 2 cups flour with ½ teaspoon baking soda and 1 teaspoon salt. Add to the flour mixture, blending with a wooden spoon. Beat 2 eggs lightly and blend in. Drop the mixture by spoonfuls on a hot, greased griddle. Flatten lightly. Brown slowly, turn, and brown the other side. Serve hot or reheated, with butter and jam.

SCONES

1⅓ cups flour
1 tsp. salt
2 tsp. double-acting baking powder
2 Tbsp. butter
⅔ cup mashed potatoes
1 egg
3 Tbsp. milk

Toss or sift 1⅓ cups flour, 1 teaspoon salt, and 2 teaspoons double-acting baking powder. Cut in 2 tablespoons butter, using a pastry blender or two knives, until mixture looks like coarse meal. Blend in ⅔ cup mashed potatoes. Beat the egg, combine with 3 tablespoons milk, and stir into the flour mixture all at once to make a dough that can be handled. If necessary, add a little more milk. Divide in half. Roll or pat out each half on a lightly floured board into a round a scant ½-inch thick. Cut each round into 6 or 8 wedge-shaped pieces. Bake on a lightly greased baking pan at 450°F. until brown, about 15 minutes.

GRIDDLE SCONES

Heat a heavy frying pan, brush lightly with fat, and cook scones over low heat until bottom is brown and the scones well risen. Turn and brown other side. Allow 10 minutes or less for each side, and turn only once.

BISCUITS

1½ cups flour
2½ tsp. double-acting baking powder
1 tsp. salt
3 Tbsp. butter
1 cup mashed potatoes
½ cup milk

164

Toss or sift 1½ cups flour, 2½ teaspoons double-acting baking powder, and 1 teaspoon salt. Cut in 3 tablespoons butter with a pastry blender. Add 1 cup mashed potatoes (leftover mashed potatoes, seasoned to your taste, add flavor). Gradually stir in about ½ cup milk, using just enough to make a soft dough. Knead lightly on a floured board. Pat or roll out about ½-inch thick and cut with a floured biscuit cutter. Bake on a lightly greased pan at 450°F., about 15 minutes, until richly browned. Serve hot. To reheat, wrap in foil and bake at 400°F. about 5 minutes.

HERB BISCUITS

Just before adding the milk in the recipe above, add any of the following: ½ teaspoon crushed, dried oregano or rosemary or basil; or 1 tablespoon fresh parsley or chives.

WAFFLES

1½ cups mashed potatoes
⅓ cup melted butter
2 eggs
1 cup sifted flour
2 tsp. double-acting baking powder
1 tsp. salt
1 cup milk

Blend 1½ cups mashed potatoes with ⅓ cup melted butter. Add 2 eggs, one at a time, beating well after each addition. Sift or toss 1 cup flour, 2 teaspoons double-acting baking powder, and 1 teaspoon salt. Add to batter alternately with portions of 1 cup milk, beginning and ending with flour. Beat well. Bake in a hot waffle iron. Serve with butter and syrup.

FOR VARIETY: Substitute bacon fat for the butter and add ¼ cup chopped onion, to make savory waffles to use instead of toast or biscuits with such favorites as chicken à la king or creamed tuna.

MUFFINS

¼ cup butter
2 Tbsp. sugar
1 egg
1 cup mashed potatoes
2 cups flour
3 tsp. double-acting baking powder
½ tsp. salt
1 cup milk

Cream ¼ cup butter and gradually work in 2 tablespoons sugar. Add 1 egg and beat until smooth and light. Blend in 1 cup mashed potatoes. Toss or sift 2 cups flour, 3 teaspoons double-acting baking powder, and ½ teaspoon salt. Add to batter alternately with portions of 1 cup milk, beginning and ending with flour. Stir after each addition just until flour is incorporated. Grease 12 medium muffin pans, or fit paper baking cups into dry muffin pans (these eliminate greasing) and divide the batter into them. Bake at 400°F. about 25 minutes. Serve hot for best flavor. To reheat, wrap in foil and bake at 400°F. about 10 minutes.

DATE MUFFINS

Fold in ½ cup finely cut dates; bake as directed.

BLUEBERRY MUFFINS

Fold in ½ cup washed and drained blueberries.

POTATO STARCH MUFFINS

½ cup potato starch
1 tsp. double-acting baking powder
½ tsp. salt
4 eggs, separated
2 Tbsp. sugar
2 Tbsp. cold water

Toss or sift together ½ cup potato starch, 1 teaspoon double-acting baking powder, and ½ teaspoon salt. Beat 4 egg whites until foamy, gradually add 2 tablespoons sugar, and continue to beat until stiff. Use the same beater (no washing is necessary) to beat 4 egg yolks. Gently but thoroughly fold in the flour mixture, a little at a time. Fold in 2 tablespoons ice-cold water. Fold in the egg whites. Bake in 12 greased and lightly floured muffin tins at 400°F., about 20 minutes, until well browned. Serve hot.

ORANGE TEA BREAD

4 cups flour
4 tsp. double-acting baking powder
½ tsp. salt
½ cup sugar
¼ cup butter
2 eggs
1⅓ cups potato water
½ cup candied orange peel
½ cup walnuts

Toss or sift 4 cups flour with 4 teaspoons double-acting baking powder, ½ teaspoon salt, and ½ cup sugar. Cut in ¼ cup softened butter (½ stick). Beat 2 eggs with 1⅓ cups cold potato water—the salted water in which potatoes were boiled—and stir until well blended. Stir in ½ cup each, chopped candied orange peel and coarsely broken walnuts. Fill a greased and floured 9-inch bread pan and set in a warm place, covered, for 15 minutes. Bake at 350°F. about 1 hour, until the bread is browned and tests done. Let stand overnight, wrapped in foil or plastic wrap, to make thin slices easier.

TIP: You can use other combinations of candied fruit, raisins, dates, and nuts, to your taste. It is potato water that makes this bread different from the standard varieties of tea bread.

BUBBLE COFFEE CAKE

2 *envelopes granulated yeast*
½ *cup very warm water*
½ *cup milk*
1 *cup butter*
1¼ *cups sugar*
1 *tsp. salt*
5 *cups flour*
2 *eggs*
1 *cup mashed potatoes*
2 *tsp. cinnamon*
  Chopped nuts (optional)

Sprinkle 2 envelopes granulated dry yeast on ½ cup warm water. Use potato water if you have it. (For cake yeast, the water should be just lukewarm.) Bring ½ cup milk to a boil with ½ cup each butter and sugar, and 1 teaspoon salt. Cool to lukewarm. Add the dissolved yeast and 2 cups flour, and beat well, using a rotary beater or the electric mixer. Beat in 2 eggs. Add 1 cup mashed potatoes and another cup of flour, and beat well. Continue to add flour, half a cup at a time, until the mixture is too thick for the mixer; then use a wooden spoon to beat in more flour (about 5 cups in all) to make a soft but not sticky dough. Turn the dough out on a lightly floured board and knead for a few minutes. Grease the mixing bowl, roll the dough in it, cover, and let stand in a warm place until it doubles in volume, about 1½ hours. Punch the dough down and let it stand for 10 minutes. With a measuring tablespoon, cut off pieces of dough and shape into balls. Dip into ½ cup melted butter and coat with a mixture of ¾ cup sugar and 2 teaspoons cinnamon. A spoonful of very finely chopped nutmeats may be added to the sugar mixture. Pile the balls into greased tubes, fluted coffee-cake pans, or loaf tins, half filling them. Leftover sugar and butter may be sprinkled on the cakes. Cover with a towel, set in a warm place, and let rise until double in bulk, 45 minutes to 1 hour. Bake at 350°F. about 35 minutes, until the cakes are well browned. Makes two or three cakes.

STREUSEL KUCHEN
(Crumb Cake)

1 envelope granulated yeast
½ cup very warm water
⅓ cup sugar
  Butter
½ cup mashed potatoes
1 egg
3 cups flour
1 tsp. salt
⅓ cup brown sugar
  Dash cinnamon
  Dash salt

Sprinkle 1 envelope granulated dry yeast on ½ cup warm water. (If you use cake yeast, crumble it into lukewarm water.) Add ⅓ cup sugar and stir to dissolve. Combine ⅓ cup butter (⅔ stick), cut into bits, with ½ cup freshly mashed or reheated potatoes. Stir until butter melts. Add 1 egg, lightly beaten. Combine with dissolved yeast. Toss or sift 2 cups flour with 1 teaspoon salt. Add potato mixture, beating well. Turn dough out on a floured board and knead until smooth. Brush with melted butter and cover with a towel; let stand in a warm place about 1½ hours, until doubled in bulk. Test by poking—if the impression of a finger remains, the dough is light. Punch down and spread in a well-greased rectangular baking pan, about 13 by 9 inches, or two 8-inch square pans. Let rise again until double, about 30 minutes. Make crumbs by stirring 1 cup flour (3 cups is used in all) with ⅓ cup dark brown sugar and dashes of cinnamon and salt. Work in ¼ cup butter with the fingertips to make a crumbly mixture. Sprinkle on cake. Bake at 350°F. for about ½ hour.

WHITE CAKE DE LUXE

⅔ cup butter
½ cup mashed potatoes
1¼ cups sugar
1 Tbsp. Cointreau
2 cups flour
2 tsp. double-acting baking powder
½ tsp. salt
½ cup milk
Grated rind of ½ orange
3 egg whites
Slivered almonds (optional)

Cream ⅔ cup butter until soft. Add ½ cup rather dry mashed potatoes and blend well. Add ¾ cup sugar and beat until very light and fluffy, about 5 minutes with the electric beater. Beat in 1 tablespoon Cointreau. Toss or sift 2 cups flour with 2 teaspoons double-acting baking powder and ½ teaspoon salt. Add the flour to the creamed mixture alternately with portions of ½ cup milk, beating well after each addition. Add the grated rind of ½ orange. Beat 3 egg whites until foamy, gradually add ½ cup sugar (1¼ cups in all), and continue to beat until stiff. Fold the egg whites into the batter. Grease a 9-inch tube pan with shortening. Sprinkle thickly with slivered blanched almonds, if desired. Pour the batter into the prepared pan and bake at 350°F. about 40 to 50 minutes, or until the cake tests done. Invert on a rack to cool. The center of the cake may be filled with whipped cream lightly sweetened and flavored with more Cointreau. If you have no orange-flavored liqueur, use 1 teaspoon vanilla and about ½ teaspoon orange flavoring in the cake, and a few drops of each in the cream.

OLD-FASHIONED CHOCOLATE CAKE

1 *cup butter*
2 *cups sugar*
2 *tsp. vanilla extract*
4 *eggs, separated*
4 *ozs. unsweetened chocolate*
1 *cup mashed potatoes*
2 *cups flour*
2 *tsp. double-acting baking powder*
½ *tsp. salt*
⅔ *cup milk*

Cream 1 cup butter, gradually add 1½ cups sugar, and beat until smooth and light. Stir in 2 teaspoons vanilla, or use 1 teaspoon almond extract. Add 4 egg yolks, beaten light, and 4 squares unsweetened chocolate, melted and cooled (or use 4 envelopes pre-melted chocolate). Blend in 1 cup mashed potatoes and beat well. Toss or sift 2 cups flour with 2 teaspoons double-acting baking powder and ½ teaspoon salt. Add flour to batter alternately with portions of ⅔ cup milk, beginning and ending with flour. Blend until smooth after each addition. Beat the egg whites fluffy, gradually beat in ½ cup sugar, and beat until stiff peaks form. Fold in. Bake in two greased and floured 9-inch layer pans, about 35 minutes at 350°F., until the cake tests done. Fill and frost with seven-minute frosting, or your favorite.

FOR VARIETY: Fold in 1 cup raisins or chopped nuts.

PECAN TORTE

5 *eggs, separated*
½ *tsp. salt*
⅔ *cup sugar*
1¼ *cups mashed potatoes*
⅔ *cup pecans*
2 *tsp. grated lemon rind*
1 *Tbsp. dark rum*

Beat yolks of 5 eggs well with ½ teaspoon salt. Gradually add all but 3 tablespoons of ⅔ cup sugar and continue to beat until light and fluffy. Blend in 1¼ cups dry, unseasoned mashed potatoes. Grind ⅔ cup pecans, or chop very finely. Blend into batter. Add 2 teaspoons grated lemon rind and 1 tablespoon dark rum or brandy. Beat the 5 egg whites with 3 tablespoons sugar until very stiff. Carefully fold in. Bake in a greased and floured 9-inch spring form or torte pan at 325°F., about 1 hour, until the torte is well risen, lightly browned, and shrinks slightly from the edges of the pan. Cool thoroughly. Remove the rim of the pan and put the torte, still on the pan bottom, on a serving plate. The torte will sink slightly as it cools. If desired, the hollow can be filled with whipped cream or fresh fruit.

DATE NUT CAKE

⅓ *cup butter*
1 *cup sugar*
2 *eggs*
⅔ *cup mashed potatoes*
1½ *cups flour*
1 *tsp. double-acting baking powder*
1 *tsp. baking soda*
½ *tsp. salt*
¾ *cup milk*
1 *tsp. vanilla extract*
½ *cup nuts*
½ *cup dates*

Cream ⅓ cup butter, gradually add 1 cup sugar, and beat until smooth. Add 2 whole eggs and beat until light and fluffy. Beat in ⅔ cup mashed potatoes. Sift or toss together 1½ cups flour, 1 teaspoon double-acting baking powder, 1 teaspoon baking soda, and ½ teaspoon salt. Add to batter alternately with portions of ¾ cup milk, beating until smooth after each addition. Stir in 1 teaspoon vanilla extract and fold in ½ cup each coarsely chopped nutmeats and finely slivered dates. Bake in a greased and floured 9-inch square pan at 350°F. about 30 minutes, until the cake tests done.

BUTTERMILK CHOCOLATE CAKE

½ *cup butter*
1½ *cups brown sugar*
1 *tsp. vanilla*
2 *eggs*
⅓ *cup mashed potatoes*
2 *cups cake flour*
1 *tsp. double-acting baking powder*
½ *tsp. baking soda*
½ *tsp. salt*
1 *cup buttermilk*
2 *ozs. unsweetened chocolate*

Cream ½ cup butter until fluffy. Gradually beat in 1½ cups well-packed brown sugar and cream until light and smooth. Add 1 teaspoon vanilla. Add 2 eggs, one at a time, beating well. Beat in ⅓ cup mashed potatoes. Toss or sift 2 cups cake flour (or 1¾ cups all-purpose flour) with 1 teaspoon double-acting baking powder and ½ teaspoon each baking soda and salt. Add to the batter alternately with portions of 1 cup buttermilk, beginning and ending with the dry ingredients. Blend well after each addition. Melt 2 squares (2 ounces) unsweetened baking chocolate, cool, and stir into batter. Bake in two well-greased and lightly floured 8-inch layer pans about 30 to 35 minutes at 350°F. Cool and frost to taste. Best of all with whipped cream on top of and between the layers.

COCOA CAKE

¾ *cup butter*
2 *cups sugar*
4 *eggs*
2 *tsp. vanilla*
1 *cup mashed potatoes*
2 *cups flour*
⅔ *cup cocoa*
2 *tsp. double-acting baking powder*
1 *tsp. baking soda*
1 *tsp. salt*
½ *cup milk*

Cream ¾ cup butter (1½ sticks), gradually add 2 cups sugar, and beat until smooth. Add 4 eggs, one at a time, beating well after each. Add 2 teaspoons vanilla. Beat in 1 cup mashed potatoes and blend well. Toss or sift 2 cups flour with ⅔ cup cocoa, 2 teaspoons double-acting baking powder, 1 teaspoon baking soda, and 1 teaspoon salt. Add flour mixture to batter alternately with portions of ½ cup milk, beginning and ending with milk. Beat until smooth after each addition. Divide into two generously greased and lightly floured 9-inch layer pans. Bake at 350°F. for 35 minutes, until the cake tests done. Fill and frost to taste—meringue or seven-minute frosting, lightly flavored with peppermint, goes well with this cake.

RICH MIX CAKES

When baking with a cake mix—devil's food, spice cake, white or yellow cake—try adding 1 cup mashed potatoes and ½ teaspoon baking soda to the dry ingredients before adding milk or water and eggs, as directed. The potato will give the mix longer-lasting freshness and a homemade moistness.

BUTTERSCOTCH RUM CAKE

1 potato
½ cup butter
1½ cups dark brown sugar
2 eggs
1¾ cups flour
1 tsp. double-acting baking powder
1 tsp. baking soda
1 tsp. salt
1 cup sour milk
1 Tbsp. dark rum

Cook 1 medium potato in a small amount of boiling salted water. Peel and mash or rice. Cool. Cream ½ cup butter until smooth and light. Gradually add 1½ cups dark brown sugar, well packed for measuring, and cream until smooth. Beat in 2 eggs, one at a time, and the mashed potato. Toss or sift 1¾ cups flour with 1 teaspoon each double-acting baking powder, baking soda, and salt. Add the flour mixture to the batter alternately with portions of 1 cup sour milk, beginning and ending with flour. Blend until smooth after each addition. Flavor with 1 tablespoon dark Jamaica rum. Bake in a well greased and lightly floured fluted turk's head pan for about 45 minutes at 350°F. Frost with ornamental frosting flavored and made quite thin with Jamaica rum, so that it drips down the sides of the cake without hiding the characteristic flutes. Or use your favorite chocolate frosting, with a little rum added for zest.

Air of Derry Derry, New Hampshire, once known as Londonderry, was settled in 1719 by Scotch-Irish immigrants who promptly planted potatoes, North America's first.

SPICE CAKE

⅔ cup butter
1¾ cups sugar
4 eggs, separated
1 cup mashed potatoes
3 cups flour
4 tsp. double-acting baking powder
½ tsp. salt
1 tsp. cinnamon
1 tsp. nutmeg
¼ tsp. allspice
1 cup milk

Cream ⅔ cup butter. Gradually add 1¼ cups sugar and cream until smooth. Add the yolks of 4 eggs and beat until very light and fluffy. Beat in 1 cup mashed potatoes, slightly warm or at room temperature rather than chilled. Sift or toss 3 cups flour with 4 teaspoons double-acting baking powder, ½ teaspoon salt, 1 teaspoon each of cinnamon and nutmeg, and ¼ teaspoon allspice. Add to batter alternately with 1 cup milk, beginning and ending with flour. Beat until smooth after each addition. Beat egg whites until fluffy, gradually beat in ½ cup sugar (1¾ cups in all), and continue to beat until stiff peaks form. Fold in carefully but completely. Bake in a greased and floured 9 by 13-inch pan at 350°F. about 45 minutes, until the cake tests done. Sprinkle with powdered sugar through a paper-lace doily, or frost, as desired. Especially good served warm.

QUICK SPONGE

3 eggs
⅞ cup sugar
1 tsp. vanilla extract
½ cup potato starch
2 tsp. double-acting baking powder
¼ tsp. salt

Beat 3 eggs well, gradually add ⅞ cup sugar (2 tablespoons less than 1 cup), and continue to beat until very light and fluffy. Add 1 teaspoon vanilla extract. Sift ½ cup potato starch, 2 teaspoons double-acting baking powder, and ¼ teaspoon salt over the egg mixture and fold in gently but thoroughly. Bake in two greased and floured 8-inch layer pans, at 350°F. about 20 minutes, until the cake tests done. Invert on a rack to cool. Perfect for fresh strawberry or peach shortcake.

PASSOVER SPONGE CAKE

6 *eggs, separated*
1 *whole egg*
1½ *cups sugar*
1½ *tsp. grated lemon rind*
2 *Tbsp. lemon juice*
¾ *cup potato starch*
¼ *tsp. salt*

Beat 6 egg yolks and 1 whole egg until very frothy. Gradually beat in 1 cup sugar, 1½ teaspoons grated lemon or orange rind, and 2 tablespoons lemon juice. Sift ¾ cup potato starch and a scant ¼ teaspoon salt directly over the egg yolk mixture and fold it in gently but thoroughly. Beat the 6 egg whites until foamy, beat in ½ cup sugar (1½ cups in all) and continue to beat until stiff. Fold into the first mixture very lightly but thoroughly. Bake in an ungreased 10-inch tube pan, at 350°F. about 55 minutes, until the cake tests done—golden brown, well risen, and firm to the touch. Invert on a rack and cool completely before attempting to remove the cake from the pan.

GATEAU MOCHA

¾ *cup butter*
1½ *cups sugar*
  4 *eggs, separated*
¾ *cup mashed potatoes*
  2 *ozs. unsweetened chocolate*
  1 *tsp. instant coffee*
1½ *cups cake flour*
  2 *tsp. double-acting baking powder*
½ *tsp. baking soda*
½ *tsp. salt*
¾ *cup finely chopped pecans or walnuts*
½ *cup milk*

Cream ¾ cup butter, gradually add 1 cup sugar, and beat until smooth and light. Beat in 4 egg yolks, one at a time, beating well after each. Add ¾ cup mashed potatoes and blend until smooth. Add 2 squares (2 ounces) unsweetened baking chocolate, melted and cooled (or use 2 envelopes pre-melted chocolate) and 1 teaspoon instant coffee. Blend. Toss or sift 1½ cups cake flour, 2 teaspoons double-acting baking powder, and ½ teaspoon each baking soda and salt. Add ¾ cup pecans or walnuts (measure nutmeats, then chop) and toss again. Add flour-nut mixture to batter alternately with portions of ½ cup milk, beginning and ending with flour. Beat until smooth after each addition. Beat 4 egg whites until fluffy, gradually add ½ cup sugar (1½ cups in all), and beat until stiff peaks form. Bake in a greased and floured 9- or 10-inch tube pan, about 1 hour at 350°F., until the cake tests done. Serve plain or with whipped cream, or drizzle with thin frosting made by mixing confectioner's sugar with strong brewed coffee, rum, or orange juice.

FRUITED DROP CAKES

⅓ cup butter
1 cup sugar
1 tsp. vanilla
2 eggs, separated
1 cup mashed potatoes
¾ cup raisins or slivered dates
1 cup flour
2 tsp. double-acting baking powder
½ tsp. salt

Cream ⅓ cup butter. Add 1 cup sugar and beat until smooth. Stir in 1 teaspoon vanilla. Add 2 egg yolks, one at a time, beating well after each. Blend in 1 cup cold mashed potatoes and ¾ cup raisins or slivered dates. (Plump the raisins in boiling water and drain well before adding—this prevents them from becoming rock-hard during baking.) Sift or toss 1 cup flour, 2 teaspoons double-acting baking powder, and ½ teaspoon salt. Add to first mixture, blending well. Beat 2 egg whites stiff. Fold in gently but thoroughly. Drop by tablespoons onto an oiled baking sheet, well apart. Bake at 350°F. about 20 minutes, until the cakes are well risen, browned around the edges, and golden on top. Cool and ice, if desired—traditionally drop cakes are iced half with chocolate and half with vanilla icing.

FOR VARIETY: Use any combination of nutmeats, chocolate morsels, raisins, and dates to make ¾ cup, instead of all raisins.

CHOCOLATE DROP CAKES

Omit raisins and add 2 ozs. unsweetened chocolate, melted and cooled, with the potatoes. Sift ½ tsp. baking soda with the flour mixture. Bake as directed.

TIP: These are designed to be eaten out of hand: sandwich them in pairs with any desired frosting, or with apricot jam for hearty lunch-box desserts. Or make them in smaller shapes and use them to flank a ball of ice cream for a party dessert.

ABRIDINES

½ cup butter
1½ cups sugar
1 tsp. almond extract
1 egg
1 cup mashed potatoes
1¼ cups flour
Apricot jam
Slivered almonds

Cream ½ cup butter. Gradually work in 1½ cups sugar and beat until smooth. Add 1 teaspoon almond extract. Add 1 egg and beat well. Beat in 1 cup rather dry, cold mashed potatoes and 1¼ cups flour. Chill for ½ hour. Drop the dough by rounded teaspoons well apart on a greased baking sheet. With the tip of a pointed spoon, press a dab of apricot jam into each cooky. Bake at 375°F. about 12–15 minutes.

FOR VARIETY: Sprinkle a few almond slivers on some of the cookies.

PEANUT BUTTER COOKIES

½ cup butter
½ cup peanut butter
1 cup mashed potatoes
1 cup sugar
1 cup brown sugar
2 eggs
1 tsp. vanilla
2½ cups flour
2 tsp. double-acting baking powder
½ tsp. salt

Cream ½ cup each butter and peanut butter until well blended. Beat in 1 cup each mashed potatoes, sugar, and brown sugar, blending well. Add 2 eggs, one at a time, beating well after each. Add 1 teaspoon vanilla. Toss or sift 2½ cups flour, 2 teaspoons double-acting baking powder, and ½ teaspoon salt. Gradually add to batter to make a firm dough. Shape into 2-inch cylinders, chill well, and slice thin. Bake on a greased baking sheet at 400°F. about 10 minutes, until firm and golden. Store in the refrigerator and bake as needed. Or you can bake at once by dropping small teaspoonfuls onto the greased baking sheet, well apart. Criss-cross with a fork dipped into water and bake as directed.

CHOCOLATE BIT COOKIES

⅔ *cup butter*
½ *cup sugar*
½ *cup brown sugar*
1 *tsp. vanilla*
2 *eggs*
1 *cup mashed potatoes, chilled*
¾ *cup chopped nuts*
¾ *cup semisweet chocolate morsels*
1 *cup flour*
1½ *tsp. double-acting baking powder*
½ *tsp. salt*

Cream ⅔ cup butter. Add ½ cup each white sugar and brown sugar, well packed, and beat until smooth. Stir in 1 teaspoon vanilla. Beat in 2 eggs, one at a time, beating well after each. Blend in 1 cup cold mashed potatoes. Add ¾ cup each chopped nuts and semisweet chocolate morsels. Sift or toss 1 cup flour with 1½ teaspoons double-acting baking powder and ½ teaspoon salt. Stir into batter. Drop by half teaspoons on an oiled baking sheet, well apart to allow for spreading. Bake at 375°F., 12–15 minutes, until lightly browned. Cool on a rack.

OATMEAL CHEWS

   1 cup flour
   1 tsp. double-acting baking powder
   ¼ tsp. baking soda
   ½ tsp. salt
   ¼ cup brown sugar
   ½ cup semisweet chocolate morsels
   ½ cup chopped nutmeats
   1 cup raw oatmeal
   1 egg
   1 small, raw potato
   1 tsp. vanilla
   ¼ cup butter, melted
   ½ cup corn syrup

Toss or sift 1 cup flour, 1 teaspoon double-acting baking powder, ¼ teaspoon baking soda, and ½ teaspoon salt. Add ¼ cup brown sugar and ½ cup each chocolate bits and nutmeats. Toss again. Add 1 cup raw oatmeal—any kind except the instant—and toss again. Beat 1 egg in the mixing bowl. Peel and grate a small potato to make ½ cup. Stir at once into the egg. Add 1 teaspoon vanilla, ¼ cup melted butter (½ stick), and ½ cup corn syrup. Add the dry ingredients and stir with a wooden spoon to blend well. Drop by teaspoons, well apart, on a greased baking sheet. Bake at 350°F. about 15 minutes, until delicately golden. Makes about 3 dozen cookies.

OATMEAL CRISPS

To make a crisper cooky, increase the brown sugar to ½ cup. Be sure that baking sheets are very well greased for each batch of cookies, and drop the dough well apart on the baking sheet.

NUT COOKIES

    1 cup butter
1½ cups confectioner's sugar
    1 cup mashed potatoes
    1 egg
1½ cups flour
    1 tsp. cream of tartar
    1 tsp. baking soda
    1 tsp. salt
    2 tsp. vanilla
      Finely chopped nutmeats

Cream 1 cup butter until smooth. Sift in 1½ cups confectioner's sugar and beat until well blended. Add 1 cup mashed potatoes and blend again. Beat in 1 egg. Toss or sift 1½ cups flour with 1 teaspoon each cream of tartar, baking soda, and salt. Stir into the first mixture and add 2 teaspoons vanilla extract, or half vanilla and half almond. For easier handling, chill the dough in the refrigerator for an hour, if you have the time; or put it in the freezer for 15 minutes. Scoop up rounded half teaspoons of the mixture, drop them into finely chopped nutmeats, and shape into balls coated with nuts. Place well apart on a well-greased baking sheet. Bake at 350°F. about 15 minutes, until the cookies begin to brown on the bottom and at the edges. Makes about 4½ dozen cookies.

FOR VARIETY: Shape the balls with flour-dusted hands and stud them with half a pecan or almond, or with semisweet chocolate morsels.

CAKE DOUGHNUTS

¼ *cup butter*
1 *cup mashed potatoes*
½ *cup sugar*
2 *eggs*
2 *cups flour*
2½ *tsp. double-acting baking powder*
1 *tsp. salt*
¼ *tsp. nutmeg*
¼ *tsp. cinnamon*

Add ¼ cup butter, cut into bits, to 1 cup hot or reheated mashed potatoes and beat until the butter melts. Add ½ cup sugar and 2 eggs. Beat well. Toss or sift 2 cups flour with 2½ teaspoons double-acting baking powder, 1 teaspoon salt, and ¼ teaspoon each nutmeg and cinnamon. Stir into potato mixture to make a soft dough that can be handled. Beat with a wooden spoon for a minute. Turn out on a lightly floured board and pat or roll out ⅓-inch thick. Cut with a doughnut cutter (you can fry the "holes" along with the doughnuts). Melt hydrogenated shortening in a saucepan or frying kettle to make a 3- to 4-inch layer of fat; or use oil. Heat the fat to 360°F., the temperature at which a 1-inch cube of day-old bread will brown in 60 seconds. Lift the doughnuts with a spatula and slide them gently into the fat. Cook as many at a time as you can without crowding the pan. When the doughnuts come to the surface of the fat, turn them with a long-handled fork. Fry until the bottom is richly browned, then turn again and brown the top. Lift from the fat with a fork, drain, and lay on a paper towel to drain thoroughly. Serve warm, sprinkled with powdered sugar or coated with a mixture of granulated sugar and cinnamon. These keep well, wrapped in plastic or foil in the refrigerator. Wrap in foil and reheat in a moderate oven to serve. Makes about 1½ dozen.

RAISED DOUGHNUTS

  1 envelope granulated yeast
  ¼ cup warm water
  2 cups milk
  ¼ cup butter
  ¾ cup sugar
  1 cup mashed potatoes
  3 eggs
  5 cups flour
  2½ tsp. salt
  1 tsp. cinnamon
  ½ tsp. nutmeg

Sprinkle 1 envelope yeast on ¼ cup very warm water. (If you use cake yeast, the water should be just lukewarm.) Bring 2 cups milk to a boil with ¼ cup butter (½ stick) and ¾ cup sugar. Cool to lukewarm. Combine 1 cup mashed potatoes with 3 eggs, beating well to make a smooth mixture, and add. Then add the dissolved yeast. Toss or sift 5 cups flour with 2½ teaspoons salt, 1 teaspoon cinnamon, and ½ teaspoon nutmeg. Beat the flour gradually into the batter, using an electric beater as long as possible, then a wooden spoon. Add more flour, if necessary, to make a soft dough. Turn the dough out on a floured board and knead until smooth. Cover with a towel and let rise in a warm place until double in bulk, 1 to 2 hours. Punch down, knead again, and roll out ¼-inch thick. Cut with a doughnut cutter and let rise until double. Fry in hot deep fat (360°F.). (Follow the frying instructions given for Cake Doughnuts.) Glaze the hot doughnuts by brushing with confectioner's sugar mixed to a paste with water or juice; or cool and frost to taste. Makes about 3 dozen.

DROP DOUGHNUTS

1 cup mashed potatoes
2 Tbsp. melted butter
2 eggs
1¼ cups sugar
4 cups flour
4 tsp. double-acting baking powder
½ tsp. salt
1 tsp. cinnamon or nutmeg
1 cup milk
1 tsp. vanilla

Use 1 cup rather dry leftover mashed potatoes. Blend the potatoes with 2 tablespoons melted butter, 2 eggs, and 1¼ cups sugar. Beat well. Toss or sift 4 cups flour with 4 teaspoons double-acting baking powder, ½ teaspoon salt, and 1 teaspoon cinnamon or nutmeg. Add the dry ingredients to the potato mixture alternately with portions of about 1 cup milk. Use enough milk to make a soft mixture that will hold its shape when mounded on a spoon. Blend in 1 teaspoon vanilla. Drop by heaping teaspoonfuls into deep hot fat and fry as directed for Cake Doughnuts (page 184). Roll in mixed sugar and cinnamon. Best served warm. Or reheat, enclosed in foil, in a moderate oven. Makes 3 to 4 dozen.

APPLESAUCE DOUGHNUTS

2 Tbsp. butter
¾ cup sugar
4 egg yolks
½ cup mashed potatoes
½ tsp. baking soda
½ cup sour cream
1 tsp. cinnamon
½ tsp. nutmeg
1 cup applesauce
3 cups self-rising flour

Cream 2 tablespoons butter with ¾ cup sugar. Add 4 egg yolks and beat until light. Add ½ cup mashed potatoes and beat well. Mix ½ teaspoon baking soda with ½ cup sour cream. Add 1 teaspoon cinnamon and ½ teaspoon nutmeg, and blend well. Add the sour cream to the potato mixture. Add 1 cup applesauce. Stir in about 3 cups self-rising flour, adding it gradually to make a soft dough that can be handled. The amount will vary with the thickness of the applesauce. Knead the dough lightly, roll out ¼-inch thick on a lightly floured board, and cut into doughnuts. Fry like Cake Doughnuts. Fry the holes separately. Roll in mixed sugar and cinnamon and serve warm. Or store, wrapped in foil or plastic, until serving time, then reheat and roll in sugar and cinnamon.

TIP: Using self-rising flour in this recipe makes it easy to adjust the amount of flour required. If you use ordinary flour, add 1 teaspoon baking powder and ½ teaspoon salt for each cup of flour.

ORNAMENTAL FROSTING

½ cup mashed potatoes
1 egg white
Dash salt
Confectioner's sugar
Flavoring

Mix ½ cup unseasoned, cold mashed potatoes with 1 unbeaten egg white, blending well. Add a dash of salt. Gradually beat in sifted confectioner's sugar, a little at a time, until the mixture is the required thickness—a thick paste to use as a spread-on icing, or a mixture thick enough to mold or force through an icing cone to decorate a cake. Add flavoring to taste: vanilla, peppermint, or almond extract, or better, brandy or rum for sophisticated flavor.

FONDANT

1 *medium potato*
1 *Tbsp. butter*
¼ *tsp. flavoring extract*
3 *cups confectioner's sugar*

Grate 1 cold, medium potato, boiled or baked, and mash it until perfectly smooth. Add 1 tablespoon butter and blend well. Add ¼ teaspoon any desired flavoring extract—vanilla, almond, rum, peppermint, or a little rum, brandy, or bourbon. Gradually beat in 3 cups sifted confectioner's sugar, to make a mixture thick enough to knead. (Sift the sugar into the mixture directly from a flour sifter you keep for this purpose. Even a recently purchased package of confectioner's sugar may contain lumps.) Knead until very smooth and satiny. Roll into small balls and coat with chopped nuts or chocolate sprinkles, or dip into melted chocolate. Or use to stuff pitted prunes or dates, or to sandwich dried apricots.

FONDANT ICING

Make Fondant above, adding only enough sugar to make a thick paste. Spread on top of a cake and let it dribble down the sides; or brush on coffee cake or sweet rolls. A slightly thicker mixture makes a frosting.

CHOCOLATE ROCKS

⅔ *cup mashed potatoes*
1 *Tbsp. butter*
1 *box (1 lb.) confectioner's sugar*
3 *Tbsp. cocoa*
1 *tsp. vanilla extract*
   Dash salt
½ *lb. moist-pack coconut*

188

Mix ⅔ cup hot mashed potatoes, unseasoned, with 1 tablespoon butter. Sift in 1 pound confectioner's sugar, beating well to combine. Add 3 tablespoons cocoa, 1 teaspoon vanilla, and a dash of salt to taste. Stir in ½ pound moist-pack coconut (available in tins). With a teaspoon shape small, irregular mounds on a foil-lined pan. Chill until firm. Store in a tightly covered tin between layers of waxed paper.

CHOCOLATE FUDGE

½ *cup heavy cream or evaporated milk*
1½ *cups sugar*
½ *cup brown sugar*
2 *Tbsp. white corn syrup*
Pinch salt
2 *squares unsweetened baking chocolate*
1 *tsp. vanilla*
1 *Tbsp. butter*
1 *cup hot, riced potatoes*
1 *cup nutmeats (optional)*

Combine ½ cup heavy cream or evaporated milk, 1½ cups white sugar, ½ cup brown sugar, 2 tablespoons white corn syrup, a pinch of salt, and 2 ounces (2 squares) unsweetened baking chocolate, cut fine. Stir over moderate heat until chocolate melts. Then boil gently without stirring until a little of the mixture dropped into cold water can be gathered into a soft ball (238°F. on a candy thermometer). Stir in 1 teaspoon vanilla. Drop 1 tablespoon butter on top of the fudge. Cool. Beat until the mixture begins to lose its gloss and is thick and creamy. Add 1 cup hot, riced potatoes (about ½ pound, freshly boiled or baked and peeled) and continue to beat until very creamy and light. Add 1 cup broken nutmeats, if desired. Spread in a buttered 8-inch square pan, and cool until firm. Cut into squares.

MOCK LEMON-CHEESE PIE

1 *cup mashed potatoes*
2 *eggs*
½ *cup sugar*
2 *tsp. grated lemon rind*
2 *Tbsp. lemon juice*
3 *Tbsp. melted butter*
⅓ *cup milk*
   Dash salt
   8-inch unbaked pie shell

Blend 1 cup cold mashed potatoes (unseasoned) with 2 eggs. Add ½ cup sugar and blend well. Add 2 teaspoons grated lemon rind and 2 tablespoons lemon juice—half a large, juicy lemon will do for this. Add 3 tablespoons melted butter. Stir in ⅓ cup milk and a dash of salt, to taste. Pour the mixture into an unbaked 8-inch pie shell with a tall, fluted rim. Bake at 450°F. for 10 minutes; reduce heat to 350°F. and continue to bake until the crust is browned and the filling firm, about 30 minutes longer.

EGGNOG PIE

   Pastry for one-crust pie
2 *eggs, separated*
¾ *cup sugar*
¼ *tsp. salt*
⅔ *cup unseasoned mashed potatoes*
2 *Tbsp. melted butter*
½ *cup milk*
2 *Tbsp. brandy or rum*
   Nutmeg

Line a 9-inch pie plate with pastry, shape a fluted standing rim, and chill. Beat 2 egg yolks with ¾ cup sugar and ¼ teaspoon salt until very light and fluffy. Beat in ⅔ cup cooked, unseasoned mashed potatoes (or use a leftover boiled or baked potato, mashed or riced) and 2 tablespoons melted butter. Beat well. Add ½ cup milk and 2 tablespoons brandy and blend thoroughly. Beat the 2 egg whites stiff and fold in. Pour the mixture into the chilled pie crust. Bake at 400°F. about 25 to 30 minutes, until the crust is browned and the custard is set.

🌿 14
🌿

Desserts

Potatoes fried in butter, sprinkled with nutmeg and lemon juice, and drizzled with warm honey—this dessert, a specialty of the Balkans, tastes better than it sounds. Our own potato desserts, most of them from Western Europe, are less strange but no less intriguing. Many of these desserts use the potato not as a principal ingredient, but as an addition that makes an important difference. Potato can be added to a pudding or custard—as to cakes, breads, and pies—without making any significant change in the flavor of the finished product. What does change, and for the better, is texture and moistness. When potatoes are among the ingredients, your desserts will be more tender, more succulent, and richer.

🌿

CREPES

¾ *cup mashed potatoes*
½ *cup flour*
2 *eggs*
½ *tsp. salt*
¾ *cup milk*
3 *Tbsp. butter*

Combine ¾ cup mashed potatoes (unseasoned if you want to use the crêpes for dessert), ½ cup flour, and 2 eggs. Beat well to make a smooth mixture. Add ½ teaspoon salt. Beat in ¾ cup milk gradually, until the batter is thick as heavy cream—if necessary, use a little less or a little more milk. Melt 3 tablespoons butter in the small skillet in which you plan to cook the crêpes —a pan measuring 5 to 6 inches across the bottom is about right. Pour the butter into the batter and blend well. The butter remaining in the pan will grease it for the first crêpe; after that you will probably not need to grease the pan again. Pour ¼ cup batter into the hot pan and tip and roll the pan to spread the batter evenly over the bottom. Cook a minute or two until the top dries and the bottom is browned. Turn the crêpe and cook the other side. Turn out on a towel and repeat until all the crêpes are baked. There will be about a dozen. Sprinkle with powdered sugar and serve with lemon quarters or with preserves, or use to make crêpe Suzettes with your favorite Suzette sauce.

BLINTZES

Make crêpes as above, but brown only one side. Prepare filling by mixing 12 ounces dry cottage cheese (1½ cups) with 1 egg, salt and sugar to taste, and a little vanilla extract or brandy if desired. Put a spoonful of this mixture on the cooked side of each crêpe, fold over the sides, and roll to enclose the filling. At serving time, brown the rolled crêpes on both sides in melted butter. Serve hot, with sour cream. Sugar and cinnamon, preserves, or applesauce are other possible accompaniments.

SHORTCAKE

¼ cup butter
½ cup sugar
2 eggs
1 cup cold mashed potatoes
1½ cups flour
2 tsp. double-acting baking powder
½ tsp. salt

Cream ¼ cup butter. Work in ½ cup sugar and beat until light and fluffy. A teaspoon of vanilla is an optional addition. Beat well 2 eggs, add 1 cup freshly cooked and cooled or leftover rather dry mashed potatoes, and beat until smooth. Toss or sift together 1½ cups flour with 2 teaspoons double-acting baking powder and ½ teaspoon salt. Add the potato mixture and the flour alternately to the butter-sugar mixture, combining well after each addition. The dough will be soft and just spreadable. Bake in a greased and floured 9-inch square baking pan at 425°F. about 30 minutes. Split and fill with sweetened fruit and top with whipped cream. The shortcake should be served warm from the oven or reheated.

NUTTED SHORTCAKE

Add ½ cup very finely chopped pecans or walnuts to the short-cake dough before baking, and add ½ teaspoon almond extract if desired. Especially good for peach, apricot, or nectarine short-cake.

TIP: In a hurry? Drop the shortcake dough by spoonfuls on a greased and floured baking sheet. Bake at 425°F. about 15 minutes.

CHRISTMAS PUDDING

 ¼ cup butter
 1 cup brown sugar
 2 eggs
 ½ lb. carrots
 ½ lb. potatoes
1¼ cups flour
 1 tsp. soda
 ½ tsp. cinnamon
 ½ tsp. powdered cloves
 ½ tsp. nutmeg
 ½ tsp. salt
 1 cup mixed candied fruits and peels
 1 cup raisins
 1 cup chopped walnuts
   Brandy for flaming (optional)

Cream ¼ cup butter with 1 cup brown sugar, firmly packed for measuring. Beat in 2 eggs, one at a time, beating well after each. Peel and grate 2 average carrots (½ pound) and 2 medium-small potatoes (½ pound) to make 1 cup gratings of each. Add to the sugar mixture. Toss 1¼ cups flour with 1 teaspoon soda and ½ teaspoon each cinnamon, powdered cloves, ground nutmeg, and salt. Reserve ½ cup flour mixture and add the rest gradually to the batter, beating well. Combine 1 cup mixed, chopped candied fruits and fruit peel with 1 cup each raisins and chopped walnuts. Dredge the fruit with the reserved flour and stir into the batter. Butter two 6-cup pudding molds, fill ⅔ full with batter, and cover tightly with foil and the lid. Place on a rack in a kettle, in boiling hot water that reaches half way up the mold. Cover the kettle and steam the pudding for 4 hours, adding more boiling water as needed to keep the level constant. Unmold, garnish with a sprig of holly, and serve with hard sauce. To serve flaming, warm ¼ cup brandy in a small pan or metal ladle, ignite it with a match, and pour it over the pudding. Makes 2 puddings, each serving 8 or more, which can be reheated in the original molds.

BRANDIED POTATO PUDDING

1 *lb. potatoes*
¼ *cup butter*
⅓ *cup sugar*
6 *eggs*
Grated rind of ½ lemon
2 *Tbsp. brandy or rum*
Salt
Nutmeg (optional)
Confectioner's sugar
Fruit preserves

Cook 3 medium potatoes (1 pound) in boiling salted water to cover. Peel and rice. Add half a stick of butter (4 tablespoons) and ⅓ cup sugar. Blend well. Cool slightly. Beat in 6 eggs, one at a time, blending well after each. Add the grated rind of ½ lemon and 2 tablespoons brandy or rum. Taste and add a dash of salt and more sugar, if you like a sweeter pudding. A little nutmeg is an optional addition. Thickly butter a baking dish and add the pudding mixture. Bake at 350°F. about 40 minutes, until the pudding is set and lightly browned. Sprinkle with sifted confectioner's sugar and serve warm or cold, with plum jam or any whole-fruit preserves. For extra zest, add the juice of half a lemon to the preserves to make them tart.

SPICE JUMBLE DESSERT

¾ cup hot mashed potatoes
6 Tbsp. butter
½ cup syrup
2 Tbsp. sugar
1 cup flour
1 tsp. double-acting baking powder
¼ tsp. baking soda
½ tsp. cinnamon
¼ tsp. ginger
¼ tsp. cloves
⅓ cup nutmeats
⅓ cup slivered dates
1 tsp. vanilla

Combine ¾ cup hot or reheated mashed potatoes with 6 table-spoons butter. Stir until the butter melts. Add ½ cup syrup—use corn or maple blend or molasses, but not pure maple, which is too thin for this purpose. Add 2 tablespoons sugar and stir well. Toss or sift in a mixing bowl 1 cup flour, 1 teaspoon double-acting baking powder, ¼ teaspoon baking soda, ½ teaspoon cinnamon, and ¼ teaspoon each ginger and cloves. If the potatoes were un-seasoned, add ½ teaspoon salt. Add the dry ingredients to the potato mixture and stir until smooth. Stir in ⅓ cup each coarsely chopped nutmeats and slivered dates. (Use a scissors, dipped oc-casionally in hot water, to snip the dates.) Grease and flour an 8- or 9-inch square baking pan. Spread batter evenly. Bake at 350°F. about 50 minutes, until browned and firm to the touch. Cut into squares. Serve hot, with whipped cream, as a dessert; or cut into small squares like a bar cooky or chocolate brownies.

SPICE JUMBLE COOKIES

Drop the dessert batter by spoonfuls on a greased baking sheet, and bake at 400°F. until browned and firm. Replace the dates with chopped raisins or semisweet chocolate morsels, and use your own favorite combination of spices.

APPLESAUCE PUDDING

½ cup butter
1 cup sugar
½ cup mashed potatoes
2 eggs
1½ cups flour
1½ tsp. double-acting baking powder
1 tsp. cinnamon
½ tsp. baking soda
½ tsp. cloves
½ tsp. ginger
½ tsp. nutmeg
1 cup applesauce
½ cup raisins

Cream ½ cup butter (1 stick). Gradually add 1 cup sugar and cream until light and smooth. Work in ½ cup cold mashed potatoes. Beat in 2 eggs, one at a time, beating well after each. Toss or sift 1½ cups flour with 1½ teaspoons double-acting baking powder, 1 teaspoon cinnamon, and ½ teaspoon each baking soda, cloves, ginger, and nutmeg. Add the flour to the batter alternately with 1 cup applesauce. Stir in ½ cup raisins. Bake in a greased and floured 8-inch baking dish, at 350°F. about 35 minutes, until the pudding shrinks from the sides of the pan and a skewer inserted in the middle comes out dry. Serve warm, with whipped cream or ice cream.

Receipt for Complexion Care (Great-grandmother's facial formula.) Wash a newly dug potato, chill it well on ice, and cut it into thick slices. Rub the slices on your face, particularly the area around the nose. You will find that this refreshing treatment cleanses the skin, discourages excess oiliness, and is a boon to skins prone to blemishes.

MAPLE PECAN PUDDING

Butter
½ *cup maple-blend syrup*
¾ *cup chopped pecans*
1½ *cups flour*
2½ *tsp. double-acting baking powder*
½ *tsp. salt*
¼ *cup butter*
1 *cup mashed potatoes*
1 *egg*
¼ *cup milk*
Sugar, cinnamon (optional)

Generously butter a 9-inch layer pan, leaving a visibly thick coating of butter on the bottom. Add about ½ cup thick maple-blend syrup, to cover. Sprinkle with ¾ cup chopped pecans or other nutmeats. Toss or sift 1½ cups flour, 2½ teaspoons double-acting baking powder, and ½ teaspoon salt. Cut in ¼ cup butter. Blend with 1 cup dry cold mashed potatoes. Beat 1 egg with ¼ cup milk and stir in. Add a little more milk, if necessary, to make a soft dough that can be handled. Turn the dough out on a floured board, pat it into a thin rectangle, brush with melted butter, and sprinkle lightly with sugar and cinnamon if desired. Roll up and cut into 1-inch slices. Lay the pinwheels side by side on the nuts and syrup in the prepared pan. Bake at 350°F. about 30 minutes, until well browned. Let the pudding stand a few minutes before turning it out on a serving platter, nutty side up. Serve warm, with whipped cream or ice cream. Any leftover pudding can be reheated and served like coffee cake.

FRESH PRUNE DUMPLINGS

1 *lb. potatoes*
2 *Tbsp. butter*
2 *eggs*
½ *tsp. salt*
2 *cups flour*
4 *Tbsp. sugar*
¼ *tsp. powdered cloves*
12 *fresh Italian prunes*

Cook 3 medium potatoes (1 pound) in a small amount of boiling salted water. Peel and force through a sieve or ricer. Or use 2 cups rather dry mashed potatoes. Add 2 tablespoons butter. Beat 2 eggs well and add. Season with about ½ teaspoon salt. Gradually work in 2 cups flour, or a little more, to make a dough that can be kneaded. Roll out ¼-inch thick on a floured board. Cut into 3-inch squares—there should be about a dozen squares. Lay a pitted blue Italian prune or other not-too-juicy variety of plum in the center of each square. If desired, the pit may be replaced with an almond half. Mix 4 tablespoons sugar with about ¼ teaspoon powdered cloves. (If you prefer cinnamon, use a little more than ¼ teaspoon.) Sprinkle a little spiced sugar over the plums. Enclose the plum in the dough and roll between the palms to seal the dumpling. Simmer, covered, in lightly salted water for about 15 minutes. Serve with melted butter and more spiced sugar.

PFLAUMEN KNÖDEL

These German dumplings are filled with cooked dried prunes rather than with the fresh. Pit and chop, or cut into small pieces, enough cooked prunes to make ¾ cup. Season with 2 tablespoons sugar and the grated rind of ¼ lemon. Add a little lemon juice, if necessary. Use to fill dumplings and cook as directed.

LEMON-NUT SOUFFLE

4 eggs, separated
½ cup sugar
½ tsp. salt
1 cup mashed potatoes
1 lemon
2 Tbsp. slivered almonds

Beat 4 egg whites until foamy. Gradually beat in ¼ cup sugar and ½ teaspoon salt, and continue to beat until the meringue is very stiff. Beat 4 egg yolks until light (no need to wash the beater) with ¼ cup sugar (½ cup in all). Beat in 1 cup mashed potatoes. Add the grated rind of a whole lemon and the juice of ½ lemon. Add ¼ the egg-white meringue to the yolks, blending thoroughly. Blend this mixture gently with the rest of the meringue. Fold in 2 tablespoons toasted slivered almonds (the canned variety are ready to use; others require prior blanching, slivering, and oven-toasting). Butter a 6-cup straight-sided soufflé dish and sprinkle it with sugar. Tap out excess sugar. Carefully pour the batter into the soufflé dish and bake at 375°F. about 30 minutes, until the soufflé is lightly browned. This is a soft soufflé; if you like it firm throughout, bake it about 10 minutes longer. Serve at once, from the baking dish. Makes 4 or 5 servings. Especially good with sugared berries or with lemon sauce.

LEMON SAUCE

Mix 2 tablespoons potato starch and 1 cup sugar. Gradually add 2 cups hot water and cook over low heat, stirring, until the sauce is thick and clear. Add the grated rind and juice of 1 lemon and 2 tablespoons butter. Serve warm, with Lemon-Nut Soufflé. Good also with plain cake or with Bread Pudding or Apple Brown Betty.

CHOCOLATE SOUFFLE

2 Tbsp. butter
2 squares baking chocolate
¼ tsp. salt
3 Tbsp. potato starch
¾ cup milk
4 eggs, separated
1 tsp. vanilla extract
⅔ cup sugar

Over low heat or in the top of a double boiler melt 2 tablespoons butter and 2 ounces (2 squares) unsweetened baking chocolate. Stir in ¼ teaspoon salt and 3 tablespoons potato starch. Cook, stirring, for a minute or two. Gradually stir in ¾ cup milk and cook, stirring constantly, until the sauce is thick and smooth. Cover closely and set aside to cool a little. Beat 4 egg yolks until light, then beat them into the cooled sauce. Flavor with 1 teaspoon vanilla extract. Beat 4 egg whites until foamy, beat in ⅔ cup sugar, little by little, and continue to beat until the mixture forms a stiff meringue that will stand up in peaks. Fold about ⅓ this meringue into the sauce, gently but very thoroughly. Fold remainder of meringue in lightly, just to incorporate it. Butter a 6-cup straight-sided soufflé dish and sprinkle it with sugar; tap the dish to shake out excess sugar. Pour the soufflé batter in the dish and set the dish in a pan of boiling water. Bake at 350°F. for 45 to 50 minutes, until the soufflé is well puffed, crusty, and lightly browned. If you like a soufflé that sauces itself, French fashion, increase the heat to 400°F. and reduce the baking time to 30 to 40 minutes. The soufflé will be well puffed but only slightly browned, and when you cut into it the center will be soft and creamy. Serve at once, in the baking dish, with whipped cream if desired.

✺ 15
✺

Garnishes

Food should be attractive to the eye as well as to the palate, for maximum appetite appeal. There are several schools of thought on how to attain that objective. One school leans toward roses carved from raw turnips, swans sculptured from ice, and similar difficult and inedible professional efforts. At the opposite end of the scale, another school relies heavily on a sprig of parsley, often tired and always uneaten, if not inedible. A more moderate school insists that some garnishes, if not all, should be comparatively easy to accomplish and generally edible. This moderate school produces fluted mushrooms, scalloped tomato shells, and scored lemon slices. A fourth school maintains that garnishes should be simple to achieve, good to eat, and decorative, although not necessarily in that order.

Garnishes made with potatoes fulfill all three of these qualifications, and add a fourth: Potatoes naturally belong on almost any menu because they go so well with almost any main dish—meat, fish, or chicken. Several examples of potatoes used as a garnish have been chosen for this chapter, but there are other decorative potato recipes in this book—tiny new potatoes rolled in butter and chopped parsley to surround sautéed or fried fish, stuffed baked potatoes to flank a platter of roast beef, and many, many more.

POMMES DUCHESSE

2 *lbs. potatoes*
½ *cup butter*
   Salt, pepper, nutmeg
4 *egg yolks*
2 *whole eggs*

Cook 6 medium potatoes (2 pounds) in boiling salted water to cover until tender. Drain, dry over the heat uncovered, peel, and mash. Beat in ½ cup butter, and salt, pepper, and a dash of nutmeg to taste. Beat 4 egg yolks and remove and reserve 2 tablespoons in a small cup. Combine the rest with 2 whole eggs and beat again. Blend the eggs well into the mashed potatoes. Force the hot mixture through a pastry bag, with a fancy tube if you like, onto a greased baking sheet. Shape rosettes, swirling cones, bows, loops, or any decorative design you fancy—it takes very little practice to become adept at shaping Pommes Duchesse, because the texture is just right and stays that way (unlike icing mixtures that can begin to harden at the critical moment). Dilute the reserved egg yolk with a little milk or water and lightly brush the high points of the shapes. Bake in a hot oven (450°F.) until the high points are golden. This makes an elegant garnish for a platter of any meat, poultry, or fish, and it is a particularly delicious way to serve potatoes.

BORDURE DE POMMES DUCHESSE

A border of Pommes Duchesse makes a fine finishing touch for casseroles of meat, fish, or vegetables. Or a hot casserole can be completely covered with a swirl of Pommes Duchesse and returned to the oven to brown the meringue-like topping. Pipe Pommes Duchesse around the edge of the board or platter on which a steak has been "planked" and brown in the oven or under the broiler.

POMMES DUCHESSE PIE SHELLS

Generously butter tart molds or a deep pie plate, or any mold you wish to use as a case for sauced mixtures, vegetables, or eggs. Spread the Pommes Duchesse mixture evenly and rather thickly on the bottom and sides of the mold. Brush with egg yolk and bake at 450°F. until the crust is firm to the touch and gilded. Unmold very carefully. Make individual shells the same way, in small pans or molds. Or spread a thick round layer of Pommes Duchesse on a greased baking sheet. Spoon more of the mixture around the edge of the circle and build it up to make a shell deep enough to hold the mixture you want to serve in it. Brush with egg yolk and bake until firm-crusted and very lightly browned. Or, make individual shells, using the same procedure.

POTATO NESTS

2 lbs. potatoes
2 Tbsp. butter
2 Tbsp. milk
1 tsp. grated onion or onion juice
Salt, pepper
2 egg yolks

Cook 6 medium potatoes (2 pounds). Peel and mash. Add 2 tablespoons each butter and hot milk, 1 teaspoon grated onion or onion juice, and salt and pepper to taste. Beat 2 egg yolks lightly. Reserve 2 tablespoons and blend the rest well with the potatoes. With an oval soup spoon, shape 6 or 8 oval mounds on a greased baking sheet. Press with the back of the spoon to make a hollow in the center, with high sides around it. Brush with the reserved egg yolk, mixed with a little milk or water. Bake at 350°F. until well browned. Use as a case for creamed ham, chicken, fish, or chipped beef, or fill with vegetables and use to garnish a roast or add glamour to a vegetable plate.

BAKED POTATOES
USED AS SHELLS

Bake large oval baking potatoes until tender. Split in half and scoop out the pulp. Fill with creamed mushrooms, or any creamed fish, meat, or poultry mixture usually served in patty shells or on toast or rice. Mash the scooped-out pulp with butter, hot milk, and salt and pepper to taste, and force it through a pastry tube to garnish the rim of the potato. Bake or not, but serve very hot.

TIP: The scooped-out potato may be cut into dice and added to the creamed mixture to extend it.

OVEN-FRIED POTATO CASES

Peel potatoes and cut them into julienne, matchlike sticks. The easiest way to make julienne without special equipment is to slice the potatoes thin, stack the slices, and cut equally thin slices across the stack. A grater that makes longish shreds can be used to grate potatoes for this purpose. Season the julienne with salt and pepper. Thoroughly butter muffin pans or small tart pans, or any molds you wish to use. Press the julienne evenly against the bottom and sides of the mold. Butter the outside of a slightly smaller mold and fit it into the first, or use a piece of double-duty foil cut to fit and press it, buttered side down, into the mold over the potatoes. Bake at 450°F. about 15 minutes. Remove the lining, press the potatoes against the mold again, and return to the oven to brown the inside. Carefully remove the cases from the molds and keep hot in a slow oven (250°F.). Use instead of patty shells or toast for creamed chicken and similar dishes, or to hold poached eggs. Or fill with vegetables and garnish a roast.

TIP: To shorten the baking time, pan-fry the potato shreds until they are soft but not brown before lining the molds with them. Just before serving time, bake at 450°F. for about 10 minutes. It will probably not be necessary to keep the cases in shape with foil or another mold.

POTATO MUFFIN PUDDINGS

    2 lbs. potatoes
    3 eggs
    1 onion, grated
    ¾ cup flour
    ¼ tsp. double-acting baking powder
    ½ tsp. salt
       Pepper
    ¼ cup melted fat

Peel and grate 6 medium potatoes (2 pounds) into cold water. Drain, press to extract as much liquid as possible, and dry on a towel. Add 3 eggs and beat well. Grate a medium onion and add. Toss ¾ cup flour with ¼ teaspoon baking powder, ½ teaspoon salt or more to taste, and a dash of pepper. Combine with the potatoes, blending well. The mixture should be stiff enough to hold its shape on a spoon (if necessary, add a little more flour). Stir in ¼ cup melted fat—preferably chicken fat or bacon drippings for best flavor. Grease a 12-cup muffin pan with the same fat and dust the cups with flour. Bake at 350°F. for about 45 minutes, until brown and crisp. Alternate these decorative "muffins" around the edge of the meat platter with small servings of carrots or asparagus or another vegetable in season.

POTATO STICKS AMANDINE

    2 lbs. potatoes
    ¼ cup butter
    2 Tbsp. milk
       Salt, pepper
    1 egg
    ⅓ cup almonds

Cook 6 medium potatoes. Peel and mash well. Add 2 tablespoons each butter and hot milk, and salt and pepper to taste. Beat a large egg and blend well with the potatoes. Shape uniform fingers of this potato mixture by rolling a spoonful between your palms. Melt 2 tablespoons butter (¼ cup in all) in a small pan and add ⅓ cup blanched almonds, rather finely chopped. Cook for a minute to brown the almonds lightly. Coat the potato sticks with the almonds and lay them side by side on a greased baking sheet. Bake at 375°F. until hot and crusty, about 15 minutes.

POTATO PORCUPINES

2 lbs. potatoes
2 Tbsp. butter
　Salt, pepper
　Milk
1 egg
2 Tbsp. water
　Cayenne pepper
　Cornflakes

Cook 6 medium potatoes (2 pounds). Peel and mash. Add 2 tablespoons butter, salt and pepper to taste, and just enough milk to moisten (the mixture should be fairly dry). Shape large spoonfuls of mixture into balls. Beat an egg with 2 tablespoons water and add a dash of cayenne pepper. Crush cornflakes coarsely (do not use the very fine prepared cornflake crumbs). Coat the potato balls with egg, roll in the crushed cornflakes, and bake on a greased baking dish at 400°F., until the balls are hot and crusty. Leftover mashed potatoes can also be treated this way.

FROSTED MEAT LOAF

Bake your favorite meat-loaf mixture in a loaf pan, as usual. Unmold on a baking sheet and frost thickly with 2 cups mashed potatoes or Potatoes Duchesse, swirling the potatoes as you would icing on a cake. Return to the oven to brown the swirls lightly.

CHIP CROQUETTES

>   4 ozs. Swiss or Cheddar cheese
>   4 cups mashed potatoes
>   4 tsp. onion juice or grated onion
>   Salt, pepper
> 1½ cups crushed potato chips

Grate 4 ounces moist Swiss or Cheddar cheese to make 1 cup. Blend with 4 cups rather dry mashed potatoes, and add seasonings to taste: 4 teaspoons onion juice or finely grated onion, salt, and a generous amount of black pepper. Shape the mixture into 12 cones or balls and coat on all sides with about 1½ cups crushed potato chips. Bake on a greased baking sheet at 400°F. for about 20 minutes, until the croquettes are crisp and brown.

NEW POTATO APPLES

Choose uniform small potatoes of apple-like shape. Scrub and scrape, if necessary. Cook in hot deep fat until brown and tender. Stick a clove in each end to simulate the stem and blossom ends of an apple, and sprinkle one cheek with paprika. Use as a garnish.

MASHED POTATO APPLES

Shape well-seasoned, rather dry mashed potatoes into apples or pears, using a clove for the blossom end and a sprig of parsley or watercress for the stem end of the fruit. The potatoes may be seasoned with grated cheese, if desired. Sprinkle one cheek of the fruit with paprika, or with grated yellow cheese in the case of the pears. Bake or not, as desired, but be sure that the "fruit" is hot when it is served.

❧ 16
❧

Main-Course
Potatoes

There are so many meat, fish, and chicken specialties in which potatoes play an important role that choosing those to be included in this book was anything but an easy task. The recipes that survived the final eliminations must serve as representatives for all the others—and as inspiration for imaginative cooks.

A Recipe for Salad

Two large potatoes, passed through a kitchen sieve,
Unwonted softness to the salad give;
Of mordant mustard add a single spoon—
Distrust the condiment which bites too soon:
But deem it not, though made of herbs, a fault
To add a double quantity of salt;
Three times the spoon with oil of Lucca crown,
And once with vinegar procured from town.
True flavor needs it, and your poet begs
The pounded yellow of two well-boiled eggs.
Let onion atoms lurk within the bowl,
And scarce suspected animate the whole;
And lastly on the favored compound toss
A magic teaspoon of anchovy sauce,
Then, though green turtle fail, though venison's tough,
Though ham and turkey are not boiled enough,
Serenely full, the epicure shall say,
Fate cannot harm me—I have dined today.

Sidney Smith

OYSTER CASSEROLE

  2 *lbs. potatoes*
  2 *Tbsp. flour*
  6 *strips bacon*
½ *cup soda cracker crumbs*
  2 *cups oysters with their liquid*
    Milk
    Salt, pepper, cayenne
  2 *Tbsp. butter*

Cook 6 medium potatoes (2 pounds) in boiling salted water. Peel and slice. Toss with 2 tablespoons flour. While the potatoes are cooking, brown 6 slices bacon. Drain and crumble. Grease a 6-cup baking dish with bacon drippings and sprinkle with ¼ cup crushed soda cracker crumbs. Fill the dish with alternate layers of floured sliced potato, 2 cups chopped raw oysters, and the crumbled bacon, finishing with potato. Measure the oyster liquid and add enough milk to make 1 cup. Season well with salt, pepper, and cayenne pepper to taste. Pour the liquid into the casserole, top with ¼ cup cracker crumbs (using ½ cup in all) and dot with 2 tablespoons butter. Bake at 350°F. about 30 minutes, until the casserole is piping hot and the topping lightly browned.

CREAMED SALMON

1½ *lbs. potatoes*
  4 *Tbsp. butter*
  4 *Tbsp. flour*
  2 *cups milk*
    Salt, pepper
  1 *canned pimiento*
  1 *Tbsp. grated onion*
  1 *can (1 lb.) salmon*
    Grated cheese (optional)

Cook 4 medium-large potatoes (1½ pounds) in boiling salted water to cover. Peel and cut into large cubes. While the potatoes are cooking, melt 4 tablespoons butter (¼ cup or ½ stick) in a saucepan, stir in 4 tablespoons flour and cook slowly, stirring, until the mixture just begins to take on color. Stir in 2 cups milk and continue to cook and stir until the sauce is thickened and smooth. Add salt and pepper to taste. Stir the potato cubes into the hot sauce and heat thoroughly. Drain and dry a canned pimiento and sliver it. Add to the sauce with 1 tablespoon finely grated onion. Discard the bones and skin from a 1-pound can of salmon and carefully break the fish into large flakes. Fold gently into the sauce. Heat and add more salt and pepper to taste. If desired, sprinkle with grated cheese and brown quickly under the broiler.

SALMON LOAF

    2 Tbsp. butter
    1 stalk celery
  ½ small onion
 1½ cups mashed potatoes
    2 Tbsp. chopped parsley
    2 Tbsp. lemon juice
      Salt, pepper, hot-pepper sauce
    3 eggs, separated
    1 small can (½ lb.) salmon

Melt 2 tablespoons butter in a skillet. Sliver a stalk of celery and half a small onion and cook until the onion is translucent. Combine the vegetables with 1½ cups mashed potatoes, freshly cooked or leftover, and add 2 tablespoons each chopped parsley and lemon juice, and salt, pepper, and hot-pepper sauce to taste. Beat in 3 egg yolks, blending well. Flake a small can of salmon (about ½ pound) and discard bones and skin. Fold the salmon into the potato mixture. Beat 3 egg whites stiff and fold in gently but thoroughly. Bake in a buttered loaf pan at 350°F. about 1 hour. Unmold and serve with chili sauce or a sauce made by mixing 1 cup green peas with 1 cup well-seasoned medium white sauce. Makes 3 or 4 servings.

FISH ON A COUCH

2 lbs. potatoes
1 cup sour cream
¼ cup minced onion
  Salt, pepper
1 egg
2 lbs. fish fillets
¼ cup butter
¼ cup crumbs
2 Tbsp. grated Parmesan cheese

Cook 6 medium potatoes (2 pounds). Peel and mash. Add ⅓ cup sour cream (⅓ of an 8-ounce container), ¼ cup minced onion, and salt and pepper to taste. Beat in 1 egg. Spread thickly on a buttered, rectangular, oven-to-table baking dish, building up the sides slightly. Cut 2 pounds white fish fillets (flounder is especially good) into uniform pieces. Brown very delicately on both sides in ¼ cup hot butter (½ stick). Do not overcook. Sprinkle with salt and pepper. Sprinkle the potato couch with 2 tablespoons bread crumbs. Arrange the fish fillets on the crumbs and sprinkle them with 2 tablespoons more bread crumbs (¼ cup in all) and 2 tablespoons grated Parmesan cheese. Spread ⅔ cup sour cream (1 cup in all) over all. Bake at 350°F. about 25 minutes. Serve in the baking dish.

BAKED FISH

2 lbs. potatoes
2 Tbsp. butter
½ cup milk
  Salt, pepper
6 fillets of sole
2 Tbsp. minced onion
2 Tbsp. minced green pepper
  Juice of ½ lemon
1 can condensed cream of celery soup

Cook 6 medium potatoes (2 pounds) in boiling salted water until tender. Peel and mash with 2 tablespoons butter, ¼ cup milk, and salt and pepper to taste. Grease a shallow bake-and-serve casserole large enough to hold 6 portions of fish in a single layer. Line it with mashed potatoes, building up the sides to make a border. (Or force some of the potatoes through a pastry bag to make a decorative border.) Lay 6 fillets of sole (or any other white-fleshed fish) on the potatoes. Scatter 2 tablespoons each minced onion and green pepper over the fish and sprinkle with the juice of ½ lemon. Heat 1 can (10½ ounces) condensed cream of celery soup with ¼ cup milk (½ cup milk in all) and pour it over the fish. (Or use cream of mushroom, Cheddar cheese or tomato soup.) Bake at 375°F. about 50 minutes, until the potato border is browned. Test the fish for doneness with a fork—it should flake easily.

SARDINE-STUFFED POTATOES

2 lbs. baking potatoes
2 Tbsp. butter
2 Tbsp. milk
2 cans sardines
1 Tbsp. grated onion
  Salt, pepper
3 hard-cooked eggs
  Parsley or chives for garnish

Bake 6 medium or 3 large baking potatoes (2 pounds). Cut a slice from the flat side of small potatoes or split larger ones vertically. Scoop out the pulp and mash it with about 2 tablespoons each butter and milk. Discard the bones from 2 cans (4 ounces each) sardines, mash, and add to the potatoes. Add 1 tablespoon or more grated onion, and salt and pepper to taste. Put half the filling back into the shells, top each with half a hard-cooked egg, and cover with the remaining filling. Bake at 400°F. until piping hot. Serve sprinkled with chopped parsley or chives.

OYSTERS ON THE POTATO
HALF SHELL

12 *large oysters*
1 *cup oil-and-vinegar salad dressing*
3 *large, oval baking potatoes*
¼ *cup butter*
¼ *cup cream*
   Salt, pepper
½ *cup soft bread crumbs*
2 *Tbsp. butter*

Marinate 12 large oysters, or 18 smaller ones, in 1 cup oil-and-vinegar salad dressing to cover for about an hour. Keep in the refrigerator and turn occasionally to season evenly. Meanwhile, bake 3 large, oval baking potatoes, weighing about 1 pound each. Split in half and scoop out the pulp. Mash with ¼ cup each butter and cream, and season with salt and pepper to taste. Pile back into the half shells, mounting high on the sides and shaping a shallow trough in the middle to hold the oysters. Put two or three marinated oysters in each shell. Toss ½ cup fine soft bread crumbs in 2 tablespoons melted butter and sprinkle over the oysters. Bake at 350°F. about 20 minutes, until the crumbs are browned. Serve hot as a main dish at luncheon or supper.

AD LIB HASH

Hash is the kind of leftover that appears on the menu at restaurants where men eat lunch—and often with a fancy price tag that attests to its popularity. At home, it falls into the budget category, but it still rates high as a family favorite. You can vary the following recipe according to what you have on hand, ad lib.

Combine equal parts of finely cut, diced or chopped (by hand) cooked potatoes and cooked meat in a bowl. Chop 1 onion for each 3 or 4 cups of mixture and cook it until golden in a little hot fat in a skillet. Add the chopped onions to the potato mixture and toss lightly. Add enough water, milk, cream, meat gravy, or bouillon (canned or made with a cube) to moisten. Season with mixed seasoning salt, garlic or onion salt, and a goodly amount of pepper. Heat more fat in the skillet and press the mixture into it. Cook slowly until the hash is browned on the bottom and hot clear through. Fold in half and serve omelet style, or sprinkle with chopped chives or parsley and serve unbrowned side up. Or cover the skillet with a large plate and invert it to unmold the hash, browned side up. Add a little more fat to the pan and slide the hash back into the skillet, browned side up, to brown the bottom. Top each serving with a poached egg and pass the chili sauce. Hash made with 4 cups mixture will serve no more than 4, and probably fewer!

CORNED BEEF HASH

Follow the pattern for Ad Lib Hash, using 2 cups each finely hand-chopped corned beef and cooked potatoes, with water as the moistening agent. A little Worcestershire sauce is a good seasoning aid.

RED FLANNEL HASH

Make Ad Lib Hash with 2 cups chopped (by hand) corned beef and an equal amount of potatoes, plus 1 cup chopped cooked or canned beets.

BAKED HASH

Prepare Ad Lib Hash as directed, spread on a buttered baking dish, and bake in a moderate oven (350°F.) until it is piping hot and crusty, about 30 minutes.

BAKED HASH WITH EGGS

When Baked Hash, above, is hot and about to brown, shape 4 hollows with the back of a tablespoon. Drop an egg into each, season with salt and pepper, and return to the oven to bake about 10 minutes longer, just until the whites are firm.

HAMBURGER HASH

3 Tbsp. fat
1 lb. ground beef
½ green pepper
1 medium onion
1 lb. potatoes
   Salt, pepper
½ cup hot water
¼ cup ketchup

Heat 3 tablespoons fat in a skillet. Add 1 pound ground beef and cook, stirring, until the meat is browned. Chop half a green pepper and 1 medium onion and add to the meat. Cook a minute or two. Peel and grate 3 medium potatoes (1 pound) directly into the skillet, stirring in the gratings as you go. Add ½ cup hot water and salt and pepper to taste. Cover the skillet and cook the hash slowly until potatoes are cooked and the bottom is crusty, about 25 minutes. Use a wide-bladed spatula to loosen and lift the hash from the bottom of the skillet, and add a little more fat if necessary. Spread ¼ cup ketchup over the hash and put the skillet under the broiler flame for a minute to glaze the top.

ROAST BEEF HASH

1 lb. roast beef
1 lb. raw potatoes
1 onion
½ green pepper
1 slice white bread
1 egg
½ cup meat juices
   Salt, pepper, garlic salt, celery salt

Put 1 pound (2 cups) leftover roast beef or pot roast (or as much as 1½ pounds, if you have it) through a food chopper. Peel 1 pound raw potatoes (about 3 medium) and a medium onion. Put these through the chopper with half a seeded green pepper and 1 large slice white bread. Blend all together and add 1 egg and ½ cup liquid—the meat juices or gravy, or bouillon made with a cube. Season to your taste—much depends on the original seasoning of the meat and gravy—with salt, pepper, and garlic or celery salt. Heat a heavy skillet, grease lightly, add the hash mixture, and cook over moderate heat until the bottom is well browned. Turn and brown the other side. If potatoes are still raw to the taste, cover the skillet and cook a little longer.

MEAT AND MUSHROOM HASH

2 *cups cooked meat*
2 *cups cooked potatoes*
1 *onion*
1 *can condensed mushroom soup*
1 *small can (4 or 6 ozs.) mushroom slices*
  Salt, pepper, soy sauce
2 *Tbsp. fat or bacon drippings*

Chop by hand, or cut finely, 1 pound any cooked meat or poultry (2 cups) and 1 pound cooked peeled potatoes. Grate 1 medium onion. Add half a can of condensed mushroom soup. Drain a small can (4 or 6 ounces) sliced mushrooms, reserving the liquid. Add the mushrooms to the hash mixture, stir to combine, and season with salt, pepper, and a dash of soy sauce to taste. Heat 2 tablespoons meat fat or bacon drippings in a skillet, add the hash, and cook over moderate heat until browned on the bottom and hot through. Heat the remaining half can of mushroom soup with the mushroom liquid, season to taste, and use as a sauce.

CREAMED CHICKEN HASH

1½ lbs. potatoes
½ onion
½ green pepper
2 Tbsp. butter
1 Tbsp. flour
1 cup chicken broth
   Salt, pepper, poultry seasoning
2 cups diced cooked chicken

Cook 4 medium-large potatoes (1½ pounds) in boiling salted
water to cover. Peel and dice. (Or use 3 cups leftover potatoes,
diced.) While the potatoes are cooking, chop half an onion and
half a green pepper (or use ½ cup celery), and cook in 2 tablespoons melted butter until golden. Sprinkle with 1 tablespoon
flour and cook a few minutes, stirring, until the roux begins to
turn golden. Gradually add 1 cup chicken broth, or 1 cup boiling
water and a chicken bouillon cube. Cook, stirring, until the sauce
is smooth. Add salt and pepper to taste and a pinch of poultry
seasoning. Stir in 2 cups cooked chicken (or turkey) cut into
small pieces. Fold in the diced potatoes, adjust the seasoning
with salt and pepper, and heat gently. Enough for 5 servings.
With the onion and green pepper (or celery) add and cook ½
pound sliced mushrooms, or use canned mushrooms, and add the
liquid to the hash, if needed, to moisten it.

FISH HASH

2 cups cooked fish
1 lb. potatoes
1 Tbsp. grated onion
3 Tbsp. butter
1 egg
   Salt, pepper

Flake 1 pound (2 cups) leftover cooked fish, discarding bones and skin. Peel and cube 3 medium potatoes (1 pound). Cook in boiling salted water to cover about 5 minutes, until just tender. Drain and add to fish with 1 tablespoon grated onion. Melt 1 tablespoon butter in a skillet and pour it over the mixture. Beat 1 egg lightly and add. Toss gently to mix, adding salt and pepper to taste. Melt 2 more tablespoons butter in the skillet. Spread the fish mixture evenly in the pan with a spatula. Cook over moderate heat until the bottom is crisply browned. Cut into wedges, turn and brown the other side. Serve in wedges with ketchup.

> *Soup Trick* Dissolve a bouillon cube or two in the boiling water used to cook potatoes, and adjust the salt accordingly. Makes a pleasant difference in color and flavor.

CLAM HASH

1 lb. potatoes
2 cups chopped clams
1 onion, chopped
6 Tbsp. butter
   Salt, pepper
½ cup cream
   Chopped parsley and lemon wedges for garnish

Cook 3 medium potatoes (1 pound) in boiling salted water to cover. Peel and cut into cubes. (Or use 2 cups leftover potatoes, diced.) Combine with 2 cups chopped clams, fresh or canned. Chop an onion and cook it for a few minutes in 4 tablespoons butter (¼ cup). Add to the clams and potatoes with salt and pepper to taste. Melt the remaining 2 tablespoons butter in a skillet. Spread the clam mixture firmly in the skillet and cook slowly until the bottom is brown. Gently pour in ½ cup cream, distributing it evenly over the hash. Continue to cook 15 minutes longer, until the cream is absorbed. Sprinkle with chopped parsley and serve with lemon wedges.

LIVER-STUFFED POTATOES

 2 *lbs. baking potatoes*
 3 *Tbsp. butter*
 2 *onions*
 1 *lb. chicken livers*
   Salt, pepper
 ¼ *cup sour cream*
   Grated cheese for garnish

Bake 6 medium uniform potatoes, or 3 large oval baking potatoes, (2 pounds) as directed. While the potatoes are baking melt 3 tablespoons butter in a skillet. Chop 2 onions and cook in the butter until translucent. Cut up 1 pound chicken livers (or use calf's liver or another, if you prefer). Add, and cook gently until no longer pink, stirring often to prevent the onions from burning. Chop finely. (You can use a meat grinder or chop the livers by hand—an electric blender makes the mixture too smooth.) Cut a slice from the flat side of the smaller potatoes, or cut the larger ones in half lengthwise. Scoop out some of the pulp, leaving a rather thick shell. Mash the pulp and combine it with the chopped liver mixture. Season well with salt and pepper to taste. Pile the liver stuffing high in the potato shells. Coat each with a little sour cream and sprinkle with grated cheese. Return the shells to the oven and bake until the cheese topping melts and browns and the potatoes are very hot.

SUPPER SPECIAL

 2 *lbs. baking potatoes*
 ½ *cup finely chopped sauerkraut*
   Pepper
 6 *frankfurters*
   Mustard

Bake 6 medium or 3 large oval potatoes (2 pounds). Cut a slice from the smaller potatoes or split the larger ones in half, and scoop out the pulp. Mash. Drain ½ cup finely chopped sauerkraut (measure after chopping) very well, pressing to force out the liquid. Combine with the mashed potatoes and add a generous amount of pepper and, if necessary, a little salt. Pile the mixture into the potato shells. Slice 6 frankfurters and place on top of the potatoes. Dab the slices with mustard. Bake at 400°F. until the frankfurters are hot and brown-edged. Or brown under the broiler.

HASH-STUFFED POTATOES

2 *lbs. baking potatoes*
2 *Tbsp. milk*
2 *Tbsp. butter*
1 *cup cooked meat*
2 *Tbsp. mayonnaise*
2 *Tbsp. chopped chives*
2 *Tbsp. chopped parsley*
   Salt, pepper
   Tabasco and Worcestershire sauce

Scrub and bake 6 medium oval baking potatoes or 3 large ones. Split the large potatoes lengthwise and scoop out the pulp; smaller potatoes should be scooped out through an opening on the flat side. Mash the pulp with 2 tablespoons each hot milk and butter. Add 1 cup leftover cooked meat, any kind, ground or finely chopped. Add 2 tablespoons each mayonnaise and chopped chives, or use 1 tablespoon each chopped parsley and ordinary onion. Season highly to taste with salt, pepper, and dashes of hot-pepper sauce and Worcestershire sauce. Pile the mixture into the shells and bake at 350°F. until hot, about 15 minutes. Good with mushroom sauce or tomato spaghetti sauce; or serve with ketchup or bottled chili sauce.

FISH STEW

½ *cup butter*
2 *onions*
2 *carrots*
3 *peppercorns*
3 *cloves*
2 *lbs. fish fillets*
2 *lbs. potatoes*
1 *tsp. salt*
  Chopped parsley for garnish

Melt ½ cup butter (1 stick or ¼ pound) in a saucepan. Chop 2 onions, and slice 2 carrots very thinly. Cook both in the butter for a few minutes without browning them. Add 3 peppercorns and 3 whole cloves. (If you tie the whole spices in a small piece of cheesecloth, they can easily be removed from the stew before serving it.) Cut 2 pounds fish fillets into serving pieces and lay the pieces on the vegetables, or use about 2½ pounds fish steaks, with the bone. (The bone adds flavor, but should be removed before serving.) Cod, haddock, or any firm-fleshed white-meated fish is good in this stew. Peel and dice 6 medium potatoes (2 pounds) and spread the dice over the fish. Add 1 teaspoon salt and enough water just to cover the potatoes. Bring the stew gently to a boil and simmer, covered, for about 15 minutes, just until the potatoes are tender and the fish flakes easily at the touch of a fork. Adjust the seasoning with salt and pepper. Discard the whole spices and the fish bones, if any, and serve the stew in soup plates. Sprinkle with chopped parsley.

SCALLOP CHOWDER

4 *slices bacon*
1 *onion*
1 *lb. potatoes*
1 *cup water*
1 *tsp. vinegar*
  Salt
1 *pint sea scallops*
1 *lb. white-fleshed fish fillets*
1 *Tbsp. butter*
1 *Tbsp. flour*
1 *cup milk*
  Salt, pepper, paprika

Cut 4 slices bacon into small pieces and cook in a saucepan until brown. Skim off the bacon bits and reserve them. Slice a small onion into the hot fat and cook for a minute or two. Peel 3 potatoes (1 pound) and cut into small cubes. Add to the pan with 1 cup water, 1 teaspoon vinegar, and a little salt. Bring to a boil, reduce the heat, and simmer, covered, about 5 minutes. Wash and dry 1 pint small sea scallops (cut larger bay scallops in half) and cut 1 pound haddock, halibut, or other white-fleshed fish fillets into matching pieces. Add the fish to the saucepan, cover, and cook about 10 minutes, just until the fish loses its translucent look. Make a white sauce in another pan: Melt 1 tablespoon butter, stir in 1 tablespoon flour, and cook a minute or two, stirring constantly. Gradually add 1 cup milk and continue to cook and stir until the sauce is smooth and thickened. Add the white sauce to the fish and heat together. Season with salt, pepper, and paprika to taste. Serve very hot, garnished with crisp bacon bits. Makes 6 meal-size servings, more stew than soup.

FISH SOUFFLE

2 cups mashed potatoes
2 eggs, separated
2 Tbsp. chopped chives
1 pkg. (10 ozs.) frozen green peas
2 Tbsp. butter
2 Tbsp. chopped onion
2 Tbsp. flour
  Milk
  Salt, pepper
1 lb. white fish fillets

Blend 2 cups seasoned mashed potatoes, freshly cooked or left-over, with 2 egg yolks and 2 tablespoons chopped chives. Spread in the bottom of a buttered 2-quart casserole that can be brought to the table. Cook 1 package (about 10 ounces) frozen green peas, as directed. Drain and reserve the liquid, and spread the peas over the potatoes. Melt 2 tablespoons butter in a saucepan, add 2 tablespoons chopped onion, and cook until the onion is translucent but not brown. Sprinkle with 2 tablespoons flour and cook for a minute or two. Gradually add the liquid drained from the peas, plus enough milk to make 1 cup in all. Cook, stirring, until the sauce is smooth and thickened. Season with salt and pepper. Cook 1 pound fish fillets in a little butter, without browning them, until just done. Break into large flakes. Add the fish to the sauce. Beat the 2 egg whites stiff and carefully fold into the sauce. Pour the sauce over the peas. Bake at 350°F. about 45 minutes, until the soufflé is puffed and browned. Serve at once in the baking dish.

MEAT LOAF

1 lb. potatoes
2 lbs. meat-loaf mixture
½ cup ketchup
1 onion
1 clove garlic
  Salt, pepper
  Oregano or marjoram
  Sage

Peel and grate 3 medium potatoes (1 pound) into 2 pounds ground meat-loaf mixture—equal parts of beef, pork, and veal. (Or use all beef.) Mix at once. Add ½ cup ketchup. Grate a medium onion and a clove of garlic and add to the meat with salt and pepper to taste. Pinches of oregano or marjoram and sage are optional additions. Shape the mixture into a loaf and bake on a greased baking sheet at 350°F. about 1½ hours, or less if all beef is used. Serve with ketchup or chili sauce. Makes 8 or more servings. Good cold, too, and great in lunch-box sandwiches with pickle relish.

VARIATIONS:

1. Substitute stewed tomatoes (the kind cooked with green pepper and onion) for the ketchup, and use the rest of the can as a sauce, to pour over the loaf at serving time or during baking.
2. Do the same with undiluted condensed tomato soup.
3. Add an egg or two to the mixture.
4. Vary seasonings to suit your taste: chili powder, poultry seasoning, and mixed seasoning salts are all good with meat loaf.
5. In short, simply add grated raw potato as an extender and binder to your favorite recipe for meat loaf, and you will enjoy a lighter, juicier, more nutritious, better-tasting loaf!

MIXED MEAT BALLS

   1 onion
   2 Tbsp. butter
   1 cup mashed potatoes
1½ lbs. meat-loaf mixture
    Flour
   2 eggs
   1 cup milk
   1 tsp. sugar
    Salt, pepper, nutmeg
    Fat

Chop a medium-large onion and cook in 2 tablespoons butter until golden. Mix with 1 cup mashed potatoes. Blend the potato mixture with 1½ pounds ground mixed meat—a combination of beef, veal, and pork (or use any two of these). Sprinkle with 4 tablespoons flour (¼ cup) and blend well. Beat 2 eggs with 1 cup milk and add with 1 teaspoon sugar, and salt, pepper, and nutmeg to season well. Chill the mixture for several hours to make it firm enough to handle. Shape small balls, coat them with flour, and fry in deep hot fat (360°F.) until browned and cooked through. Serve with tomato sauce or ketchup.

TIP: For a party, pierce each with a cocktail pick and serve hot with any dipping sauce. A mixture of sour cream and horseradish is good with these.

RAPEE WITH HAM

   4 eggs
  ⅓ cup milk
   3 ozs. Swiss or Cheddar cheese
   1 bunch scallions
   4 Tbsp. butter
  ½ lb. cooked ham
   1 lb. potatoes
    Salt, pepper, mustard

Beat 4 eggs with ⅓ cup milk. Add 3 ounces grated cheese (about ¾ cup), Swiss or Cheddar, as you prefer. Slice the white parts of a bunch of scallions, and chop the green parts separately. Add the green to the egg mixture. Melt 4 tablespoons butter in a skillet, add the white scallion slices (there should be about ½ cup), and cook until translucent. Sliver ½ pound sliced cooked ham (or use about 1 cup finely diced leftover ham) and toss with the scallions and butter until hot. Combine with the eggs. Peel and grate 3 medium potatoes (1 pound) directly into the egg mixture. Season to taste with salt, pepper, and a little mustard if desired. Bake in a buttered, shallow oven-to-table casserole at 375°F. about 35 minutes, or until the top is browned and the potatoes cooked.

HAM PUDDING

2 lbs. potatoes
⅓ cup hot milk
4 Tbsp. butter
  Salt, pepper
3 egg yolks
½ lb. ham
3 Tbsp. bread crumbs
3 Tbsp. grated Parmesan cheese

Cook 6 medium potatoes (2 pounds) in boiling salted water to cover. Peel and mash. Beat in ⅓ cup hot milk, 4 tablespoons butter (¼ cup or ½ stick) and salt and pepper to taste. Add 3 egg yolks and beat well. Cut ½ pound cooked sliced ham into slivers (or chop leftover ham to make 1 cup). Fill a buttered baking dish with alternate layers of potato mixture and ham, beginning and ending with potato. Sprinkle with a mixture of 3 tablespoons each bread crumbs and grated Parmesan cheese. Bake at 400°F. about 25 minutes, until the top browns.

Farmhouse Medicine Long before the word *vitamin* came into our vocabularies, our ancestors stored potatoes for the winter as a preventive against scurvy. They may have thought that potatoes had some magic quality, but we know it is the ascorbic acid content.

HAM SCALLOP

    2 *lbs. potatoes*
    ¼ *cup grated onion*
    ½–1 *lb. cooked ham*
        Pepper, salt
        Mustard (*optional*)
    2 *cups milk*

Peel and thinly slice 6 medium potatoes (2 pounds). Fill a greased 2-quart casserole with alternate layers of potatoes, ¼ cup grated onion, and ½ to 1 pound thinly sliced or slivered cooked ham. (If leftover ground ham is used, 1 to 2 cups are needed.) Season as you go with pepper, and if the ham is not excessively salty, use a very little salt. Mustard may be added to taste. Heat 2 cups milk to the boiling point and add to the baking dish. The milk should barely show through the potatoes. Cover the casserole and bake at 350°F. for 50 minutes. Add more hot milk if necessary. Remove the cover, increase the heat to 450°F., and bake about 10 minutes longer, until the scallop is brown and crusty and the potatoes tender.

HAM-AND-CHEESE SCALLOP

Substitute ¼ pound grated cheese for ½ cup of the ham in the recipe above. Sprinkle the top with 2 tablespoons grated cheese and bake as directed.

HAM STEAK SCALLOP

     2 *lbs. potatoes*
     1 *medium onion*
     ¼ *cup flour*
         Salt, pepper
     2 *lbs. ham steak*
     1 *can consommé*
     ½ *cup milk*
     2 *Tbsp. butter*

Peel and thinly slice 6 medium potatoes (2 pounds). Chop 1
onion and combine with the potatoes. Sprinkle with ¼ cup flour,
and salt and pepper to taste. Toss well to distribute the flour and
seasonings. Spread half this mixture in a casserole large enough
to hold a tenderized, but not cooked, ham steak weighing about
2 pounds. Taste the ham for saltiness—if necessary, cover it with
cold water, bring it to a boil, and drain. Lay the ham steak on the
potatoes and cover it with the remaining potatoes, spreading
evenly. Mix 1 can (about 10 ounces) condensed chicken or beef
consommé with ½ cup milk. (Or use a bouillon cube, plus 1 cup
boiling water and ¾ cup milk.) Pour this mixture over the potatoes. Dot with 2 tablespoons butter and bake, covered, at
375°F. about 1 hour. Remove the cover and continue to bake
until the potatoes are tender and browned, 20 minutes or longer.

GOLDEN BAKE

1½ lbs. potatoes
2 Tbsp. butter
Salt, pepper
⅓ cup milk
1 lb. chopped lean pork
1 onion
1 garlic clove
½ tsp. thyme or sage
1 tsp. chopped parsley
1 egg

Cook 4 medium-large potatoes (1½ pounds). Peel and mash with 2 tablespoons butter and salt and pepper to taste. Add ⅓ cup hot milk and beat well. While the potatoes are cooking, brown slowly 1 pound chopped lean pork in a skillet with salt and pepper to taste. Stir with a fork to separate the grains and keep them from sticking. Chop a medium onion and a small garlic clove, and cook with the meat for about 10 minutes, covered, stirring often. Season with ½ teaspoon thyme or sage. Spread the pork in an 8-inch baking dish, sprinkle with 1 teaspoon chopped parsley, and cover with the freshly mashed and seasoned potatoes. (Or use 3 cups reheated mashed potatoes.) Beat 1 egg with a rotary beater until frothy and add salt and pepper to taste. Pour the egg over the potatoes. Bake at 375°F. about 10 minutes, until brown. Good with other meats, too, freshly cooked or leftover.

GROUND BEEF STEW

½ cup butter
3 onions
½ lb. ground beef
1 can (8 ozs.) tomatoes
Salt, pepper
2 lbs. potatoes
2 cups water

Heat ¼ cup butter in a saucepan (or use another flavorful fat).
Chop 3 onions and cook a few minutes until golden. Add 1 cup
ground beef (½ pound). Cook, stirring, until the meat loses its
red color. (Or use 1 cup finely chopped cooked meat, or leftover
hamburger.) Add a small can (8 ounces) solid-pack tomatoes
and cook slowly for 10 minutes. Season well with salt and pepper.
Peel 6 medium potatoes (2 pounds) and cut them in quarters.
Melt ¼ cup butter (½ cup in all) in a skillet and brown the potato quarters lightly on all sides. Add them to the saucepan with
2 cups water. Bring the mixture to a boil and simmer 30 minutes,
until the potatoes are tender.

HAMBURGER SCALLOP

2 Tbsp. fat
1 lb. ground beef
1 onion
  Salt, pepper
1 Tbsp. butter
1 Tbsp. flour
1½ cups milk
1 lb. potatoes

Heat a skillet with 2 tablespoons bacon or meat drippings. Add 1
pound ground beef and 1 onion, chopped. Cook, stirring with a
fork, until the meat loses its red color. Pour off excess fat. Season
to taste with salt and pepper. In a saucepan, melt 1 tablespoon
butter, stir in 1 tablespoon flour, and cook a minute or two, stirring. Add 1½ cups milk and continue to cook and stir until the
sauce is thickened and smooth. Add salt and pepper to taste. Peel
3 medium potatoes (1 pound) and cut into thin slices. Fill a
greased baking dish with alternate layers of beef, potatoes, and
sauce, ending with potatoes and sauce. Cover and bake at 350°F.
about 1 hour, until the potatoes are tender. Remove the cover
and bake 5 to 10 minutes longer at 450°F.—or put the dish under
the broiler for a few minutes to brown the top.

SHEPHERD'S PIE

Shepherd's Pie is traditionally made with leftover potatoes and other vegetables, along with the leftover lamb and gravy that inspired its creation. But it is often necessary to supplement meager leftovers with some freshly cooked vegetables. Freshly cooked and mashed potatoes make a lighter crust for the pie. The following recipe is intended to be used as a rule of thumb and a general guide.

> 2 *cups leftover roast lamb*
> 2 *cups gravy*
> 1 *cup cooked vegetables*
> *Salt, pepper, rosemary*
> 1 *lb. potatoes*
> 2 *Tbsp. butter*
> ¼ *cup hot milk*

Cut cooked lamb (or other meat) into 2 cups small dice. Heat 2 cups gravy. (Leftover gravy can be supplemented with the canned product, or a sauce made with bouillon cubes.) Add 1 cup cooked vegetables—carrots, green beans, or peas are most usual. Heat this mixture, simmer a few minutes, and adjust the seasoning with salt, pepper, and a pinch of rosemary, thyme, or sage. Add the meat. Meanwhile, boil 3 medium potatoes (1 pound). Peel and mash. Add 2 tablespoons butter, ¼ cup hot milk, and salt and pepper to taste. Put the meat mixture into a 6-cup casserole and top with a swirl of mashed potatoes. Brush with milk. An egg can be beaten into the potatoes, if you wish, or the potatoes can be brushed with egg yolk. Bake at 400°F. about 15 minutes, until the topping browns and puffs a little. Serve in the casserole.

FOR VARIETY: Some cooks prefer to toss the diced meat in hot fat before combining it with the gravy. Roasted meat will toughen if it is heated too long, so avoid over-cooking.

STEAK AND KIDNEY PIE

2 *beef kidneys*
1 *lb. round steak*
  Salt
  Flour
1 *onion, chopped*
3 *cups water*
3 *bouillon cubes*
  Pepper, Worcestershire sauce
1 *lb. potatoes*
  Pie pastry for 1 crust

Trim the fat from 2 beef kidneys and render it in a skillet. Leave 3 or 4 tablespoons fat in the pan and reserve the rest for another purpose. Peel the membranes from the kidneys with a sharp knife and cut out the tough white veins. Cover with cold water and chill in the refrigerator for half an hour. Cut into strips. Cut 1 pound round steak into matching strips. Drain the kidneys and dredge kidney and steak strips heavily with lightly salted flour. Add a chopped onion to the kidney fat in the skillet and cook until translucent. Add the floured kidneys and steak strips and brown on all sides, turning often. Stir in 3 cups hot water and 3 bouillon cubes—two beef and one vegetable, or all beef. Cook, stirring, until the sauce is smooth. Cover the skillet and simmer until meat is nearly tender, about 1½ hours. Adjust the seasoning with pepper and Worcestershire sauce. Add 3 medium potatoes (1 pound), peeled and cut into cubes, and cook until meat and potatoes are tender. Transfer the mixture to a deep baking dish. There should be enough thinnish sauce barely to cover. Cover with the pie pastry (your favorite type) and bake at 450°F. until the pastry is brown, 15 to 20 minutes.

PORK CHOPS EN CASSEROLE

> 6 *double-thick loin chops*
> *Salt, pepper*
> 1 *clove garlic*
> 2 *lbs. potatoes*
> 2 *onions*
> 2 *apples*
> 6 *slices Canadian bacon*
> ½ *cup dry white wine*
> *Chopped parsley for garnish*

Trim the fat from 6 double-thick loin pork chops and season the chops well with salt and pepper. Render the fat in a heavy skillet. Add a clove of garlic, finely chopped, and brown the pork chops well on both sides. Meanwhile, peel and slice 6 medium potatoes (2 pounds), 2 onions, and 2 large apples. Grease a casserole fitted with a lid and fill it with layers of potato and onion slices, seasoning lightly with salt and pepper. Lay the browned chops on top and cover them with 6 thin slices Canadian bacon. Pour ½ cup dry white wine into the casserole. Cover tightly with the lid and bake at 350°F. about 1 hour and 15 minutes, until potatoes and meat are tender. Spoon off any excess fat, sprinkle with chopped parsley, and serve in the casserole.

PORK CHOP SCALLOP

> 6 *double-thick pork chops*
> *Salt, pepper*
> 1½ *lbs. potatoes*
> 1 *onion*
> 2 *Tbsp. flour*
> ¼ *tsp. poultry seasoning or sage*
> 1 *cup milk*

Trim excess fat from 6 double-thick pork chops, preferably loin chops. Season with salt and pepper. Rub a heated skillet with the fat and brown the chops slowly on both sides. Grease a large shallow casserole with the drippings in the skillet. (The casserole should have a tightly fitting cover.) Peel and thinly slice 4 medium-large potatoes (1½ pounds) and 1 large onion. Fill the casserole with alternate layers of potato slices and onion, sprinkling each layer with flour (2 tablespoons or less in all), salt and pepper, and about ¼ teaspoon poultry seasoning or sage. You can increase the herbs to taste. Add 1 cup hot milk. Taste and add a little more salt and pepper, if desired. Lay the browned chops on top of the potatoes and cover the casserole. Bake at 350°F. about 1 hour or longer, until potatoes and meat are tender and thoroughly cooked. Remove the lid and bake a few minutes longer to crisp the chops a little.

SAUSAGE SOUFFLE

½ lb. fresh pork sausages
1½ lbs. potatoes
2 Tbsp. butter
1 cup milk
Salt, pepper
3 eggs, separated

Put ½ pound fresh pork sausage links in a small skillet. Cover with water, bring to a boil, and cook rapidly until the water boils away. Continue to cook slowly until the sausages are lightly browned on all sides, turning often. Cut into small slices. Cook 4 medium-large potatoes (1½ pounds) in boiling salted water to cover. Peel and mash with 2 tablespoons butter, 1 cup hot milk, and salt and pepper to taste. Stir in the browned sausage slices. Beat 3 egg whites stiff, and with the same beater (no need to wash it) beat the 3 egg yolks until light. Stir the egg yolks into the potato mixture, blending well. Fold in the beaten egg whites gently. Bake in a buttered 6-cup baking dish at 350°F. for about 40 minutes, until the soufflé is well puffed and lightly browned.

SKILLET PORK-POTATO STEW

1 lb. lean pork shoulder
3 onions
1 Tbsp. flour
4 cups water
  Salt, pepper
1 bay leaf
  Parsley
1 stalk celery
2 lbs. potatoes

Trim the fat from 1 pound lean boneless pork shoulder and render it in a large heavy skillet. Discard the cracklings and all but 2 tablespoons of the fat. Cut 3 onions into eighths. Cut the pork meat into 1-inch cubes. Brown together in the pork fat remaining in the skillet, stirring often. Sprinkle with 1 tablespoon flour and stir for a minute or two to brown the flour. Gradually stir in 4 cups hot water and cook, stirring, until the mixture comes to a boil. Add salt and pepper to taste. Tie a bay leaf, a sprig of parsley, and a stalk of celery (with the leaves) with thread, and add this bouquet to the pot. Simmer 15 minutes, tightly covered. Peel 6 medium potatoes (2 pounds) and cut into quarters. Add to the stew, cover the skillet, and simmer about 30 minutes, until the meat is tender and the potatoes cooked. Shake the skillet occasionally to prevent sticking. Discard the herb bouquet, add more salt and pepper to taste, and sprinkle with fresh parsley.

VEAL CHOPS GRAND'MERE

6 loin veal chops
  Salt, pepper
  Flour
¼ cup beef fat
1 jar (1 lb.) boiled onions
1 can (6 ozs.) whole button mushrooms
1 bouillon cube
1 lb. potatoes

Season 6 thick, meaty loin veal chops with salt and pepper and dredge with flour. Heat ¼ cup rendered beef fat or other shortening in a flame-proof casserole or a deep skillet large enough to hold the chops side by side. Brown the chops on both sides, very slowly, and remove to a plate to keep warm. Drain and reserve the liquid from a 1-pound jar of boiled onions and a 6-ounce can of button mushrooms. Add onions and mushrooms to the fat in the pan and cook, stirring, until the onions are golden. Remove to the plate with the chops. Add the onion and mushroom liquid to the pan, with enough water to make 1 cup, and a bouillon cube. Cook for a few minutes, stirring and scraping in the brown bits clinging to the pan. Return the chops to the pan. Peel and cut 3 medium potatoes (1 pound) into large cubes. Cook potatoes and meat together, covered, until the potatoes are barely tender, about 15 minutes. Return the onions and mushrooms to the pan and continue to cook 5 to 10 minutes longer, until meat and potatoes are tender. Taste and adjust the seasoning.

BAKED FRANKS AND POTATO SALAD

2 *lbs. potatoes*
6 *Tbsp. oil*
3 *Tbsp. vinegar*
½ *tsp. prepared mustard*
  Salt, pepper
½ *onion*
½ *green pepper*
6 *frankfurters*

Cook 6 medium potatoes (2 pounds) in boiling salted water to cover. Peel and slice. Mix 6 tablespoons oil with 3 tablespoons vinegar, ½ teaspoon prepared mustard (or more to taste), and salt and pepper. Pour over the warm potatoes and turn gently to coat. Chop ½ onion and ½ green pepper. Fill a greased 6-cup casserole with alternate layers of potato salad, chopped onion and pepper, and 6 frankfurters, skinned, split, and cut into bite-size chunks. Bake at 375°F. about 35 minutes, until piping hot. Serve with thickly sliced tomatoes.

TURKEY POT PIE

1 *can cream of mushroom soup*
¼ *cup milk*
1 *cup cooked green peas*
1 *cup cooked sliced carrots*
2 *cups diced cooked turkey*
2 *Tbsp. sherry*
  Salt, pepper
  Pot Pie Crust (recipe below)

Heat 1 can (about 10 ounces) condensed cream of mushroom soup with ¼ cup milk, stirring with a whisk to make a smooth sauce. Add 1 cup each cooked, drained green peas and sliced carrots, or the equivalent in other freshly cooked or leftover vegetables, and 2 cups diced cooked turkey or chicken. Heat gently. Add 2 tablespoons sherry and adjust the seasoning with salt and pepper to taste. Pour the creamy mixture into a 6-cup baking dish and cover with Pot Pie Crust, below. Cut several gashes in the crust and bake at 400°F. about 20 minutes, until the crust is brown and the pie bubbling hot.

POT PIE CRUST

1 *cup mashed potatoes*
  Salt, pepper
1 *egg*
2 *Tbsp. melted butter, fat, or bacon drippings*
1½ *tsp. double-acting baking powder*
  Flour

Season 1 cup dry mashed potatoes, freshly cooked or leftover, with salt and pepper to taste. Beat in 1 egg and 2 tablespoons melted butter, poultry fat, or bacon drippings. Sprinkle with 1½ teaspoons double-acting baking powder and blend. Stir in just enough flour to make a dough that can be handled, about ⅔ cup. Pat or roll out between sheets of well-floured waxed paper, to make a circle or rectangle that fits the baking dish. Use to top Turkey Pot Pie, Shepherd's Pie, or any similar hot mixture.

CHICKEN BONNE FEMME

4 lbs. chicken parts
Salt, pepper
8 bacon strips
1 jar (1 pound) boiled onions
1½ lbs. small new potatoes
¼ cup butter
Bay leaf, parsley

Use about 4 pounds meaty chicken parts—breasts and legs in the combination preferred by your family. Wipe, dry, and sprinkle chicken with salt and pepper. Cover 8 bacon strips with boiling water, let stand 5 minutes, and drain. Cover with cold water, drain, and dry. Cook the bacon in a skillet until it is limp and just beginning to brown. Remove the bacon. In the bacon fat, cook the chicken pieces until golden on all sides. Meanwhile, drain the boiled onions. Peel or scrub the skins from 1½ pounds new potatoes of uniform size—the smaller the better. Remove the chicken to a casserole. Pour off the remaining bacon drippings and add ¼ cup butter to the skillet. Toss the potatoes and onions in the hot butter in the skillet to glaze them slightly. Sprinkle with a little sugar, if desired. Add to the casserole. Lay the bacon strips over the chicken. Add a bit of bay leaf and a few parsley sprigs. Cover the casserole tightly and roast at 350°F. about 1 hour, until the chicken is tender. Baste the chicken and vegetables occasionally with the pan juices. If the casserole seems dry, add a very little hot water or bouillon.

SOUR CREAM OMELETTE

1½ *lbs. potatoes*
3 *Tbsp. butter*
1 *onion*
  Salt, pepper
4 *eggs*
3 *Tbsp. sour cream*

Cook 4 medium-large potatoes (1½ pounds) in boiling salted water to cover. Peel and dice. (Or use leftover boiled or baked potatoes.) Melt 3 tablespoons butter in a skillet and cook a small onion, finely minced, until translucent. Add the potato dice and cook, turning often with a spatula, until the dice are lightly browned. Season with salt and pepper. Beat 4 eggs with 3 tablespoons sour cream and salt and pepper to taste. Stir the eggs into the pan and cook, stirring gently, over low heat until the egg is set, but still creamy and moist. Serves 4.

OMELETTE SOUFFLE

1 *potato*
3 *Tbsp. butter*
3 *eggs, separated*
3 *Tbsp. milk*
1 *Tbsp. chopped chives or parsley*

Grate a leftover or freshly cooked medium potato (about ⅓ pound) and mash it to a paste with 1 tablespoon butter. (Or use ⅔ cup leftover mashed potatoes.) Beat in 3 egg yolks and 3 tablespoons milk. Add 1 tablespoon chopped chives or parsley, and salt and pepper to season generously. Beat 3 egg whites stiff and fold in gently but thoroughly. Melt 2 tablespoons butter (3 tablespoons in all) in a 10-inch skillet. Roll and tip the pan to coat it with butter. Fill the pan with omelette mixture and bake at 400°F. until puffed and lightly browned. Check after 10 minutes. Serve with crisp bacon or with ham, as a hearty lunch for two.

SCRAMBLED EGGS

4 eggs
¼ cup milk
1 cup mashed potatoes
Onion salt, pepper
2 Tbsp. butter

Beat 4 eggs with ¼ cup milk (or use cream if you like a richer scramble). Stir in 1 cup cold mashed potatoes. Add onion salt and pepper to taste. Melt 2 tablespoons butter in a heavy pan over low heat or in the top of a double boiler over hot water. Add the egg mixture and cook, stirring constantly, until the mixture is set but still creamy and soft. Serve with crisp browned sausages, bacon, or ham, as a deliciously different breakfast, luncheon, or supper dish for two.

SUPPER SCRAMBLE

2 lbs. potatoes
6 slices bacon
1 onion
4 eggs
¼ cup milk
Salt, pepper

Cook 6 medium potatoes (2 pounds) in boiling salted water to cover. Peel and cut into dice. (Or use leftover cooked or baked potatoes.) Cook 6 slices bacon in a skillet until crisp. Drain and crumble. Pour off all but 4 tablespoons of the bacon fat. Chop an onion and cook it in the fat until translucent but not brown. Add the potato cubes and toss gently over low heat to mix. Beat 4 eggs with ¼ cup milk and salt and pepper to taste. Pour the eggs into the pan and cook slowly, stirring with a fork, until the eggs are just set, but still soft and creamy. Serve at once, garnished with crumbled bacon.

241

DELMONICO CASSEROLE

   2 *lbs. potatoes*
   3 *Tbsp. butter*
   2 *Tbsp. flour*
1½ *cups milk*
   1 *canned pimiento*
      Salt, pepper
   6 *hard-cooked eggs*
   4 *ozs. Cheddar cheese*

Cook 6 medium potatoes (2 pounds) in boiling salted water to cover. Peel and cut into slices. While the potatoes are cooking, melt 3 tablespoons butter and stir in 2 tablespoons flour. Cook for a minute or two, stirring, without letting the roux take on color. Gradually stir in 1½ cups milk and cook, stirring, until the sauce is thickened and smooth. Dry and mince 1 canned pimiento and add. Season highly with salt and pepper to taste. Fill a buttered 2-quart baking dish with alternate layers of potatoes, slices of 6 hard-cooked eggs, sauce, and 4 ounces grated Cheddar cheese (1 cup), ending with sauce and cheese. Bake at 375°F. until the casserole is bubbling hot and browned, about 20 minutes.

EGG AND SOUR CREAM CASSEROLE

   2 *lbs. potatoes*
   6 *hard-cooked eggs*
¼ *cup butter*
   2 *cups dairy sour cream*
   6 *slices bread, toasted*
      Salt, pepper, paprika

Cook 6 medium potatoes (2 pounds) in boiling salted water. Peel and slice. Cut 6 hard-cooked eggs into lengthwise quarters. Melt ¼ cup butter (½ stick) and stir in 2 cups sour cream (a pint container). Keep warm, but do not boil. Crush 6 slices toasted dry bread to make fine crumbs. Fill a buttered 2-quart casserole with alternate layers of potatoes, eggs, sour-cream mixture, and crumbs, ending with sour cream and crumbs, and seasoning as you go with salt, pepper, and paprika. Bake at 350°F. until the casserole is bubbling hot, about 25 minutes.

CURRIED EGG CASSEROLE

2 *lbs. potatoes*
1¼ *cups milk*
6 *Tbsp. butter*
Salt, pepper
6 *hard-cooked eggs*
2 *Tbsp. flour*
1 *tsp. curry*
Chopped parsley for garnish

Cook 6 medium potatoes (2 pounds) in boiling salted water to cover. Peel and mash with ¼ cup hot milk and 4 tablespoons butter (½ stick). Add salt and pepper to taste. Spread in a shallow 6-cup baking dish. Cut 6 hard-cooked eggs into quarters and arrange over potatoes. Melt 2 tablespoons butter (6 tablespoons in all) in saucepan. Stir in 2 tablespoons flour and 1 teaspoon curry. Cook, stirring, for a few minutes. Gradually add 1 cup milk (1¼ cups in all) and cook, stirring, until the sauce is thick. Taste and add salt, pepper, and more curry to taste. Pour the sauce over the eggs. Bake at 400°F. about 20 minutes, until the mixture is bubbling hot and beginning to brown. Sprinkle with parsley and serve in the baking dish.

EGGS IN CREAM

2 lbs. potatoes
3 Tbsp. butter
1 onion, chopped
¾ cup half-and-half or light cream
   Salt, pepper
6 hard-cooked eggs
   Canadian bacon and tomato halves for garnish

Cook 6 medium potatoes (2 pounds) in boiling salted water to cover. Peel and cut into cubes. Melt 3 tablespoons butter in a skillet and add 1 onion, finely chopped, and the potatoes. Cook over moderate heat, turning often with a spatula, until the potatoes are lightly browned. Add more butter, if necessary. Add ¾ cup half-and-half or light cream, stir gently, and heat. Add salt and pepper to taste. Cut 6 (or more) hard-cooked eggs into wedges and arrange on a serving platter. Pour the potato mixture over the eggs. Sprinkle with parsley and garnish with Canadian bacon and broiled tomato halves.

FARMER'S OMELETTE

2 cups diced cooked potatoes
3 Tbsp. bacon drippings or butter
½ onion
½ green pepper
   Salt, pepper
4 eggs
2 Tbsp. water or milk

Use freshly cooked or leftover cooked potatoes to make 2 cups uniform dice. Heat 3 tablespoons bacon drippings or butter in a skillet, and brown the potatoes lightly. Add half a small onion and half a small green pepper, both finely chopped, and cook for a few minutes, until the onion is translucent. Season with salt and pepper. Beat 4 eggs with 2 tablespoons water or milk, and salt and pepper. Pour the eggs over the mixture in the skillet and cook quickly, like a plain omelette, pulling the cooked edges into the center as they set. When the egg is no longer liquid but still creamy and moist, slide the omelette down toward the handle of the pan and fold one-third over with a spatula. Slide it toward the other side of the pan and fold over the remaining third. Invert onto a heated serving dish. This makes the classic oval omelette shape. If you cannot manage this rather tricky procedure, simply fold the omelette in half and slide it onto a serving dish. Serve with sliced tomatoes and crusty bread, as luncheon for 2 or 3.

FOR VARIETY: Use chives instead of onion and pepper; or well-drained chopped spinach or other leftover vegetables. Grated cheese may be added for extra flavor, and the omelette may be served with a rich tomato sauce.

FILLED POTATO BALLS

Shape cold mashed potatoes into large balls and scoop a spoonful of potato out from the top, to make a hollow. Fill the hollow with well-seasoned chopped or finely cut leftover meat, or mixed meat and vegetables. Cover with potato, top with butter, and arrange on a greased baking sheet. Bake at 400°F. until brown and crusty.

FOR VARIETY: Pack the potatoes into well-greased custard cups or muffin tins, fill and bake as above, and turn out to serve.

PIZZA BALLS

Fill the Potato Balls (above) with shredded Mozzarella cheese and a bit of anchovy; or with the cheese, a dab of tomato sauce, and a pinch of oregano; or with crumbled cooked sausage flavored Italian-style with basil and oregano; or with the sausage and mushrooms sautéed in butter or with crumbled bacon. Sprinkle with grated Parmesan cheese, bake, and serve with tomato sauce.

STUFFED EGGPLANT

3 *medium eggplants*
¼ *cup oil*
1 *clove garlic*
1 *onion*
½ *lb. ground lamb*
1 *can (8 ozs.) tomato sauce*
2 *Tbsp. chopped parsley*
  Salt, pepper, oregano
3 *cups mashed potatoes*
½ *cup fresh bread crumbs*

Split 3 medium eggplants in half lengthwise and cut out the pulp with a sharp knife, leaving shells ¾-inch thick. Cut the eggplant pulp into cubes. Heat ¼ cup oil in a skillet. Roll the shells in the oil, then set aside. Add to the skillet the eggplant dice, a large clove of crushed garlic, and a medium-large onion, finely chopped. Cook, stirring, until the eggplant dice and onion begin to look translucent. Add 1 cup (½ pound) ground raw lamb and cook, stirring, until the lamb is no longer pink. Discard the garlic. Moisten by adding 2 or 3 tablespoons tomato sauce from an 8-ounce can of Spanish-style tomato sauce, and add 2 tablespoons parsley. Season with salt, pepper, and oregano to taste. Blend lightly with 3 cups mashed potatoes, freshly made or leftover, and adjust the seasoning again. Pile the mixture into the reserved oiled eggplant shells. Sprinkle with ½ cup fine, soft fresh bread crumbs and drizzle with the remainder of the tomato sauce. Bake at 350°F. for about 45 minutes, until the eggplant shells are tender and the topping browned.

🌿 17
🌿

Potatoes
for
the
Barbecue

Anyone who has ever eaten a Mickey—a potato buried in the hot ashes of a bonfire to roast until the skin is charred black and the inside white, fluffy, and inimitably delicious—will swear that potatoes never taste better than they do outdoors. He may also insist that Mickeys, and perhaps their almost-equivalents, foil- and grill-roasted potatoes, are the best possible potatoes to eat outdoors. And he may be right. But a great many potato dishes normally cooked atop a range can also be cooked on a backyard grill, or over a wood fire or a Coleman stove at a campsite, without changing a step of the recipe. The difference, if any, is in the appetites that seem to burgeon outdoors. The recipes segregated in this chapter were chosen for their extra-hearty flavor and for their ability to complement or to stand up to the spicy seasoning characteristic of outdoor food in general. You will discover that given a heavy iron skillet and/or pot in addition to the usual barbecue grills and broilers, it is as easy (and maybe quicker) to prepare potato stews, fries, and scallops outdoors as to simply bake or broil the potatoes.

TIP: It is an unimaginative cook who does not add a package or two of "instant" dehydrated potatoes to her camp larder. The manufacturer's suggestions for making use of these versatile products for everything from plain mashed potatoes and endless variations thereof to "breading" for fried chicken or fish are very sound and helpful. One ingenious camper-cook of our acquaintance uses the potatoes as a thickener for a mock cream sauce. And her clean-the-larder soups, made at packing-up time with what's on hand plus dehydrated potatoes, are a wonder!

COAL-ROASTED POTATOES

Bury large baking potatoes in hot coals—at the ashy gray stage, not the red stage—for about 45 minutes. Test by piercing with a fork. The skins will become inedibly charred and black. Pass butter, salt, and the pepper grinder. Or offer any of the baked potato toppings suggested for oven-baked potatoes.

FOIL-ROASTED POTATOES

Scrub the potatoes, wrap them in double-thick foil, and roast them in ashy gray coals for 45 minutes. The skins are soft and edible this way—you can brush them with salad oil or bacon fat before roasting if you wish. Serve at once, if possible. Cut a cross in the flat side of the potato, squeeze it to force some of the pulp up through the gap, and pass butter, salt, and pepper.

GRILL-ROASTED POTATOES

Wrap the potatoes in foil or not, as you prefer, and lay them on the grill, close to the coals but not in them. This method takes longer, of course. Test for tenderness after 1 hour.

ROSIN BAKED POTATOES

Rosin baked potatoes exemplify barbecuing in a big way. They are likely to share the spotlight with a huge, crowd-size roast cooked on a revolving spit over a charcoal pit. But the technique can be used, on a smaller scale, over your backyard grill. Buy rosin at the local hardware store—it is a by-product of turpentine. Pour it into a large pot, can, or bucket that you can devote to this use permanently. Bring it to a boil over gentle heat. (Be careful not to let it boil over or splash.) Lower baking potatoes into the rosin and boil about 40 minutes, or until they come to the surface and float. At this point they are cooked. Cut newspapers into squares large enough to wrap the potatoes, allowing several thicknesses for each. Remove the cooked potatoes from the rosin with a perforated spoon—do not pierce them by using a fork. Drain. Wrap the potatoes in the paper, then with a sharp knife cut them in half. The skins will stick to the paper, and the pulp will have a texture and flavor that devotees say is worth the trouble. Let the rosin cool in the cooking vessel and store it away to use another time.

SALT-BOILED POTATOES

Scrub 6 medium, all-purpose potatoes and cover with boiling water. Add 1 cup salt—yes, 1 cup—and simmer over the grill until tender, about 30 to 45 minutes. (The salt raises the boiling temperature of the water.) These have the texture of baked potatoes, rather than of ordinary boiled potatoes, so treat them like baked potatoes by cutting a cross in the top, pressing to force some of the pulp through the gash, and serving with butter or any of the toppings suggested for baked potatoes. This method is particularly useful when your cooking must be done on a camp stove rather than over a campfire.

TOASTED NEW POTATOES

Cook new potatoes in boiling salted water to cover until tender. Season with salt and pepper, roll in melted butter or salad oil, and coat with dry bread crumbs. At the grill, arrange the potatoes side by side in a hinged broiling basket. Toast, turning occasionally, until they are brown and crusty.

CHILI WEDGES

Cook uniform potatoes in boiling salted water until barely tender. Do not peel, but cut each into four lengthwise wedges. Make several cuts down each wedge, halfway to the skin side. Brush with melted butter or salad oil and season with salt and pepper and with chili powder to taste. Broil on the grill, turning to brown both cut sides, about 15 minutes.

BARBECUED BROILS

Peel long, oval baking potatoes and split lengthwise. Score the cut sides with a small diamond pattern. Brush with salad oil or butter. Broil very slowly, at the back of the grill, turning often to cook evenly. Brush again with oil or butter if they seem dry. Test with a skewer after 35 minutes (the time can vary considerably). Sprinkle with seasoned salt and serve piping hot. Pass the pepper mill and more butter.

LOW-CAL BROILED POTATOES

Cover a broiling rack with aluminum foil. Dip a pastry brush or sprig of celery leaves into a dish of oil and very lightly brush the foil. Scrub potatoes and cut them into ¼-inch slices. Do not peel —the crisped peel adds flavor. Brush the potatoes very lightly with oil. (This oil may be omitted, thus reducing the calorie count still further.) Broil over moderate heat until brown, then turn and brown the other side, about 20 minutes in all. Sprinkle with seasoned salt and pepper.

LOW-CAL OVEN-BROILED POTATOES

Follow the recipe above, using the oven broiler pan. Cook under the broiler flame at moderate heat until brown.

GRILLED POTATO SLICES

Scrub large baking potatoes, preferably uniformly oval in shape. Cut crosswise, peel and all, into thickish slices. Dip into melted butter or salad oil, and arrange side by side in a hinged double broiler. Cook not too close to the coals until brown. Turn and cook until brown and tender. Sprinkle with salt and pepper and serve piping hot. A large baker, weighing nearly a pound, makes two extra-hearty or three middling servings.

POTATOES SURPRISE

Scrub 6 medium, oval baking potatoes (2 pounds). With an apple corer remove a cylinder from the center of each potato. Fill the hollow with grated cheese, chopped cooked meat or bacon, a frankfurter, or a whole link sausage, partly cooked. Close both ends of the hollow with the ends of the cylinder. Wrap in foil and bake in the ashes or on the grill close to the coals until the potatoes are tender, about 45 minutes to 1 hour.

OREGANO TOASTIES

Cook potatoes in their jackets in boiling salted water to cover until just tender. Do not overcook. For 6 to 8 potatoes, season ½ cup oil with 1 teaspoon salt and ¼ teaspoon dried oregano or tarragon, crushed to release the flavor. Brush the skins with the oil. Lay the potatoes on the grill, unwrapped, directly over the heat, and toast, turning often, until brown on all sides, about 15 minutes. Brush with the seasoned oil as you turn.

> *Low-Salt Diet*   Potatoes have such a low sodium content, and such a high satiety value, that they are commonly prescribed for low-sodium diets. Good eating, too!

CAMPFIRE FRIES

2 *lbs. potatoes*
½ *cup bacon drippings*
   Salt, pepper, paprika

Peel 6 medium potatoes (2 pounds) and cut into thin slices. Heat ½ cup bacon drippings in a large skillet and cook the potatoes on the grill close to the coals, turning often, until they are browned and tender. Sprinkle with salt, pepper, and paprika— or use garlic, onion, or a mixed seasoned salt.

CURRIED FRIES

2 *lbs. potatoes*
3 *onions, chopped*
1 *green pepper*
⅓ *cup bacon drippings*
2 *tsp. curry powder*
2 *tsp. prepared mustard*
   Salt, pepper

Cook 6 medium potatoes (2 pounds) in boiling salted water to cover. Cool, peel, and cut into thickish slices. Chop 3 onions finely with a green pepper. At cooking time, melt ⅓ cup bacon drippings in a skillet over the grill. Add the potatoes, onions, and green pepper and cook until brown, turning carefully with a spatula. Add more fat if necessary. Mix 2 teaspoons curry powder with 2 teaspoons prepared mustard and stir the paste into the pan, being careful not to break up the potatoes. Add salt and pepper and cook a few minutes longer. Particularly good with plain grilled chicken.

QUICK POTATOES FOR
THE GRILL

Canned boiled potatoes, or any of the frozen deep-fried specialties—most of these are seasoned mashed-potato mixtures that
have been breaded and fried to make small croquettes—can be
heated on the grill, on skewers, or in a hinged broiler. The fried
specialties need extra seasoning, but no more fat. Dry the canned
boiled potatoes, roll them in salad oil or bacon drippings, and
season. Brown over the coals, turning often.

GRILLED POTATO PATTIES

Brush frozen potato patties on both sides with melted butter,
bacon fat, or salad oil. Arrange on greased grid, about 4 inches
from the coals. Cook until brown on the bottom and cooked
through. Turn and brown the other side, if you like. Or simply
sprinkle with salt and paprika and serve.

SPUDBURGERS

   1 onion
 ⅔ lb. potatoes
   2 eggs
 1½ lbs. ground beef
   Garlic salt, pepper

Grate 1 medium onion. Peel and grate 2 medium-large potatoes
into a bowl of cold water (1½ cups gratings). Drain, add 2 eggs,
and combine well. Blend with 1½ pounds ground beef—lean
chuck makes the best and most economical "hamburger." Season
with garlic salt and pepper to taste. Shape into patties and cook
on a greased broiling rack, not too close to the coals, until crusty
and cooked through. These should not be rare. Serve on hot
toasted rolls or French bread. Pickle relish, ketchup, sliced sweet
onion, and the other usual hamburger accompaniments go well
with Spudburgers, too.

CHEESE STRATA

Cook potatoes in their jackets in boiling salted water to cover
until just tender. Do not overcook. Cool, peel, and slice lengthwise. Sprinkle the slices with salt and pepper and drizzle lightly
with oil or melted butter. Reshape the potatoes with a thin slice
of cheese or a little grated cheese between the slices, and wrap
in foil. To serve, heat thoroughly over the coals, turning often,
about 15 minutes.

> *Receipt for Silver Polish* Save the water in which po-
> tatoes have been boiled, add a little salt, and let it stand
> in a warm place for several days to sour. On silver-polishing
> day, warm the potato water, dip a soft cloth in it, and rub
> the silver clean. Rinse with clear warm water.

CHILI-STUFFED POTATOES

2 lbs. baking potatoes
3 Tbsp. butter
1 Tbsp. grated onion
1 tsp. chili powder
Salt, pepper
1 Tbsp. milk

Bake 6 oval bakers in the oven until tender (about an hour at
450°F., longer at lower temperatures). Split the potatoes in half
and carefully scoop out the pulp and mash it. Season with 3 tablespoons butter, 1 tablespoon grated onion, 1 teaspoon chili powder, and salt and pepper to taste. Add about 1 tablespoon milk,
or just enough to make the mixture smooth. Pack the shells with
the mixture and reshape the potatoes. Wrap in foil. Reheat on the
back of the grill, about 20 minutes.

BACON-STUFFED POTATOES

2 *lbs. baking potatoes*
6 *slices bacon*
3 *Tbsp. butter or bacon drippings*
  Onion salt, pepper

Scrub and bake 6 oval baking potatoes until tender (about an hour at 450°F., longer at lower temperatures). Meanwhile, cook 6 strips bacon until crisp. Split the potatoes in half, scoop out the pulp, mash, and season with 3 tablespoons butter or bacon drippings, and onion salt and pepper to taste. Crumble the bacon and add. Fill the shells, reshape the potatoes, and wrap in foil. Reheat on the back of the grill, about 20 minutes.

HOT BARBECUE POTATO SALAD

2 *lbs. potatoes*
1 *onion*
½ *cup salad dressing*
  Salt, pepper
6 *strips bacon*
6 *squares aluminum foil*

Cook 6 medium potatoes (2 pounds) in boiling salted water to cover. Peel and dice while still warm. Grate an onion and sprinkle it on the potatoes. Add ½ cup or more French or Italian bottled salad dressing. Let stand in a cool place to absorb the dressing. If necessary, add more dressing. Season with salt and pepper to taste. Cook 6 strips bacon until crisp and crumble them. Drain any excess dressing and divide the potato salad onto 6 squares of aluminum foil. Sprinkle each portion with crumbled bacon. Fold the foil to make a loosely fitting package and seal the seams. Heat on the back of the grill, about 15 minutes. Serve piping hot. Especially good with grilled frankfurters, sausages, or ham.

CAMPFIRE POTATO STEW

　3 Tbsp. oil
　1 onion
　2 garlic cloves
1½ cups water
　　Pinch marjoram
　1 tsp. chili powder
　　Dash hot-pepper sauce
　　Salt, pepper
1½ lbs. new potatoes

Heat 3 tablespoons oil in a pan fitted with a lid. Chop a medium onion coarsely and add with 2 garlic cloves, very finely sliced. Cook gently at the back of the grill just until the onion becomes translucent. Add 1½ cups water and bring to a boil. Add a generous pinch of dried marjoram, crushing the leaves to release the flavor, about 1 teaspoon (or more) chili powder, a dash of hot-pepper sauce, and salt and pepper to taste. Peel 1½ pounds new potatoes and cook gently in this spicy mixture, covered, about 25 minutes. Check frequently to make sure the liquid does not entirely boil away, and shake and roll the potatoes so that they cook evenly. Toward the end of the cooking time, taste the sauce again and adjust the seasoning—you may want to add more chili powder and salt at this point. Good with frankfurters instead of potato salad.

GRILL PAN SCALLOP

6 strips bacon
2 lbs. potatoes
2 lbs. onions
　Salt, pepper

Dice 6 strips bacon and cook very slowly in a skillet at the back of the grill until limp. Remove and dice the bacon, but leave the drippings. Peel and slice 6 medium potatoes (2 pounds) and 6 medium onions (2 pounds). Fill the skillet with alternate layers of potato and onion slices, seasoning the layers with salt and pepper to taste, and sprinkling each with some of the bacon dice. Add water to cover the potatoes half way. Cover the skillet and cook at the back of the grill, very slowly, until the potatoes are cooked through.

TIP: Creamed potatoes, scalloped potatoes, or any moist and saucy potato dish can be prepared ahead and reheated over the grill. Add a little more liquid if the mixture seems dry. Be sure to use a casserole that is resistant to direct heat (which eliminates glass bakers).

SCALLOPED POTATOES EN PAPILLOTE

6 *large squares of heavy foil*
¼ *cup butter*
2 *lbs. potatoes*
¾ *cup half-and-half or light cream*
  Salt, pepper
  Chopped parsley for garnish

On the center of each square of double-duty aluminum foil (6 squares in all) spread 1 teaspoon butter. Peel and slice 6 medium potatoes (2 pounds) and arrange the slices in overlapping layers on each square. Carefully add 2 tablespoons half-and-half or light cream (¾ cup in all) to each square. Sprinkle with salt and pepper and top with a second teaspoon of butter (¼ cup in all). Fold the foil to cover the potatoes, not too tightly, and seal. Cook over the coals, about 25 minutes, turning often. Test the potatoes by piercing them with a skewer, through the top layer of foil. A little grated cheese is an optional addition, as is chopped onion. Serve in the foil packet. Garnish with chopped parsley.

18

Choice for the Buffet

With the increasing scarceness of household help and the limitations in seated dining space of most modern homes, buffet dinners continue to grow more popular. Special foods for the buffet include a variety of potato dishes in addition to the ubiquitous potato salad.

A potato dish for the buffet, like all food served on the buffet, should be especially good to look at and to eat, as befits a party food. In addition, it should retain its good taste and keep hot or cold, as the intent may be, until the last peripatetic diner has enjoyed a second portion. This final stricture eliminates—or at least makes it more difficult—to serve plain baked or fried potatoes and all the soufflés and puddings that begin to sink as soon as they are taken from the oven. Otherwise, almost any potato dish can hold its own on the buffet with other specialties of your house.

This chapter includes a sampling of recipes especially good for the buffet. There are many more throughout the book. Keep hot dishes hot on an electric tray, or over a candle warmer or hot water, uncovered if the dish has a crisp crusty top, covered if the top is soft and creamy.

POTATOES ANNA

Butter for the skillet
2 *lbs. potatoes*
Salt, pepper
½ *cup melted butter*
Watercress for garnish

Generously butter the bottom and sides of a deep 10-inch skillet
fitted with an oven-proof lid and handle. Peel and slice 6 medium
potatoes (2 pounds) into uniform thin discs. Line the bottom of
the skillet with overlapping slices, arranging them in an orderly
pattern and using the most perfect slices, since this will be the
top of the finished mold. Fill the skillet with three more layers of
potato slices, seasoning each with salt and pepper, and sprinkling
each with a generous 2 tablespoons of melted butter (1 stick
butter in all). Cover the skillet and bake at 425°F. about 40 minutes. When the potatoes shrink from the sides of the pan and are
almost tender, remove the cover and return to the oven to finish
cooking and brown the top. To serve, drain off any extra butter,
release the cake with a spatula, invert on a hot platter, and garnish with watercress.

NUT-AND-OLIVE STUFFED
POTATOES

2 *lbs. baking potatoes*
2 *Tbsp. butter*
¼ *cup chopped pimiento-stuffed olives*
Salt, pepper
¼ *cup chopped nutmeats*

Bake 6 medium or 3 large baking potatoes (2 pounds). Scoop
out the pulp and leave the shells intact, cutting large potatoes in
half and removing a slice from the flat side of smaller potatoes.
Mash the pulp with 2 tablespoons butter. Add ¼ cup stuffed
olives, chopped coarsely, and salt and pepper to taste. Pile back
into the potato shells and sprinkle thickly with ¼ cup very finely
chopped nutmeats. Heat in the oven before serving.

MUSHROOM-STUFFED POTATOES

2 lbs. baking potatoes
2 Tbsp. butter
1 onion
½ lb. mushrooms
  Salt, pepper

Bake 6 medium or 3 large, oval baking potatoes (2 pounds).
Open the smaller potatoes by removing a slice from the flat side;
split the larger ones in half. Scoop out the pulp, leaving the shells
intact, and mash. Meanwhile, melt 2 tablespoons butter and sauté
1 onion, very finely chopped, until golden. Add ½ pound fresh
mushrooms, sliced, and cook a few minutes, or use a 6-ounce can
of mushrooms, thoroughly drained. (Use the mushroom liquid in
gravy or add it to soup—do not throw it away!) Combine potato, butter, onions, and mushrooms. Season well with salt and
pepper and pile back into the shells. Return to the oven to heat.

PROVENCALE SCALLOP

3 onions
4 Tbsp. olive oil
5 tomatoes
  Salt, pepper
6 anchovies
2 cloves garlic
½ tsp. oregano
2 lbs. potatoes
¼ cup grated Parmesan cheese

Slice 3 large onions and cook in 2 tablespoons olive oil until translucent. Peel 5 tomatoes by dipping them for a moment in boiling
water to loosen the skin. Cut the tomatoes in half crosswise and
scoop or squeeze out the seedy pulp. Cut the rest of the tomato
into uniform strips. Add to the onions. Season with a little

salt and pepper—easy on the salt, because anchovies can be very salty. Drain 6 anchovies, the flat type, and mash them. Puree or mash 2 garlic cloves. Blend anchovies and garlic with 2 more tablespoons olive oil (4 tablespoons in all), ½ teaspoon oregano, and more pepper to taste. Peel and thinly slice 6 medium potatoes (2 pounds). Fill an oiled 2-quart casserole with alternate layers of onion and tomato, potatoes, and anchovy mixture, beginning and ending with onion and tomato. Bake at 400°F. about 40 minutes, until the potatoes are cooked. At the half-way point, sprinkle with ¼ cup grated Parmesan cheese. Serve hot with hot roast lamb or beef, or cold with cold roasts, or hot with cold roasts for that matter!

SAVORY SCALLOP

2 Tbsp. butter
1 clove garlic
2 lbs. potatoes
4 ozs. Parmesan cheese, grated
1 egg
1 can condensed consommé
    Salt, pepper, cayenne
    Chopped parsley for garnish

Mash 2 tablespoons butter with 1 garlic clove and spread on bottom and sides of a shallow 5-cup baking dish. Chill, peel, and thinly slice 6 medium potatoes (2 pounds). Spread half the potatoes over the butter. Sprinkle with ½ cup grated Parmesan cheese and add the remaining potatoes. Beat 1 egg lightly with 1 can (10½ ounces) consommé, undiluted. Pour the consommé over the potatoes. Sprinkle with remaining ½ cup cheese (1 cup in all). Bake at 350°F. about 1¼ hours (covered for the first half hour) until the potatoes are cooked through. If the scallop seems dry, add a very little water. Taste the sauce and add salt, pepper, and cayenne to taste. Sprinkle with chopped parsley and serve in the baking dish.

CHEDDAR SCALLOP

2 lbs. potatoes
1/4 cup butter
6 ozs. Cheddar cheese
2 medium onions
1/2 cup chopped parsley
  Salt, pepper
1 tsp. savory
2 cups half-and-half or light cream
  Paprika for garnish

Peel 6 medium potatoes (2 pounds) and slice very thin. Fill a buttered 2-quart casserole with alternate layers of potato slices, 1/4 cup butter (1/2 stick), 1 1/2 cups grated Cheddar cheese (6 ounces), 2 medium onions (chopped), and 1/2 cup chopped parsley. Begin and end with potatoes, and season each layer of potatoes with salt, pepper, and savory, using 1 teaspoon savory in all. Add about 2 cups hot half-and-half or light cream, barely covering the potatoes. Bake at 350°F. about 1 hour, until the potatoes are tender. Sprinkle with 1/4 cup more cheese, if desired, and bake until the topping browns. Garnish with paprika.

RED AND GOLD CASSEROLE

2 lbs. potatoes
1 onion
1 can (8 ozs.) pimientos
2 cups milk
2 Tbsp. potato starch or flour
8 ozs. Cheddar or American cheese
  Salt, pepper

Cook 6 medium potatoes (2 pounds) in boiling salted water to cover until tender. Peel and dice. Grate 1 onion. Drain 1 can (about 8 ounces) pimientos and cut into slivers. Reserve a few slivers for garnish, and add the rest to the potato dice with the onion. Measure 2 cups milk into a saucepan. Stir ¼ cup of this milk with 2 tablespoons potato starch or flour to make a smooth paste. Return it to the pan. Cook, stirring, until the sauce is smooth and thickened. Grate ½ pound Cheddar or American cheese (or use 2 cups grated cheese). Add the cheese to the sauce and cook, stirring, until it melts. Combine sauce and potatoes in a baking dish and add salt and pepper to taste. Bake at 350°F. about ½ hour, until the mixture is bubbling hot and beginning to brown. Arrange the reserved pimiento slivers on top of the casserole and bake a few minutes longer.

COTTAGE CHEESE PIE

1 lb. potatoes
1 lb. cottage cheese
½ cup sour cream
  Salt, white pepper
  Pastry for 1-crust pie
  Chopped chives for garnish

Cook 3 medium potatoes in boiling salted water to cover. Peel and cut into dice. (Or use 2 cups leftover cooked potatoes, diced.) Force 2 cups cottage cheese (a 1-pound container) through a sieve with ½ cup sour cream, or whirl in a blender to make a smooth mixture. If the cottage cheese is very dry, add a little more cream; if it is very creamy, use less sour cream. Add the potatoes and season with salt and white pepper to taste. Line a deep 9-inch pie plate with pastry and shape a standing fluted edge. Fill with the cheese mixture. Bake at 350°F. about 45 minutes, until brown. Sprinkle with chopped chives and serve very warm, but not directly from the oven. Good with a hearty fruit or vegetable salad as a main dish at a luncheon buffet.

POTATO CHEESE PIE

1½ *lbs. potatoes*
  3 *Tbsp. grated onion*
  1 *tsp. prepared mustard*
    Salt, pepper
  2 *eggs*
  1 *cup milk*
  1 *cup grated Cheddar cheese*
  1 *Tbsp. chopped parsley*
  2 *Tbsp. butter*

Cook 4 medium-large potatoes (1½ pounds) until tender. Peel
and mash. Add 3 tablespoons finely grated onion, 1 teaspoon (or
more) prepared mustard, and salt and pepper to taste. Butter a
10-inch glass pie plate. Spread the potato mixture evenly in the
plate, building up the sides to make a rim. Make the filling: Beat
2 eggs with 1 cup milk, 1 cup grated Cheddar or other cheese,
1 tablespoon chopped parsley, salt and pepper to taste. Pour the
cheese mixture into the pie plate. Melt 2 tablespoons butter and
brush the potato rim; pour remaining butter over the filling.
Bake at 325°F. until the filling is set and the potatoes golden,
about 35 minutes. Sprinkle the filling with buttered bread crumbs,
if you like.

TIP: You can make a potato chicken pie, or fish pie, or seafood
pie by filling the mashed potato shell with creamed mixtures.
Use about 2 cups chicken, fish, or seafood in 1 cup medium-thick
white sauce, with seasonings to suit your taste.

POTATO PIE

  Pastry for 2-crust pie
  2 *lbs. potatoes*
  1 *large onion*
  1 *Tbsp. chopped parsley*
    Salt, pepper, paprika
  3 *Tbsp. butter*
  ½ *cup half-and-half*

Line a 9-inch pie plate with pastry. Chill. Peel and thinly slice 6 medium potatoes (2 pounds) and 1 large onion. Toss with 1 tablespoon chopped parsley, and salt, pepper, and paprika to taste. Spread the mixture in the prepared pie shell and dot with 3 tablespoons butter cut into small bits. Cover with pastry and pinch the rim to seal. Cut two or three slits in the top crust to allow steam to escape. Bake at 375°F. about 1¼ hours, until the potatoes are tender and the crust browned. Pour at once into the pie, through the slits in the crust, ½ cup half-and-half. Let stand 5 minutes in a warm place. If all the cream has been absorbed, add a little more—it should be moist but not runny. Serve hot. Very good with cold meats and a salad.

CLAM PIE

2 lbs. potatoes
6 scallions
½ cup slivered celery
1 Tbsp. flour
2 cups chopped clams
½ cup clam liquid
½ cup cream
Salt, pepper
Pastry for 1-crust pie

Cook 6 medium potatoes in boiling salted water to cover. Peel and slice into a mixing bowl. Add 6 finely chopped scallions, with the greens, and ½ cup slivered celery. Sprinkle with 1 tablespoon flour. Add 2 cups chopped or whole clams, fresh or canned, ½ cup clam liquid, and ½ cup cream or more. Season with salt and pepper to taste and toss lightly. Fill a greased 2-quart baking dish. Cover with pie pastry and slash the pastry to allow the steam to escape. Bake at 400°F. about 30 minutes, until the crust is browned.

SESAME POTATO NOODLES

    2 lbs. potatoes
    3 eggs
      Salt, pepper, onion salt
    ½ cup flour or more
    ¼ cup melted butter
      Sesame seeds for garnish

Cook 6 medium potatoes (2 pounds) in boiling salted water to cover. Peel, mash, and cool. Beat in 3 eggs and a generous amount of salt, pepper, and onion salt, if desired, to season well. Add enough flour, beginning with a scant half cup, to make a soft dough that can be rolled or patted out into a thin sheet. (Use as little flour as possible.) Butter a large, shallow baking dish or pie plate. Divide the mixture in half and roll each half into a rectangle on a floured board. Cut into broad noodles as long as the baking dish you plan to use, and about 1-inch wide. Fill the dish lightly with layers of noodles arranged in lattice style. Sprinkle with ¼ cup melted butter and add a generous scattering of sesame seeds. Bake at 375°F. about 35 minutes, until top and bottom are browned. Cut into squares or pie-like wedges to serve. Can be reheated, at 375°F., if necessary.

TOMATO POTAGE

    3 Tbsp. butter
    3 onions
    3 large tomatoes
    1 qt. water
    2 tsp. sugar
    1 Tbsp. monosodium glutamate
    5 potatoes
      Salt, pepper
    1 cup cream
      Croutons for garnish

Melt 3 tablespoons butter in a saucepan. Slice 3 onions and cook in butter until translucent. Peel 3 large tomatoes by scalding them in boiling water so that the skins easily slip off. Discard the seedy pulp and chop them coarsely. Add tomatoes to the saucepan and simmer a few minutes. Add 1 quart water and bring to a boil. Season with 2 teaspoons sugar and 1 tablespoon monosodium glutamate. Peel and dice 5 potatoes directly into the soup. Cook until potatoes are soft, about 20 minutes. Adjust the seasoning with salt and pepper. Force the soup through a sieve or food mill, or whirl it in an electric blender. Heat 1 cup cream and add slowly to hot soup. Serve very hot, with croutons.

ICED GREEN SOUP

2 Tbsp. butter
½ small onion
1 qt. half-and-half
2 potatoes
1 pkg. (10 ozs.) frozen chopped spinach
1 tsp. salt
½ tsp. garlic salt
White pepper
Sour cream for garnish

Melt 2 tablespoons butter in a saucepan. Mince half an onion and cook it in the butter until translucent but not brown. Add 1 quart half-and-half (or 1 pint each milk and light cream). Peel 2 potatoes and grate directly into the milk. Add 1 package frozen spinach, preferably the chopped variety. Season with 1 teaspoon salt, ½ teaspoon garlic salt, and a dash of white pepper. Heat slowly. Separate the frozen spinach with a fork to hasten thawing. When milk reaches the boiling point, reduce the heat and simmer the soup for about 10 minutes longer, until the potatoes are cooked. Force the soup through a food mill or a ricer, or whirl it in a blender to make a smooth puree. Adjust seasoning with more salt and pepper to taste. Chill. Serve with a spoonful of whipped cream or sour cream.

℀ 19
℀

Profitable
Potatoes
for a
Crowd

Women's clubs and other organizations interested in fund-raising know one sure way to extract money for good causes and make the donors enjoy it: feed 'em. Strawberry festivals, pancake breakfasts, harvest suppers—any occasion when people are invited to come and eat together is an almost certain success, financially and socially.

Because potatoes as salad, casserole, scallop, or soup, or in rolls and doughnuts, are universally popular, always in season, and so inexpensive that they always bring substantial profit, they deserve a place on the menu. Servings for fifty are as much as amateur cooks, working with large but nonprofessional pans, can manage at a time; therefore the recipes given here are for fifty. The recipes specify amounts of ingredients in ordinary supermarket sizes, but if commercial sizes are available they will reduce costs and increase profits still further. Of course, it is possible to ask many members to make normal household-size recipes rather than to have a few cook in quantity, but the latter method assures consistency of flavor and texture. Save the many-contributions method for a potluck supper on another fund-raising occasion.

MASHED POTATOES FOR FIFTY

18 lbs. potatoes
½ lb. butter
3 Tbsp. salt
½ tsp. white pepper
1½ qts. milk

Cook 18 pounds potatoes in their jackets in boiling salted water until tender. Pour off the water and leave the potatoes over low heat, shaking often, until all the water has evaporated. Peel the potatoes while hot, holding them on a two-pronged fork. Mash at once, using an electric mixer to make a smooth puree. Add ¼ pound (½ cup or 1 stick) butter or margarine bit by bit, and season with 3 tablespoons salt and about ½ teaspoon white pepper. Beat in 1½ quarts hot milk. Pile lightly on heated serving pans. Cut 1 stick butter into thin shavings and sprinkle over the potatoes (½ pound used in all). Makes 50 or more servings, ⅔ cup each.

TIP: For extra flavor, season the mashed potatoes with grated onion, about ¾ cup. For richer potatoes, double the amount of butter.

SUGGESTION: Since mashed potatoes do not stay light and fluffy if they must stand, it is a good idea to prepare them in amounts as needed—perhaps 6 pounds at a time to make about 18 servings. For 6 pounds potatoes, use ⅓ stick butter or margarine, 1 tablespoon salt, and 2 cups milk. Add ¼ cup grated onion, if desired. Top with a second ⅓ stick butter cut into thin shavings.

SCALLOPED POTATOES FOR FIFTY

½ *lb. butter*
½ *cup flour*
3 *qts. milk*
2 *Tbsp. salt*
1 *Tbsp. monosodium glutamate*
  White pepper
15 *lbs. potatoes*
2 *lbs. onions*
1 *qt. dry bread crumbs*

Melt ½ cup butter (1 stick) in a large pan. Stir in ½ cup flour
and cook, stirring, for a few minutes, without allowing the butter
to brown. Heat 3 quarts milk and add slowly, stirring. Cook,
stirring constantly, until the sauce is thick and smooth. Simmer
10 minutes, stirring occasionally. Add 2 tablespoons or more salt,
1 tablespoon monosodium glutamate, and white pepper to taste.
While the sauce is cooking, peel and thinly slice 15 pounds potatoes and 2 pounds onions. Separate the onion rings. Divide
the potatoes and onion rings into 3 baking pans, about 9 by 13
inches. Pour the prepared sauce over the potatoes, dividing it
evenly. Melt ½ cup butter (1 cup in all), add 4 cups dry bread
crumbs, and toss well. Sprinkle the crumbs evenly over the potatoes. Bake at 350°F. about 1½ hours, until the potatoes are
tender. Makes about 50 servings, ⅔ cup each.

DELMONICO POTATOES FOR FIFTY

15 *lbs. potatoes*
¾ *lb. butter*
1½ *cups flour*
3 *qts. milk*
2 *Tbsp. salt*
½ *tsp. white pepper*
16 *ounces grated cheese*
  Pimientos (optional)

Cook 15 pounds potatoes in boiling salted water to cover. Peel
and slice or cube while hot. While the potatoes are cooking, melt

¾ pound butter (3 sticks) in a large kettle, stir in 1½ cups flour, and cook, stirring, for a few minutes. Do not let the mixture brown. Gradually add 3 quarts hot milk, stirring well, and cook, stirring constantly, until the sauce boils and thickens. Simmer, stirring occasionally, for 10 minutes. Season with 2 tablespoons or more salt and ½ teaspoon white pepper. Divide the hot sliced potatoes into 3 baking pans, about 9 by 15 inches. Pour the hot sauce over the potatoes, dividing it evenly. Sprinkle each pan with ⅔ cup grated cheese—Cheddar, Swiss, or Parmesan (about 1 pound in all). Broil until the cheese topping melts and the casserole is piping hot. A can or two of pimientos, well drained and slivered, is an optional addition. Makes 50 servings.

POTATO SALAD FOR FIFTY

    10 *lbs. waxy potatoes*
    ½ *lb. onions*
     1 *bunch celery*
     1-*qt. jar sweet gherkins*
     3 *Tbsp. salt*
    ½ *tsp. pepper*
     1 *pint French or Italian dressing*
     1 *qt. mayonnaise or salad dressing*
    12 *hard-cooked eggs*
     1 *bunch parsley*

Cook 10 pounds waxy new-crop potatoes in their jackets in boiling salted water. Peel and cut into slices or dice while still hot. Finely chop ½ pound onions and sprinkle on the potatoes. Sliver a medium-to-large bunch celery, with the green leaves, and add. Slice a 1-quart jar of gherkins (small sweet pickles) and add. Sprinkle with 3 tablespoons salt and ½ teaspoon pepper. Add 1 pint well-seasoned French or Italian dressing and toss gently to mix. Mellow by setting in a cool place, but not the refrigerator, for an hour. Drain off any excess dressing. Spread in 3 flat pans about 9 by 13 inches. Spread each pan with 1⅓ cups mayonnaise or salad dressing (1 quart). Chop together 12 hard-cooked eggs and 1 bunch parsley. Sprinkle on the salad. Mark each pan in 18 squares to make 54 portions.

HOT POTATO SALAD FOR FIFTY

12 lbs. waxy potatoes
2 lbs. bacon, diced
1 cup distilled vinegar
4 cups water
⅓ cup salt
½ tsp. pepper
1 lb. sweet red onions
1 bunch celery
1 bunch parsley

Cook 12 pounds waxy new-crop potatoes in their jackets in boiling salted water to cover. Peel and cut into cubes or slices. While the potatoes are cooking, dice 2 pounds bacon and cook in a stew pan until the dice are just crisp. (Do not let the fat burn.) Add 1 cup full-strength distilled vinegar (not a mild seasoned vinegar), 4 cups water, ⅓ cup salt, and ½ teaspoon pepper. Heat the sauce and keep it hot. Thinly slice 1 pound sweet, small red onions and separate the rings. Sliver a medium-to-large bunch of celery into thin crescents (about 4 cups). Chop the fresh green celery leaves. Chop a medium bunch of parsley (about ½ cup). Add onions, celery, celery leaves, and parsley to the hot cubed or sliced potatoes. Add the hot vinegar dressing and toss gently to mix. Taste for seasoning and add more salt and pepper if desired. Cover and set aside in a warm place to mellow for half an hour before serving. Reheat, if necessary. The salad should be served very warm. Makes 50 servings, ⅔ cup each.

OLD-FASHIONED POTATO SALAD

10 lbs. waxy potatoes
1 cup chopped onion
Hot Salad Dressing
1 cup chopped green pepper
4 cups finely slivered celery
2 cups diced cucumber
Salt, pepper, cayenne
12 hard-cooked eggs

Cook 10 pounds waxy new-crop potatoes in salted boiling water to cover. Peel and dice. Spread in 3 serving pans, 9 by 15 inches. Sprinkle with 1 cup finely chopped onion. Cover evenly with Hot Salad Dressing [following]. With wide spatula turn potatoes carefully in the dressing to coat completely. Let stand in a warm place, covered, for half an hour. At serving time, sprinkle with 1 cup chopped green pepper, 4 cups finely slivered celery, and 2 cups diced cucumber. Carefully toss to mix ingredients. Adjust seasoning, if necessary, with salt, pepper, and cayenne. Separately grate the yolks and whites of 12 hard-cooked eggs and sprinkle on the salad in patterns through a paper doily, keeping the colors separate. Makes about 50 servings, ⅔ cup each.

HOT SALAD DRESSING FOR FIFTY

½ *cup flour*
¼ *cup sugar*
1 *Tbsp. dry mustard*
1 *Tbsp. salt*
½ *tsp. pepper*
  Cayenne
1 *qt. milk*
4 *eggs*
1 *cup distilled vinegar*
¼ *cup butter*

Put a 2-quart pan into a roasting pan with hot water in it. In the pan, mix together ½ cup flour, ¼ cup sugar, 1 tablespoon each dry mustard and salt, ½ teaspoon pepper, and a generous dash of cayenne. Gradually add 1 quart hot milk, stirring until smooth. Cook, stirring, until the sauce bubbles and thickens. Cook 10 minutes, stirring often. Beat 4 eggs lightly, warm them with a little hot sauce, and stir them into the pan. Cook for a minute or two. Remove the pan from the hot water and add 1 cup full-strength distilled vinegar (not the mild seasoned type). Swirl in ¼ cup butter (½ stick). If the sauce seems too thick, add a few tablespoons of water to thin it as desired. Taste and adjust the seasoning with more salt and pepper to taste. Makes 1½ quarts.

POTATO SOUP FOR FIFTY

5 *lbs. potatoes*
3 *qts. water*
2 *Tbsp. salt*
1 *Tbsp. monosodium glutamate*
3 *lbs. onions*
½ *lb. butter or margarine (2 sticks)*
½ *cup flour*
4 *qts. milk*
1 *pint cream*
  White pepper
1 *cup chopped chives or scallion greens*

Peel 5 pounds potatoes and cut into small dice. Cover with 3 quarts water, add 2 tablespoons salt and 1 tablespoon monosodium glutamate, and cook, covered, until the potatoes are mushy. Whisk or beat until the mixture forms a puree. Meanwhile, chop 3 pounds onions. Melt ½ pound butter or margarine (2 sticks) in a heavy pan, add the chopped onions, and cook, stirring often, until golden. (Do not allow the onions to brown.) Sprinkle with ½ cup flour and cook, stirring, for a few minutes. Heat 4 quarts milk and add gradually to the onion mixture, stirring. Cook, stirring, until the sauce is smooth and thickened. Simmer 10 minutes, stirring often. Combine the sauce with the potato puree. Heat well. Add 1 pint cream and heat gently (or use all milk). Taste and adjust the seasoning with more salt and a little white pepper. Finely chop fresh chives or scallion greens to make about 1 cup. Serve the soup with a ladle, about ¾ cup to a portion, and sprinkle each serving with about ½ teaspoon chopped chives. Serves 50 or more.

POTATO PUFFS FOR FIFTY

12 *lbs. potatoes*
½ *lb. butter or margarine*
1 *qt. milk*
¼ *cup grated onion*
3 *Tbsp. salt*
½ *tsp. pepper*
9 *eggs, separated*

Cook 12 pounds potatoes in boiling salted water to cover. Peel and mash while hot. Use an electric mixer to make a very smooth purée. Blend in ½ pound (1 cup or 2 sticks) butter or margarine bit by bit. Gradually beat in 1 quart hot milk to make a very light and fluffy mixture. Add ¼ cup finely grated onion. Season with about 3 tablespoons salt and ½ teaspoon pepper, to taste. Beat 9 medium egg whites until fluffy. With the same beater (no need to wash it) beat the 9 egg yolks until light. Beat the egg yolks into the potato mixture, blending thoroughly. Gently but thoroughly fold in the beaten egg white. Butter 3 baking pans about 9 by 15 inches, and divide the mixture into them. Bake at 400°F. until puffed and browned, about ½ hour. Serves 50.

SUGGESTION: Potato puffs do not stand up well, so it is a good idea to make them as needed. The basic potato and egg-yolk mixture can be divided into three portions, and the egg whites beaten 3 at a time and folded in as required just before baking.

Thickener   To thicken a soup without adding flour or eggs, simmer it for a few minutes with a little grated raw potato.

POTATO ROLLS FOR FIFTY

    2 pkgs. granulated yeast
    ½ cup very warm water
    1 qt. milk
    1 cup butter or margarine
    1 cup sugar
    1½ Tbsp. salt
    1 cup mashed potatoes
    12 cups flour
    1 tsp. soda
    2 tsp. double-acting baking powder

Dissolve 2 packages granulated yeast in ½ cup warm water. (If you use cake yeast, the water should be just lukewarm.) Bring 1 quart milk to a boil with 1 cup butter or margarine, 1 cup sugar, and 1½ tablespoons salt. Add 1 cup rather dry mashed potatoes, freshly mashed or leftover. Cool to lukewarm and add yeast. Stir well. Toss or sift 6 cups flour with 1 teaspoon soda and 2 teaspoons double-acting baking powder. Add to the yeast mixture, beating well. Add more flour, about 5 or 6 cups, to make a soft dough. Mix well, using an electric bread mixer if possible. Divide the dough into three or four parts and knead each part on a floured board until smooth. Roll in a greased bowl, cover, and let rise until double in bulk, about 1½ hours. Punch down, knead briefly again, and shape into rolls—Parker House rolls are handy because they can easily be opened to make small sandwiches (see below). Let rise in a warm place until double in bulk, about 1 hour or more. Then bake at 400°F. until browned, about 20 minutes. Makes about 5 to 6 dozen rolls. Serve hot or reheated.

SHAPING PARKER HOUSE ROLLS

Roll out Potato Roll Dough about ⅓-inch thick on a lightly floured board. Cut 3-inch rounds or ovals. With the back of a knife make a crease through the center of the shape, brush the center with butter, fold, and press to seal.

POTATO DOUGHNUTS FOR FIFTY

1½ lbs. potatoes
 3 cups sugar
 2 large cans evaporated milk
 6 eggs
 1 Tbsp. vanilla
10 cups flour
 2 Tbsp. double-acting baking powder
 2 tsp. salt
 ½ tsp. nutmeg (or 1 tsp. cinnamon)

Cook 4 medium-large potatoes (1½ pounds) and mash to make 2 cups. Add 3 cups sugar to the hot potatoes and stir until smooth. Cool slightly. Add 2 cans (about 14 ounces each) evaporated milk. Beat in 6 eggs, one at a time, blending well after each. Flavor with 1 tablespoon vanilla. Toss or sift 10 cups flour with 2 tablespoons double-acting baking powder, 2 tablespoons salt, and ½ teaspoon powdered nutmeg or 1 teaspoon cinnamon. Gradually add the flour to the milk mixture, combining with an electric mixer at first, then with a wooden spoon. The dough should be soft, but firm enough to roll out. Divide into four parts and roll each part ¼-inch thick on a lightly floured board. Cut doughnuts with a cutter. Fry in deep hot fat (360°F.). Do not crowd the fryer. Turn the doughnuts with a long-handled fork when they come to the surface, and often thereafter until they are richly browned. (Fry the "holes" separately.) Drain on paper towels. Serve as is, or roll in a mixture of sugar and cinnamon, or dust with powdered sugar. Makes 6 dozen doughnuts, 6 dozen "holes."

Conservation If potatoes must be peeled for cooking, wash, dry, and chill them beforehand. Chilling helps to conserve Vitamin C content and discourages darkening.

⚜ 20
⚜

National
Specialties

Potato recipes have traveled so fast and so far, and have made themselves so thoroughly at home in every nation, that it is often difficult to say for sure that a certain recipe originated in a certain country. The following recipes have distinctive touches that identify them reasonably closely with the countries that claim them as native dishes. There are undoubtedly many other recipes, also foreign in origin, that are less easily attributed to one country or another. These are scattered elsewhere throughout this book, where they will taste just as good as part of the melting-pot that is American cooking.

IRISH LAMB STEW

3 *lbs. neck of lamb*
3 *lbs. potatoes*
2 *lbs. onions*
  Salt, pepper, thyme
  Bay leaf, sprigs of parsley, green celery top

Have the butcher trim the excess fat from 3 pounds neck of lamb and cut the necks into 3- or 4-inch sections. Peel 9 medium potatoes (3 pounds) and cut 4 of them into thick slices. Put the potato slices into the bottom of a heavy kettle or Dutch oven. Slice 6 medium onions (2 pounds) and cover the potatoes with half of them. Add the lamb chunks and season with salt, pepper, and a pinch of thyme. Cover the lamb with the remaining onion slices. Cut the 5 remaining potatoes into quarters and lay them on the onions. Season again with salt, pepper, and thyme. Tie together with string a bit of bay leaf, a few sprigs of parsley, and a green celery top and add. Then add 2 cups cold water and bring the liquid slowly to a boil. Skim off and discard the scum that arises to the top. (Do not stir and disturb the arrangement of the ingredients.) Cover the kettle tightly and simmer gently for 2 hours, or longer, until the lamb is very tender.

DUTCH STEW
(Hotchpotch)

2 *lbs. brisket of beef*
1 *tsp. salt*
3 *cups water*
2 *lbs. carrots*
3 *lbs. potatoes*
1 *lb. onions*
   Salt, pepper

Put a 2-pound piece of brisket of beef, or other soup meat, into a kettle. Add 1 teaspoon salt and 3 cups water. Bring to a boil, skim, cover, and simmer for 1½ hours. Peel and dice 8 medium carrots (2 pounds) and add to the kettle. Cook half an hour. Peel and dice 9 medium potatoes (3 pounds) and add to the kettle with 3 medium onions (1 pound), also peeled and diced. Continue to cook until the meat is tender and the vegetables very soft. Remove the meat to a platter in a slow oven (250°F.) and brush with a little fat to keep the surface moist. Cook the vegetables rapidly, stirring often, until the liquid has all but evaporated. Season with salt and pepper to taste. Serve meat and vegetables together. This Dutch national dish is variously called Hotchpotch, Hodgepodge, and Hutspot.

This is the famous French country soup from which the even more famous Vichyssoise was derived. Louis Diat, for many years chef of the old Ritz-Carlton Hotel in New York, improved on his mother's recipe by using chicken stock instead of water for the liquid, and enriching the soup with cream. Then he had the ultimate inspiration, and served the soup icy cold. He called it Crème Vichyssoise, in honor of his home town.

POTAGE PARMENTIER

4 leeks, white parts only
1 onion
2 Tbsp. butter
4 potatoes
4 cups water
1 tsp. salt
2 cups hot milk
1 Tbsp. butter

Thoroughly wash the white parts of 4 leeks and cut finely. Chop 1 onion. Melt 2 tablespoons butter in a saucepan, add the vegetables, and cook slowly until the onions are translucent. Peel and dice 4 potatoes and add with 4 cups (1 quart) water and 1 teaspoon salt. Bring to a boil and simmer for 30 minutes or longer, until the potatoes are very soft. Rub the soup through a sieve or food mill, or whirl it in an electric blender. Reheat the soup, add 2 cups hot milk and 1 tablespoon butter, and heat slowly together, without boiling. Serve hot or cold. Makes 8 or more servings.

WATERCRESS SOUP

Wash and trim the stems from 2 bunches watercress. Reserve a few perfect sprigs for garnishing. Add the rest to the Potage Parmentier 5 minutes before the soup is sieved or blended into a puree. Garnish each serving with a sprig of watercress.

CAPETOWN CURRIED BEEF SOUP

3 *Tbsp. beef suet*
1 *lb. beef soup meat*
3 *onions, diced*
1 *Tbsp. curry powder*
1 *bay leaf*
3 *peppercorns*
1 *tsp. salt*
2 *quarts water*
1 *lb. potatoes*
1 *Tbsp. vinegar*

Cut 3 tablespoons suet into small dice and render in a soup kettle; remove the crisp bits. Brown a 1-pound piece of soup meat, and a soup bone if you have one, in the fat remaining in the kettle. Add 3 diced onions and cook, stirring often to prevent scorching, until golden. Add 1 to 2 tablespoons curry powder (the amount is a matter of taste) and cook and stir for a minute longer. Add a bay leaf, 3 peppercorns, and 1 teaspoon salt. Add 2 quarts cold water and bring to a boil. Remove any scum that rises, as necessary. Cover the kettle and simmer about 1 hour, until beef is nearly tender. Peel and dice 3 medium potatoes (1 pound) and add to the soup with 1 tablespoon vinegar. Cook until the potatoes and beef are tender. Discard bay leaf. Adjust the seasoning with more salt, pepper, and vinegar. Cut the beef into bite-size pieces and garnish each plate of soup. Makes hearty main-dish servings for 6 or more.

Housecleaning Receipt Grandmother used a piece of raw potato to wash fingerprints from painted surfaces—the high alkaline content makes it a fine cleaner.

GERMAN BUTTERMILK SOUP

1 lb. potatoes
4 cups buttermilk
1 Tbsp. flour
3 strips bacon
1 onion
  Salt, white pepper
  Parsley for garnish

Peel and dice 3 potatoes and cook in a very small amount of salted water until tender. Pour ¼ cup buttermilk into a jar and the rest of the quart into a saucepan. To the jar add 1 tablespoon flour and shake until smooth. Stir this into the buttermilk in the saucepan and bring slowly to the boiling point, without allowing it to boil. Meantime, dice 3 strips bacon and chop 1 onion. Cook together until bacon bits are crisp and onion golden. Drain and add to the buttermilk. Add potatoes and their liquid and heat to the boiling point once again. Add salt and white pepper to taste. Serve garnished with chopped parsley.

POLISH SAUSAGE CASSEROLE

2 Tbsp. butter
1 onion
3 Tbsp. flour
1 Tbsp. paprika
1 Tbsp. vinegar
2 cups water
2 bouillon cubes
2 lbs. potatoes
1½ lbs. kielbasa

Melt 2 tablespoons butter. Add 1 onion, chopped, and cook until the onion is golden. Stir in 3 tablespoons flour and 1 tablespoon paprika and cook the roux for a few minutes, without allowing it to brown. Add 1 tablespoon vinegar, 2 cups boiling water, and 2 bouillon cubes. Cook, stirring, until the sauce is smooth. Peel and quarter 6 medium potatoes (2 pounds) and add to the sauce.

Cover the pan and cook gently until the potatoes are almost tender, about 20 minutes. Shake the pan occasionally to prevent sticking. Slice about 1½ pounds kielbasa into chunks and add. Cook 5 minutes longer, until sausage is hot and potatoes tender.

MURGH I MUSSALAM
(Pakistani Stuffed Chicken)

1 *roasting chicken* (4 *lbs.*)
1 *onion*
1 *oz. green ginger root*
1 *cup* (8 *ozs.*) *yogurt*
1 *Tbsp. pepper*
1 *lb. potatoes*
   Juice of 1 lemon
2 *hard-cooked eggs*
2 *Tbsp. slivered almonds*
¼ *cup raisins*
½ *cup butter*

Choose a plump roasting chicken weighing about 4 pounds. Grate a small onion and a piece of fresh, or green, ginger root weighing about 1 ounce. (Oriental stores have this, or you may be able to buy a piece from your favorite Chinese restaurateur.) Blend with 1 cup yogurt (an 8-ounce container). Add 1 table-spoon pepper (use less if you find this amount frightening). Rub the chicken with the yogurt mixture and pierce well with a fork so that the marinade will penetrate the flesh. Let stand in a cool place for 2 hours or longer. Meanwhile, make the stuffing: Cook 3 medium potatoes (1 pound) in boiling salted water. Peel, dice, and sprinkle with the juice of 1 lemon. Chop 2 hard-cooked eggs and add to the potatoes with 2 tablespoons slivered almonds. Cover ¼ cup raisins with boiling water and let stand for 10 minutes. Drain and add. Pack stuffing into chicken, filling both neck and body cavities. Sew or skewer the openings closed. Melt ½ cup butter (¼ pound or 1 stick) in a range-to-oven casserole. Brown the chicken on all sides in the butter. Transfer the bird to the oven and roast until tender and cooked through, from 1 hour 15 minutes to 2 hours, depending on the quality of the bird.

SWEDISH MEAT BALLS

1 lb. ground beef
1 lb. ground lean pork
1 cup mashed potatoes
½ cup bread crumbs
1 large onion
6 Tbsp. butter
2 eggs
1 Tbsp. onion salt
  Pepper
1 cup water
⅓ cup flour
2 cans condensed consommé
1 cup heavy cream

Blend 1 pound each ground beef and ground lean pork, 1 cup mashed potatoes, and ½ cup soft bread crumbs. Finely chop a large onion and cook it in 2 tablespoons butter until translucent. Add to the meat. Beat in 2 eggs and add 1 tablespoon or more onion salt, to taste, and a dash of pepper. Add 1 cup cold water and blend well. Shape small balls between wet palms and brown slowly on all sides in a ¼-inch layer of oil. Remove. Make the sauce: Pour off any oil remaining in the pan after the meat balls have been browned. In the same pan, melt ¼ cup butter (½ stick) and stir in ⅓ cup flour. Cook, stirring, for a few minutes to cook and brown the flour a little. Gradually add 2 cans (10½ ounces each) undiluted beef consommé. Cook, stirring in the brown bits, until the sauce is thick and smooth. Add 1 cup heavy cream and bring to the simmering point. Add the meatballs to the sauce and cook slowly about 30 minutes. The meatballs can be made ahead. Reheat before serving and keep hot in a chafing dish on the buffet.

MEAT BALLS STROGANOFF

Substitute sour cream for the sweet cream in the recipe for Swedish Meat Balls, and add to the sauce ½ pound sliced mushrooms, lightly sautéed in 2 tablespoons butter. The meat used may be all beef, or part beef, part veal, and part pork.

FRICADELLEN
(German Meat Cakes)

3 *cups mashed potatoes*
2 *cups cooked beef, chopped*
1 *onion*
2 *Tbsp. butter*
1 *tsp. chopped parsley*
  Salt, pepper
1 *egg*
  Flour
  Fat for frying

Mix 3 cups seasoned mashed potatoes (1½ pounds, leftover or freshly cooked) with about 2 cups chopped or slivered cooked beef. Chop a large onion and cook it until golden in 2 tablespoons butter. Add to the potato mixture with 1 teaspoon chopped parsley and adjust the seasoning with salt and pepper. Beat in 1 egg. Shape the mixture into flat cakes, dip into flour, and brown slowly on both sides in ¼ inch of hot fat (use chicken or beef fat, if possible, for flavor).

SCANDINAVIAN FISH SCALLOP

    1 large onion
    2 Tbsp. butter
    1 lb. mackerel fillet
 1½ lbs. potatoes
    2 eggs
    2 cups milk
     Salt, pepper
    ¼ cup bread crumbs
    2 Tbsp. melted butter

Chop a large onion and cook in 2 tablespoons butter until golden. Cut 1 pound or more filleted mackerel into bite-size pieces. (Or use salmon, blue fish, or any rich dark-fleshed fish.) Peel and very thinly slice 4 medium-large potatoes (1½ pounds). Cover with salted boiling water and cook 5 minutes. Drain. Fill a greased casserole with alternate layers of parcooked potatoes, fish, and onions. Begin and end with potatoes. Beat 2 eggs with 2 cups milk, and add salt and pepper to taste. Pour over the potatoes. Sprinkle with ¼ cup fine bread crumbs tossed with 2 tablespoons melted butter. Bake at 350°F. about 50 minutes, until the potatoes are tender. A sliced tomato may be added to the layers, if desired.

BACALHAU A LA GOMES DE SA
(Portuguese Codfish Stew)

 1½ lbs. fresh codfish steaks
     Salt, pepper
    3 onions
    1 lb. potatoes
    1 cup olive oil
    1 clove garlic
    2 hard-cooked eggs
    ½ cup chopped parsley

Cover 1½ pounds fresh codfish steaks (or use frozen fillets) with boiling water. Add salt and half an onion, sliced, and cook for about 10 minutes, until the fish loses its transparent look and becomes white and opaque. Drain and flake the fish, discarding bones and skin. Cook 3 medium potatoes (1 pound) in boiling salted water to cover. Peel and cut into thick slices. (Or use leftover cooked potatoes.) Cut the remaining half onion and two more onions into thin slices. Heat 1 cup olive oil in a large skillet with a crushed garlic clove. Discard the garlic. Fry the potato slices in the oil until golden. Add the onions and cook until the onions are golden. Carefully stir in the codfish flakes, season with salt and pepper to taste, and cook over low heat for about 10 minutes, shaking the pan often. With a slotted spoon lift the fish and vegetables from the skillet, allowing the oil to drain back into the pan. Transfer to a heated serving dish. Rice or grate 2 hard-cooked eggs, mix with ½ cup chopped parsley, and sprinkle over the fish.

PATATES PILASKISI
(Turkish Potato Ragout)

½ cup olive oil
1 large onion
1 clove garlic
1 small can (8 ozs.) tomato sauce
3 cups water
  Salt
2 lbs. potatoes
  Pepper
½ cup chopped parsley

Heat ½ cup olive oil in a saucepan. Add a large onion, thinly sliced, and a large garlic clove, minced. Cook gently until the onion is lightly browned—be careful not to scorch it. Add half a small can of tomato sauce (the thick kind usually seasoned with basil). Add 3 cups water and a little salt and bring to a boil. Simmer a few minutes. Peel and cut into uniform dice 6 medium potatoes (2 pounds). Add to the stew and cook, covered, about 30 minutes, until tender. Add more tomato sauce and salt and pepper to taste, and finish with ½ cup chopped parsley.

CARIUCHO
(Ecuadorian Creamed Potatoes)

2 *lbs. potatoes*
2 *Tbsp. butter*
1 *onion*
1 *cup half-and-half*
1 *Tbsp. peanut butter*
   Salt, pepper
   Hard-cooked egg for garnish

Cook 6 medium potatoes (2 pounds) in boiling salted water to
cover, until tender. Peel and cut into eighths. While the potatoes
are boiling, melt 2 tablespoons butter and cook 1 onion, chopped,
until golden. Add 1 cup half-and-half and simmer over low heat
for 5 minutes. Stir in 1 tablespoon peanut butter, and salt and
pepper to taste. Add the potatoes to the sauce, heat for a minute,
and pour into a heated serving dish. Sprinkle with chopped hard-
cooked egg.

ITALIAN POTATO AND
PEPPER STEW

1 *cup olive oil*
2 *cloves garlic*
3 *large green peppers*
6 *scallions*
2 *lbs. potatoes*
1 *can (8 ozs.) tomato puree*
   Salt, pepper
   Oregano or basil

Heat ¼ cup olive oil in a large skillet with 2 cloves garlic,
crushed, but in one piece. Cook for a few minutes until the garlic
just begins to color. Discard the garlic. Clean 3 large peppers,
discarding pith and seeds. Cut into strips. Cut 6 plump scallions

into 1-inch lengths, green and all. Peel and cut 6 medium potatoes (2 pounds) into strips about the same length as the peppers and less than ½-inch thick. Add the vegetables to the oil and cook for a few minutes, stirring carefully to coat all with oil. Add 1 cup (an 8-ounce can) tomato puree (not sauce, but the lightly seasoned puree) and bring to a boil. Add a little salt and pepper to taste. Cover the pan and simmer gently for about 25 minutes, until the potatoes are tender. Shake or stir often to prevent sticking, and add a little water if the mixture seems dry. Adjust the seasoning with salt, pepper, and a generous pinch of oregano or basil.

BALKAN POTATO GIVETCH

1 lb. tomatoes
1 lb. carrots
2 stalks celery
1 lb. onions
2 cloves garlic
2 lbs. potatoes
Salt, pepper
2 cups water
¼ cup olive oil

Peel 4 solid ripe tomatoes (1 pound) by dipping them into boiling water for a moment to loosen the skins. Cut in half, squeeze out and discard the seedy pulp, and cut into pieces. Slice 3 or 4 carrots (1 pound) into thin slices. Sliver 2 large stalks celery and mince 3 medium onions. Chop 2 cloves garlic. Mix these vegetables and add salt and pepper to taste. Peel 6 medium potatoes (2 pounds) and slice thinly into an oiled casserole. Season with salt and pepper to taste. Cover the potatoes with the vegetables. Add 2 cups boiling hot water. Bake at 400°F. for 35 minutes. Sprinkle with ¼ cup olive oil (neutral oils add no flavor, of course, but they can be used) and bake until tender, about 10 minutes longer. Good hot as a vegetable, or cold as a relish salad.

POTATOES ROESTI
(Swiss Fries)

2 lbs. potatoes
½ cup butter
Salt, pepper

Peel and grate 6 medium potatoes (2 pounds) into a pan of cold water. Drain and dry. Melt 4 tablespoons butter in a skillet, add the potatoes, and season with salt and pepper. Cover and cook over low heat until the potatoes are tender and the bottom crusty. Serve as is, or turn and brown the other side. To turn, cover the pan with a large plate and invert to unmold the potatoes. Melt 4 tablespoons more butter (½ cup in all) in the pan, slide the cake into the pan, and brown the cake on the other side.

FOR VARIETY: Potatoes roesti can be made with partly cooked potatoes: Boil the potatoes for 10 minutes, then peel and grate. Use half again as much butter for cooking—6 tablespoons rather than 4 for each side. The advantage of this method, if there is one, is that it may be a little easier to peel and grate partly cooked potatoes rather than raw ones. The dish requires more fat, however, and does not have the texture of the Swiss original.

SENF KARTOFFELN
(Austrian Mustard Potatoes)

2 lbs. potatoes
½ cup butter
½ onion
2 Tbsp. flour
1 can condensed consommé
¼ cup prepared mustard
Salt, pepper
3 Tbsp. bread crumbs

Cook 6 medium potatoes (2 pounds) in boiling salted water to cover. Peel and slice thickly. Lay the slices in a greased 9-inch bake-and-serve casserole. Melt ¼ cup butter (4 tablespoons or ½ stick) in a small pan. Add half a small onion, finely chopped, and cook until the onion is translucent. Sprinkle with 2 tablespoons flour and cook, stirring, for a few minutes. Gradually add 1 can (10½ ounces) condensed consommé or bouillon and continue to cook, stirring, until the sauce is smooth and thick. Add about ¼ cup prepared mustard (the mild salad style or a stronger type, depending on your preference) and blend well. Taste and add salt and pepper if needed. Pour the mustard sauce over the potatoes. Sprinkle with 3 tablespoons bread crumbs and dot with 4 more tablespoons butter (1 stick butter in all). Bake at 350°F. about 25 minutes, until the top is brown. Serve in the baking dish.

ALUKO ACHAR
(Nepalese Potatoes)

2 *lbs. potatoes*
2 *Tbsp. dry mustard*
¼ *cup lemon juice*
½ *cup salad oil*
1 *tsp. salt*
2 *Tbsp. chopped hot pepper*

Cook 6 medium potatoes (2 pounds) in boiling salted water to cover. Peel and cut into cubes. While the potatoes are cooking, blend 2 tablespoons powdered mustard to a paste with ¼ cup lemon juice. Gradually stir in ½ cup salad oil and 1 teaspoon salt. Pour the sauce over the hot potatoes and sprinkle with 2 tablespoons chopped, fresh, hot red peppers. (The last are very hot indeed for Western palates—a milder version substitutes fresh sweet red peppers or canned pimientos for the hot peppers, and adds a dash of cayenne.)

KUGEL
(Jewish Potato Pudding)

    3 *eggs*
    3 *Tbsp. flour*
    ½ *tsp. double-acting baking powder*
    1 *tsp. salt*
       Pepper
    ½ *onion*
    1½ *lbs. potatoes*
    ¼ *cup rendered chicken fat*

Beat 3 eggs well and beat in 3 tablespoons flour, ½ teaspoon double-acting baking powder, 1 teaspoon or more salt, and a generous sprinkling of black pepper. Finely grate half a medium onion and add. Peel and grate 4 medium-large potatoes (1½ pounds) to make 3 cups gratings. Drain and add. Then add ¼ cup rendered chicken fat for the authentic middle-European flavor (or use butter or beef drippings). Grease the baking dish with the same fat. Bake at 350°F. about 1 hour, until the kugel is well browned. Serve hot, as a side dish with pot roast or other meats.

QUENELLES
(French Potato Dumplings)

    1 *lb. potatoes*
    2 *eggs*
       Salt, pepper, nutmeg
    ¾ *cup flour*

Cook 3 medium potatoes (1 pound) and mash well with 2 eggs. Add salt, pepper, and a dash of nutmeg to taste. (Nutmeg frequently appears in potato dishes of French origin.) Add ¾ cup flour, to make a soft mixture that can be shaped into ovals with a dessert spoon. Poach in simmering salted water about 10 minutes. Serve with gravy from poultry or meat, or with melted butter and bread crumbs.

GNOCCHI
(Italian Dumplings)

½ cup milk
⅓ cup butter
1 cup flour
1 tsp. salt
¼ tsp. white pepper
    Dash paprika
2 eggs
1 cup mashed potatoes
¼ cup grated Parmesan cheese
2 Tbsp. melted butter

Heat ½ cup milk and ⅓ cup butter (⅔ stick) until the milk boils and the butter melts. Add 1 cup flour, all at once, and stir until the mixture forms a ball and leaves the sides of the pan. Remove the pan from the heat. Stir in 1 teaspoon salt, ¼ teaspoon white pepper, and a dash of paprika. Beat in two eggs, one at a time, to make a smooth mixture. Add 1 cup mashed potatoes and combine well. This should make a soft dough that can be shaped; if necessary, thicken the mixture by adding more flour and blending it in well. Dust a sheet of waxed paper well with flour, turn the dough on it to coat both sides, and pat into a rectangle ½-inch thick. Cut the rectangle into 5 or 6 strips. Roll each strip with the palm of the hand to make a cylinder thick as your thumb. Cut the cylinder into thumb lengths. Drop into boiling salted water and simmer, uncovered, for 10 minutes. Drain well. Spread in a buttered baking dish and sprinkle with ¼ cup grated Parmesan or Romano cheese and 2 tablespoons melted butter. Bake at 400°F. until the cheese browns a little. Serve piping hot, as is, or with meat gravy or tomato sauce.

IRISH BOXTY CAKE

2 lbs. potatoes
1½ tsp. salt
1½ tsp. baking soda
¾ cup flour

Cook 3 medium potatoes (1 pound) in boiling salted water to cover. Peel and mash. While the potatoes are cooking, peel and grate 3 medium raw potatoes (2 pounds in all) into cold water. Drain and combine with the mashed potatoes. Add about 1½ teaspoons salt, to taste. Toss 1½ teaspoons baking soda with ¾ cup flour and work into the potatoes. Add more flour, as needed, to make a firm dough. Knead to blend well. Divide in half and roll or pat each half into a round ½-inch thick. Cut into wedges and bake on a hot lightly greased griddle, over low heat, about 20 minutes. Turn and brown the other side, about 20 minutes longer. Serve hot, with butter.

SUBRICS
(French Potato Cakes)

2 Tbsp. butter
2 Tbsp. grated onion
2 Tbsp. flour
1½ cups milk
Salt, pepper, nutmeg
1 lb. potatoes
3 egg yolks
1 egg

Melt 2 tablespoons butter in a saucepan. Add 2 tablespoons grated onion and cook over low heat, stirring, until the onion is just golden. Sprinkle with 2 tablespoons flour and cook and stir for a moment or two. Gradually add 1½ cups milk to this roux, and cook, stirring constantly, until the sauce is smooth and thickened. Continue to cook, stirring, until the sauce reduces to about 1¼ cups. Add salt, pepper, and a dash of nutmeg to taste. This is a true Béchamel Sauce Maigre—without meat. Peel 3 medium potatoes (1 pound) and dice them directly into a pan of boiling salted water. Cook for 5 minutes until just tender. Drain and dry on towels. Combine the potatoes with the Béchamel Sauce. Beat 3 egg yolks and 1 whole egg and add to the potato mixture. Drop spoonfuls of mixture well apart on a hot griddle generously coated with butter. Turn with a spatula to brown both sides. Especially good with simple broiled fish dishes.

LATKES
(Jewish Potato Pancakes)

1 *lb. potatoes*
½ *onion*
2 *eggs*
1 *tsp. salt*
   Pepper
2 *Tbsp. matzo meal*

Peel and coarsely grate 3 medium potatoes (1 pound) and half a medium onion. Add 2 eggs and beat well. Season with about 1 teaspoon salt and a dash of pepper to taste. Sprinkle with 2 tablespoons matzo meal and blend. Fry by spoonfuls in ¼-inch hot fat—use rendered chicken fat for the classic Middle European flavor. Turn to brown both sides. The latkes should be thin and crisp-edged. Serve as a side dish with pot roast or other meats and poultry, or as a luncheon or supper dish with applesauce. Except during the Passover holiday, when flour is forbidden, Jewish cooks sometimes substitute it for the matzo meal.

BLENDER LATKES

Following the recipe above, first put the eggs into the electric blender. Then add the potatoes, peeled and cut into smallish chunks, and the onion, also cut up. Sprinkle with matzo meal and seasonings and blend at low speed just until the potatoes are uniformly grated. Scrape the sides of the blender often. Or put 1 cup water into the blender, add the cut-up potatoes, and blend until grated. Drain off the water and proceed as directed above.

FRENCH POTATO PANCAKES

½ *cup flour*
1 *tsp. salt*
2 *eggs*
1¾ *cups milk*
2 *Tbsp. butter*
2 *Tbsp. minced onion*
1 *lb. potatoes*

Toss ½ cup flour and 1 teaspoon salt in a mixing bowl. Beat 2 eggs well with 1¾ cups milk and gradually beat into flour. Melt 2 tablespoons butter and cook 2 tablespoons minced onion until translucent. Add to batter. Peel 3 medium potatoes (1 pound) and grate them directly into the batter. Blend well. Bake on a hot, lightly greased griddle, or in a 5-inch crêpe pan or skillet. Makes a thin, foldable pancake that can be used like a French crêpe and filled with creamed chicken, seafood, or mushrooms as a luncheon dish.

LEFSE
(Scandinavian Pancakes)

2 *cups mashed potatoes*
1½ *Tbsp. melted butter*
1 *Tbsp. milk*
2 *tsp. sugar*
½ *tsp. salt*
⅞ *cup flour*

Blend 2 cups mashed potatoes, freshly cooked and cooled or leftover, with 1½ tablespoons melted butter and 1 tablespoon milk. Season with 2 teaspoons sugar and about ½ teaspoon salt, to taste. Work in 1 cup flour less 2 tablespoons (⅞ cup) and knead until smooth. Chill for half an hour. Divide the dough into 12 equal parts. Roll each out on a floured board to make very thin rounds. Bake slowly on a griddle, turning to brown both sides lightly.

PAPAS RELLENAS
(Peruvian Potato Balls)

2 *lbs. potatoes*
4 *Tbsp. butter*
   Salt, pepper
1½ *lbs. ground meat*
1 *clove garlic*
1 *onion*
3 *hard-cooked eggs*
1 *small can black olives*
   Egg yolk

Cook 6 medium potatoes (2 pounds) in boiling salted water to cover. Peel and mash. Add 4 tablespoons butter, and salt and pepper to taste. Cool. Heat a large skillet and lightly brown 1½ pounds ground pork or beef, or a combination, stirring with a fork to separate the pieces. Add a crushed garlic clove and 1 large onion, chopped. Cook, still stirring, until the onion is translucent. Discard the garlic clove. If pork is used, cover the pan and simmer a few minutes to cook thoroughly. If beef alone is used, add a little fat to the skillet. Chop 3 hard-cooked eggs and combine with the meat. Drain a small can (4 or 6 ounces) chopped or sliced black olives and add. Season well with salt and pepper. Shape the potatoes into 8 large balls, press a hollow in each with a spoon, and fill with some of the meat mixture. Reshape the potato balls around the meat. Arrange on a lightly greased baking sheet, brush with beaten egg yolk, and bake in a moderate oven (375°F.) until browned. Or roll the balls in beaten egg yolk mixed with 1 tablespoon water, then in flour, and fry in hot deep fat (380°F.).

PATATAS CON QUESO
(Spanish Stuffed Potatoes)

  2 *lbs. uniform boiling potatoes*
½ *lb. cheese*
  1 *egg*
  1 *Tbsp. water*
    Flour
    Salt, pepper
    Olive oil for frying

Cook 6 medium potatoes (2 pounds) in boiling salted water to cover. Drain and peel. Remove a cylinder from the center of each with a potato corer and reserve. Cut ½ pound cheese, any kind you favor, into small chunks. Fill the potatoes with cheese and seal the openings with the cylinders, trimming them to fit. Roll the potatoes in an egg beaten with 1 tablespoon water, then in flour seasoned with salt and pepper. Brown in hot olive oil, turning to brown all sides evenly.

IRISH CHAMP

  2 *lbs. potatoes*
  8 *scallions*
1½ *cups milk*
    Salt, pepper
  6 *pats butter for garnish*

Cook 6 medium potatoes (2 pounds) in boiling salted water. Peel and mash. Meanwhile, finely chop 8 whole plump scallions. Pour boiling water over them and drain at once. Add the blanched scallions to 1½ cups milk and bring the milk to the boiling point. Add milk and scallions to the mashed potatoes, beating well, and season with salt and pepper to taste. Serve very hot, with a pat of butter in the center of each serving.

IRISH COLCANNON

1½ lbs. potatoes
½ medium cabbage
1 Tbsp. butter
1 Tbsp. chopped parsley
   Salt, pepper
1½ cups milk
6 scallions

Cook 4 medium-large potatoes (1½ pounds) in boiling salted water to cover. Meanwhile, chop half a medium head of cabbage and cook in a small amount of salted water, covered, for just 7 minutes. (There should be half as much cabbage as potato—about 1½ cups.) Drain and season with 1 tablespoon each butter and parsley, plus salt and pepper to taste. Peel and mash the potatoes, and beat in 1½ cups very hot milk. Chop 6 scallions, with the greens, and add. Combine with the cabbage and add salt and pepper to taste. Serve very hot—very Irish!

NEW POTATOES DANISH STYLE

1½ lbs. new potatoes
3 Tbsp. sugar
¼ cup butter
   Salt, pepper

Cook 1½ pounds uniform, tiny new potatoes in boiling salted water to cover. Peel. Meanwhile, stir 3 tablespoons sugar in a heavy skillet large enough to hold all the potatoes at once in a single layer. When the sugar is melted and lightly browned, add ¼ cup (½ stick) butter. Stir until the syrup is well blended. Add the peeled potatoes, and tip and roll the pan to coat them without breaking them. Cook a few minutes, shaking often, until the potatoes are glazed. Sprinkle with salt and pepper.

FRITTATA
(Italian Potato Omelette)

1 lb. potatoes
3 eggs, separated
  Salt, pepper
  Chopped parsley

Cook 3 medium potatoes (1 pound) in boiling salted water to cover. Peel and mash. (Or use 2 cups rather dry leftover mashed potatoes.) Add 3 egg yolks and season with salt and pepper to taste. Beat 3 egg whites stiff and fold in. Brown in butter in an omelette pan, without stirring. Turn and brown the other side. Sprinkle with 1 tablespoon chopped parsley. Serves 3.

PERSIAN POTATO OMELETTE

¼ cup butter
1 lb. potatoes
  Salt, pepper
1 onion
  Juice of 1 lemon
3 large tomatoes
6 eggs
½ tsp. cinnamon

Heat ¼ cup butter in a large skillet. Peel and cut 3 medium potatoes (1 lb.) into ¼-inch slices. Fry in the butter until nearly tender and brown on both sides. Sprinkle with salt and pepper. Remove from the skillet and set aside. Add more butter to the pan, if necessary, and cook 1 large onion, chopped, until it is golden. Skim the onion from the butter with a perforated spoon. Transfer the onion to a bowl and sprinkle with a little salt and cover with the juice of 1 small lemon (about 2 tablespoons).

Return the fried potatoes to the pan. Dip 3 large tomatoes into hot water and remove the skins. Slice ¼-inch thick and arrange over the potatoes. Spread onions and lemon juice over all. Cover the skillet and cook slowly, without stirring, for 10 minutes, until the potatoes are cooked through. Beat 6 eggs with salt to taste and a scant ½ teaspoon cinnamon. Pour the eggs over the vegetables, cover the skillet, and cook very slowly until the eggs are set.

INDEX

Abridines, 180
Ad Lib Hash, 214
Almond Baked, 11
Aluko Achar, 291
Amandine Croquettes, 49
Amandine Potato Sticks, 206
Anchovy Savory, 120
Anchovy Turnovers, 114
Anna, 259
Antipasto, 119
Appetizers
    Anchovy Savory, 120
    Anchovy Turnovers, 114
    Antipasto, 119
    Cheese Crackers, 114
    Cocktail Meat Balls, 118
    Codfish Balls, 117
    Codfish Cakes, 117
    Cornish Pasties, 112
    Cream Cheese Turnovers, 113
    Frozen Snacks, 110
    Herring, 118
    Knishes, Liver, 115
    Knishes, Potato, 115
    New Potato Snacks, 110
    Pigs in Blankets, 111
    Quiche, 116
    Roll-Up Snacks, 110
    Seedy Sticks, 116
    Stuffed Pigs, 111
    Tender Pastry, 112
Apple Stuffing, 91
Apples, Mashed Potato, 208
Apples, New Potato, 208
Applesauce Doughnuts, 186
Applesauce Pudding, 197
Aroostock Baked, 12
Asparagus Soup, 123
Austrian Mustard, 290

Bacalhau (Codfish Stew), 286
Bacon-Stuffed, 255
Baked Fish, 212
Baked Hash, 215

Baked Hash with Eggs, 215
Baked Puffs, 26
Baked Potatoes
    Almond, 11
    Aroostock, 12
    Crunchy, 12
    Franconia, 10
    in a Hurry, 10
    on the Half Shell, 9
    Oregano, 11
    Oven Browned, 10
    Surprise, 13
    Used as Shells, 205
    Stuffings (see Stuffed Potatoes)
    Toppings, 8
Balkan Givetch, 289
Balls, 22
Basquaise, New Potatoes, 88
Barbecue, Potatoes for the
    Bacon-Stuffed, 255
    Broils, 250
    Campfire Fries, 252
    Campfire Stew, 256
    Cheese Strata, 254
    Chili-Stuffed, 254
    Chili Wedges, 250
    Coal-Roasted, 248
    Curried Fries, 252
    Foil-Roasted, 248
    Grill Pan Scallop, 256
    Grill-Roasted, 248
    Grilled Patties, 253
    Grilled Slices, 251
    Hot Barbecue Salad, 255
    Low-Cal Broiled, 250
    Low-Cal Oven Broiled, 250
    Oregano Toasties, 251
    Quick Potatoes for the Grill, 253
    Rosin Baked, 248
    Salt-Boiled, 249
    Scalloped en Papillote, 257
    Spudburgers, 253
    Surprise, 251
    Toasted New Potatoes, 249

302

Barbecued Broils, 250
Basic Stuffing, 90
Basquaise, 88
Biscuits, 164
Biscuits, Herb, 165
Blintzes, 192
Blue Cheese Salad, 142
Blueberry Muffins, 166
Bordure de Pomme Duchesse, 203
Boston Clam Chowder, 132
Boulangère, 65
Brandied Pudding, 195
Breads
 Biscuits, 164
 Blueberry Muffins, 166
 Buttermilk Scones, 163
 Country Wheat Bread, 157
 Crescents, 159
 Date Muffins, 166
 Griddle Scones, 164
 Herb Biscuits, 165
 Muffins, 166
 Orange Tea Bread, 107
 Pioneer Cinnamon Roll, 161
 Potato Starch Muffins, 166
 Refrigerator Rolls, 158
 Rich Raisin Bread, 162
 Scones, 164
 Sweet Roll Dough, 160
 Waffles, 165
 White Bread, 156
Bread Crumb Scallop, 65
Bread Dumplings, 97
Bubble Coffee Cake, 168
Buffet, Potatoes for the, 258-267
Butter, Clarified, 29
Butter-Fried, 28
Butter-Frying, 29
Butterscotch Rum Cake, 175
Buttermilk Pancakes, 106
Buttermilk Chocolate Cake, 173
Buttermilk Scones, 163
Buttermilk Soup, 282

Cabbage Soup, 124
Cakes (Dessert)
 Bubble Coffee Cake, 168
 Buttermilk Chocolate, 173
 Butterscotch Rum, 175
 Cocoa, 174
 Crumb, 169
 Crumb Topping, 169
 Date Nut, 172

Gateau Mocha, 178
 Old-Fashioned Chocolate, 171
 Passover Sponge, 177
 Pecan Torte, 172
 Quick Sponge, 176
 Rich Mix, 174
 Spice, 176
 Streusel Kuchen, 169
 White de Luxe, 170
Cake Doughnuts, 184
Calorie Chart, 6
Campfire Fries, 252
Campfire Stew, 256
Candies
 Chocolate Fudge, 189
 Chocolate Rocks, 188
 Fondant, 188
Capetown Curried Beef Soup, 281
Caraway Dumplings, 102
Cariucho, 288
Carrot Charlotte, 68
Casseroles
 Custard, 70
 Custard Stuffing, 95
 Delmonico, 242
 Egg and Olive, 70
 Givetch, 289
 Golden Bake, 230
 Mustard, 290
 Oyster, 210
 Red and Gold, 262
 Sour Cream, 72
 Stuffing, 96
 Tomato, 71
Celery Stuffing, 91
Chantilly, 38
Château, 29
Charlotte, 68
Cheddar Cheese Soup, 128
Cheddar Scallop, 262
Cheese
 Balls, 46
 Crackers, 114
 Cream, Puff, 75
 Pie, 264
 Salad, 146
 Scallop, 67
 Soufflé, 73
 Strata, 254
Cheesed New Potatoes, 83
Chicken Bonne Femme, 239
Chicken Liver Patties, 45

Chicken Liver Stuffing, 92
Chili-Stuffed, 254
Chili Wedges, 250
Chip Croquettes, 208
Chocolate Chips, 22
    Bit Cookies, 181
    Drop Cakes, 179
    Fudge, 189
    Rocks, 188
    Soufflé, 201
Christmas Pudding, 194
Citron, New Potatoes, 79
Clam
    Cakes, 44
    Hash, 219
    Pie, 265
Clarified Butter, 29
Classic Creamed Potatoes, 53
Classic Salad, 136
Coal-Roasted Potatoes, 248
Cocktail Meat Balls, 118
Cocoa Cake, 174
Codfish
    à la Gomes de Sa, 86
    Balls, 117
    Cakes, 117
Cookies and Small Cakes
    Abridines, 180
    Chocolate Bit Cookies, 181
    Chocolate Drop Cakes, 179
    Fruited Drop Cakes, 179
    Nut Cookies, 183
    Oatmeal Chews, 182
    Oatmeal Crisps, 182
    Peanut Butter Cookies, 180
Corn Chowder, 132
Corned Beef Hash, 215
Cornish Pasties, 112
Cottage Cheese Pie, 263
Cottage Cheese Salad, 145
Cottage Fried Potatoes, 31
Country Wheat Bread, 157
Crabmeat Salad, 149
Crackers, Cheese, 114
Crackers, Seedy, 116
Cream Cheese Puff, 75
Cream Cheese Topping, 9
Cream Cheese Turnovers, 113
Cream Fries, 34
Cream of Onion Soup, 127
Cream of Vegetable Soup, 126
Creamed Chicken Hash, 218

Creamed Potatoes
    Cariucho, 288
    Classic, 53
    Delmonico, 54
    Grated Pan-Creamed, 55
    Maître d'Hôtel, 54
    Old Fashioned, 55
    Pan-Creamed, 55
    Quick, 56
    with Sour Cream, 56
Creamed Salmon, 210
Creamy French Dressing, 154
Crème, à la (mashed), 38
Crêpes, 192
Crescents, 159
Crinkle Cuts, 22
Crisp Cakes, 104
Croquettes
    Amandine, 49
    Chip, 208
    Crunch Balls, 51
    Fritters, 50
    Home Style, 48
    Hot Potato Balls, 50
    Puffs, 51
    Tuna, 43
Crumb Cake, 169
Crumb Topping, 169
Crunch Balls, 51
Crunchy Baked Potatoes, 12
Curls, 22
Curried
    Bisque, 125
    Egg Casserole, 243
    Fries, 252
Custard
    Casserole, 70
    Stuffing Casserole, 95

Danish Style New Potatoes, 299
Date Muffins, 166
Date Nut Cake, 172
Dauphine, Pommes, 26
Dauphinoise, 64
Delmonico Potatoes, 54
Delmonico Casserole, 242
Delmonico for Fifty, 270
Delmonico Quick Scallop, 66
Desserts
    Applesauce Pudding, 197
    Blintzes, 192
    Brandied Pudding, 195
    Chocolate Soufflé, 201

Desserts (*cont'd*)
  Christmas Pudding, 194
  Crêpes, 192
  Fresh Prune Dumplings, 199
  German Prune Dumplings, 199
  Lemon-Nut Soufflé, 200
  Lemon Sauce, 200
  Maple Pecan Pudding, 198
  Nutted Shortcake, 193
  Pflaumen Knödel, 199
  Shortcake, 193
  Spice Jumble Cookies, 196
  Spice Jumble Dessert, 196
Dilled New Potatoes, 80
Dilled Potatoes and Beans, 81
Dilled Stuffed, 16
Doughnuts
  Applesauce, 186
  Cake, 184
  Drop, 186
  for Fifty, 277
  Raised, 185
Drop Doughnuts, 186
Dumplings
  Bread, 97
  Caraway, 102
  Gnocchi, Easy, 100
  Gnocchi, Puffed, 99
  Prune, Fresh, 199
  Prune, German, 199
  Quenelles, 292
  Steamed, 101
  Steamed Raw, 100
  Surprise, 98
Dutch Stew, 279

Easy Gnocchi, 100
Ecuadorian Creamed, 288
Egg
  in Cream, 244
  Curried Casserole, 243
  Delmonico Casserole, 242
  Farmer's Omelette, 244
  Frittata, 300
  Mayonnaise, Mashed with, 41
  Olive Casserole, 70
  Omelette Soufflé, 240
  Persian Omelette, 300
  Scrambled, 241
  Sour Cream Casserole, 242
  Sour Cream Omelette, 240
  Supper Scramble, 241
Eggplant, Stuffed, 246

Family Style Stewed, 61
Farmer's Omelette, 244
Filled Balls, 245
Fish and Seafood
  Baked Fish, 212
  Clam Cakes, 44
  Codfish Stew, 286
  Creamed Salmon, 210
  Fish on a Couch, 212
  Fish Hash, 218
  Fish Scallop, 286
  Fish Soufflé, 224
  Fish Stew, 222
  Oyster Casserole, 210
  Oysters on Half Shell, 214
  Salmon Loaf, 211
  Sardine-Stuffed Potatoes, 213
  Scallop Chowder, 223
Foil-Roasted Potatoes, 248
Fondant, 188
Fondant Icing, 188
Forester's Potatoes, 31
Franconia Potatoes, 10
Franks, Baked Salad, 237
Freezer Vichyssoise, 122
French Potato Cakes, 294
French Dumplings, 292
French Fries, 21
French Fries, various shapes, 22
French Pancakes, 296
Fresh Prune Dumplings, 199
Fricadellen, 295
Friday Chowder, 134
Fried, Deep (*see also* Croquettes,
    Mashed Potato Cakes)
  French Fries, 21
  In Various Shapes, 22
  Mock Pommes Soufflés, 24
  Oven "Fried" Wedges, 27
  Oven "Fries," 27
  Pennsylvania Fries, 25
  Peruvian Balls, 97
  Pommes Dauphine, 26
  Pommes Soufflés, 23
  Puffed Fritters, 26
  Quick Oven Fries, 27
  Southern-Fried, 24
  Tempura, 25
  Twice-Fried French Fries, 21
Fried, Skillet
  Butter-Fried, 28
  Campfire Fries, 252
  Cottage Fries, 31

Fried, Skillet (*cont'd*)
    Cream Fries, 34
    Curried, 252
    Forester's, 31
    Hashed Brown, 35
    Landaise, 30
    Lyonnaise, 30
    Onion Cake, 34
    Patties, 35
    Provençale, 32
    Roesti, 290
    Sour Cream Fries, 32
    Sweet and Sour Fries, 33
Frittata, 300
Fritters, 50
Frosted Meat Loaf, 208
Frozen Potato Snacks, 110
Fruited Drop Cakes, 179

Garden-Stuffed, 18
Gâteau Mocha, 178
Gaufrettes, 22
German Buttermilk Soup, 282
German Meat Cakes, 285
German Prune Dumplings, 199
German Salad, 142
Gnocchi, Easy, 100
Gnocchi, Puffed, 99
Golden Bake, 230
Golden Salmon Salad, 150
Golden Vegetable Soup, 129
Goose Liver Stuffing, 92
Grated Pan-Creamed Potatoes, 55
au Gratin, New Potatoes, 87
Green Stew, 60
Griddle Crumb Cakes, 45
Griddle Scones, 164
Grill Pan Scallop, 256
Grill Roasted Potatoes, 248
Grilled Patties, 253
Grilled Slices, 251
Ground Beef Stew, 230

Ham
    and Cheese Scallop, 228
    Patties, 44
    Pudding, 227
    Salad, 148
    Scallop, 228
    Steak Scallop, 229
    Stuffed Potatoes, 16
Hamburger
    Hash, 216

Scallop, 231
Harlequin Salad, 147
Hash
    Ad Lib, 214
    Baked, 215
    Baked with Eggs, 215
    Cakes, 42
    Clam, 219
    Corned Beef, 215
    Creamed Chicken, 218
    Egg, 218
    Fish, 218
    Hamburger, 216
    Meat and Mushroom, 217
    Red Flannel, 215
    Roast Beef, 216
Hashed-Brown Potatoes, 35
Hash-Stuffed Potatoes, 221
Herb Biscuits, 165
Herb Garden Mash, 42
Herbal Salad, 137
Herring Salad, 152
Herring Hors d'Oeuvre, 118
Home Style Croquettes, 48
Hot Barbecue Potato Salad, 255
Hot Potato Balls, 50
Hot Salad Dressing, 273
Hot Salad for Fifty, 272
Hotchpotch, 279
Hungarian New Potatoes, 86
Hurry, Baked, 11

Iced Green Soup, 267
Icings
    Fondant Icing, 188
    Ornamental Frosting, 187
Irish Boxty Cake, 294
Irish Champ, 298
Irish Colcannon, 299
Irish Lamb Stew, 278
Italian Dumplings, 293
Italian Omelette, 300
Italian Potato and Pepper Stew, 288

Jewish Pancakes, 295
Jewish Pudding, 292
Julienne Potatoes, 22

Knishes
    Liver, 115
    Potato, 115
Kugel, 292

Landaise, 30
Latkes, 295
Latkes, Blender, 295
Leek Scallop, 67
Lefse, 296
Lemon Nut Soufflé, 200
Lemon Sauce, 200
Links and Bolts, 22
Liver-Stuffed, 220
Luncheon Pancakes, 108
Lyonnaise, 30

Maine Cracknels, 47
Maine Pancakes, 105
Maine Scallop, 64
Maître d'Hôtel Butter, 10
Maître d'Hôtel Creamed Potatoes, 54
Manhattan Clam Chowder, 133
Maple Pecan Pudding, 198
Mashed Potato Cakes (see also Meat
    and Poultry, Fish)
    Basic, 42
    Cheese Balls, 46
    Griddle Crumb, 45
    Maine Cracknels, 47
    Mock Fillets, 47
    Nutted Puffs, 46
    Pancakes, 106
    Seedy Puffs, 46
    Sour Cream Diamonds, 107
Mashed Potatoes
    Champ, 298
    Chantilly, 38
    Colcannon, 299
    à la Crème, 38
    with Egg Mayonnaise, 41
    for Fifty, 269
    Herb Garden Mash, 42
    Mont d'Or, 39
    Peanutty, 41
    Riced, 37
    Smetana, 40
    Snow, 38
    Varieties, 37
    Vintner's, 40
    with Vegetables, 39
    Whipped, 37
Meat and Poultry Main Dishes (see
    also Hash)
    Baked Franks and Potato Salad,
      237
    Chicken Bonne Femme, 239
    Chicken Liver Patties, 45

Filled Potato Balls, 245
Fricadellen, 285
Golden Bake, 230
Ground Beef Stew, 230
Ham and Cheese Scallop, 228
Ham Patties, 45
Ham Pudding, 227
Ham Scallop, 228
Ham Steak Scallop, 229
Hamburger Scallop, 231
Hash Cakes, 42
Hash-Stuffed Potatoes, 221
Hotchpotch, 279
Irish Lamb Stew, 278
Liver-Stuffed Potatoes, 220
Polish Sausage Casserole, 282
Meat Balls Stroganoff, 285
Meat Loaf, 225
Mixed Meat Balls, 226
Pizza Balls, 245
Pork Chop Scallop, 234
Pork Chops en Casserole, 234
Pot Pie Crust, 238
Rapée with Ham, 226
Sausage Soufflé, 235
Shepherd's Pie, 232
Skillet Pork Stew, 236
Steak and Kidney Pie, 233
Stuffed Chicken, 283
Stuffed Eggplant, 246
Supper Special, 220
Swedish Meat Balls, 284
Turkey Pot Pie, 238
Veal Chops Grand'Mere, 236
Meat and Mushroom Hash, 211
Meat Loaf, 225
Meat Loaf, Frosted, 208
Meat Balls Stroganoff, 285
Menthe, New Potatoes à la, 78
Mixed Meat Balls, 226
Mocha, Gâteau, 178
Mock Fillets, 47
Mock Lemon Cheese Pie, 190
Mock Pommes Soufflés, 24
Mold, Salad, 141
Monday Lunch, 131
Mont d'Or, 39
Muffin Puddings, 206
Muffins
    Blueberry, 166
    Date, 166
    Potato Starch, 166

P

Murgh I Mussalam (Stuffed Chicken), 283
Mushroom
    Scallop, 66
    Soup, 124
    Stuffed, 260
Mustard Potatoes, 290

Nepalese Potatoes, 291
Nests, 204
New Brunswick Pork Stuffing, 94
New Potato Apples, 208
New Potato Snacks, 110
New Potatoes
    with Anchovies, 82
    Basquaise, 88
    Cheesed, 83
    to Cook, 78
    au Citron, 79
    Danish, 299
    Dilled, 80
    Dilled with Beans, 81
    à la Française, 83
    au Gratin, 87
    aux Herbes, 80
    Hungarian, 87
    Maître d'Hôtel, 78
    à la Menthe, 79
    and Peas, 81
    Pittsburgh, 84
    Printemps, 84
    Salad, 86
    Savory Browned, 82
    Scramble, 85
Niçoise Salad, 152
Noodles, Sesame, 266
Nut-and-Olive Stuffed Potatoes, 259
Nut Cookies, 183
Nutted Puffs, 46
Nutted Short Cake, 193

Oatmeal Chews, 182
Oatmeal Crisps, 182
O'Brien Potatoes, 31
Old-Fashioned Chocolate Cake, 171
Old-Fashioned Creamed Potatoes, 55
Old-Fashioned Mashed Salad, 140
Old-Fashioned Pork Stuffing, 94
Old-Fashioned Salad for Fifty, 272
Old-Fashioned Vegetable Chowder, 130
Omelette Soufflé, 240
Onion Cake, 34
Onion Soufflé, 72

Orange Tea Bread, 167
Oregano Baked Potatoes, 11
Oregano Toasties, 251
Ornamental Frosting, 187
Oven-Browned, 10
Oven-Fried Cases, 205
Oven-Fried Wedges, 27
Oven-Fries, 27
Oven-Fries, Quick, 27
Oven Temperature Chart, 5
Oyster Casserole, 210
Oysters on the Potato Half Shell, 214

Pakistani Stuffed Chicken, 283
Pan-Creamed, 55
Pancakes
    Boxty Cake, 294
    Buttermilk Breakfast, 106
    Crêpes, 192
    Crisp, 104
    French, 296
    Latkes, 295
    Latkes Blender, 295
    Lefse, 296
    Luncheon, 108
    Maine, 105
    Mashed, 106
    Sour Cream, 108
    Sour Cream, Diamonds, 107
    Subrics, 294
    Sweet Cream, 105
    Variety, 104
Papas Rellenas, 297
Paprikasch Potato Stew, 58
Parisienne Potatoes, 29
Parker House Rolls, 276
Parmigiana Puff, 76
Passover Sponge Cake, 177
Pastry, Tender, 112
Pastry, Pot Pie, 238
Patatas Con Queso, 298
Patates Pilaskisi (Potato Ragout), 287
Patties
    Chicken Liver, 45
    Ham, 44
    Salmon, 43
    Skillet Fried, 35
Peanut Butter Cookies, 180
Peanutty, 41
Peas and New Potatoes, 81
Pecan Torte, 172
Pennsylvania Dutch Salad, 144

Pennsylvania Dutch Fries, 25
Persian Omelette, 300
Peruvian Balls, 297
Pflaumen Knödel, 199
Pies
    Cheese, 264
    Clam, 265
    Cottage Cheese, 263
    Eggnog, 190
    Mock Lemon Cheese, 190
    Potato, 264
    Shepherd's, 232
    Steak and Kidney, 233
Picnic Salad, 138
Pigs in Blankets, 111
Pioneer Cinnamon Roll, 161
Pioneer Scalloped, 63
Pittsburgh, 84
Pizza Balls, 245
Polish Sausage Casserole, 282
Pommes
    Dauphine, 26
    Duchesse, 203
        Bordure, 203
        Pie Shells, 204
    Soufflés, 23
Porcupines, 207
Pork Chop Scallop, 234
Pork Chops en Casserole, 234
Portuguese Codfish Stew, 286
Potage
    Parmentier, 280
    Printanière, 126
    Tomato, 267
Potatoes
    Buying, 2
    Calories, 3
    Nutrients, 3
    Storing, 3
Potato Starch Muffins, 166
Pot Pie Crust, 238
Poultry (see Meat and Poultry)
Printemps, New Potatoes, 84
Profitable Potatoes for a Crowd
    Delmonico for Fifty, 270
    Doughnuts for Fifty, 277
    Hot Dressing for Fifty, 273
    Hot Salad for Fifty, 272
    Mashed for Fifty, 269
    Old-Fashioned Salad for Fifty, 272
    Puffs for Fifty, 275
    Rolls for Fifty, 276
    Salad for Fifty, 271
    Scalloped for Fifty, 270
    Soup for Fifty, 274
Provençale, 32
Provençale Scallop, 260
Prune Stuffing, 93
Puddings
    Brandied, 195
    Carrot Charlotte, 68
    Charlotte, 68
    Cheese, 67
    Christmas, 194
    Ham, 227
    Kugel, 292
    Maple Pecan, 198
    Rapée with Ham, 226
    Squares, 69
Puff Parmesan, 176
Puff Pie, 74
Puffed Dumplings, 99
Puffed Fritters, 26
Puffed Gnocchi, 99
Puffs, 51
Puffs for Fifty, 275

Quantity Cooking (see Profitable Potatoes)
Quenelles, 292
Quiche, 116
Quick Creamed Potatoes, 56
Quick Delmonico Scallop, 66
Quick Dumplings, 98
Quick Oven Fries, 27
Quick Potatoes for the Grill, 253
Quick Sponge Cake, 176

Raised Doughnuts, 185
Rapée with Ham, 226
Recipe Seasoning, 5
Recipe Yields, 5
Red and Gold Casserole, 262
Red Flannel Hash, 215
Refrigerator Rolls, 158
Rich Mix Cake, 174
Rich Raisin Bread, 162
Rissolée, 29
Roast Beef Hash, 216
Roesti, 290
Roll, Salad, 138
Roll-Up Snacks, 110
Rolls
    Crescents, 159
    for Fifty, 276

Rolls (cont'd)
    Parker House, 276
    Refrigerator, 158
Rosin Baked Potatoes, 248
Russian Salad, 148

Salad Dressings
    Creamy French, 154
    Tartar Mayonnaise, 154
Salads
    Basic, 135
    Blue Cheese, 142
    Cheese, 146
    Classic, 136
    Cottage Cheese, 145
    Crabmeat, 149
    Creamy French Dressing, 154
    for Fifty, 271
    German, 142
    Golden Salmon, 150
    Ham, 148
    Harlequin, 147
    Herbal, 137
    Herring, 152
    Hot Barbecue, 255
    Mashed, 140
    Mold, 141
    Niçoise, 152
    Old-Fashioned Mashed, 140
    Pennsylvania Dutch Hot, 144
    Picnic, 138
    Roll, 138
    Russian, 148
    Salmon, 150
    Sardine, 151
    Spanish, 143
    Tuna Crunch, 153
    Vintner's, 139
    Waldorf, 144
    Zucchini, 146
Salmon
    Creamed, 210
    Loaf, 211
    Patties, 43
    Puff, 17
    Salad, 150
Salt-Boiled, 249
Sardine Salad, 151
Sardine-Stuffed, 213
Sauerkraut Stew, 58
Sauerkraut Stuffing for Goose, 92
Sausage Casserole, 282
Sausage Soufflé, 235

Savory Browned New Potatoes, 82
Savory Scallop, 261
Savoyard, 65
Scallop Chowder, 223
Scalloped Potatoes
    Anna, 259
    Boulangère, 65
    Bread Crumb, 65
    Cheddar, 262
    Cheese, 67
    Dauphinoise, 64
    Delmonico, Quick, 66
    for Fifty, 270
    Ham, 228
    Ham and Cheese, 228
    Ham Steak, 229
    Hamburger, 231
    Leek, 67
    Maine, 64
    Mushroom, 66
    en Papillote, 257
    Pioneer, 63
    Pork Chop, 234
    Provençale, 260
    Savory, 261
    Savoyard, 65
    Variations, 63
Scandinavian Fish Scallop, 286
Scandinavian Pancakes, 296
Schneider Potatoes, 57
Scones, Buttermilk, 163
Scones, Griddle, 164
Scramble, New Potato, 85
Scrambled Eggs, 241
Seafood (see Fish and Seafood)
Seedy Puffs, 46
Seedy Sticks, 116
Senf Kartoffeln, 290
Sesame Noodles, 266
Shepherd's Pie, 232
Shoestrings, 22
Shortcake, 193
Skillet Pork Stew, 236
Smetana, 40
Snow, 38
Soufflés and Puffs
    Cheese, 73
    Cream Cheese, 75
    Onion, 72
    Parmigiana, 76
    Puff Pie, 74
    Spinach, 74
    Tapioca, 75

Soups
    Asparagus, 123
    Boston Clam Chowder, 132
    Buttermilk, German, 283
    Cabbage, 124
    Capetown Curried Beef, 281
    Cheddar Cheese, 128
    Corn Chowder, 132
    Cream of Onion, 127
    Cream of Vegetable, 126
    Curried Bisque, 125
    for Fifty, 274
    Freezer Vichyssoise, 122
    Friday Chowder, 134
    Golden Vegetable, 129
    Iced Green, 267
    Manhattan Clam Chowder, 133
    Monday Lunch, 131
    Mushroom, 124
    Old-Fashioned Vegetable
      Chowder, 130
    Potage Parmentier, 280
    Potage Printanière, 126
    Tomato, 266
    Turnip, 128
    Vichyssoise, 122
    Watercress, 280
Sour Cream
    Casserole, 72
    Diamonds, 107
    Fries, 32
    Omelette, 240
    Pancakes, 108
    Potatoes with, 56
Southern-Fried, 24
Spanish
    Salad, 143
    Stuffed, 298
Spice Cake, 177
Spice Jumble Cookies, 196
Spice Jumble Dessert, 196
Spinach and Potato Soufflé, 74
Spudburgers, 253
Squares, 69
Steak and Kidney Pie, 233
Steamed Dumplings, 101
Steamed Raw Potato Dumplings, 100
Stewed Potatoes
    au Jus, 57
    Family Style, 61
    Green, 60
    Paprikasch, 58
    Pepper, Italian, 288

    Sauerkraut, 58
    Schneider, 57
    Tomato, 60
    Turkish Potato Ragout, 287
    Vegetable, 59
Sticks, Amandine, 206
Streusel Kuchen, 169
Stroganoff, Meat Balls, 285
Stuffed Eggplant, 246
Stuffed Pigs, 14
Stuffed Potatoes
    Bacon, 255
    Chili, 254
    Dilled, 16
    Frank, 220
    Garden, 18
    Ham, 16
    Hash, 221
    Liver, 220
    Mushroom, 260
    Nut and Olive, 259
    Papas Rellenas, 297
    Salmon Puff, 17
    Sardine, 213
    Spanish, 298
    Surprise, 251
    Tuna Puff, 17
    Turnip, 18
    Variations, 14
    Vegetable, 15
Stuffings
    Apple, 91
    Basic, 90
    Casserole, 96
    Celery, 91
    Custard, 95
    Goose Liver, 92
    New Brunswick Pork, 94
    Old-Fashioned Pork, 94
    Prune, 93
    Sauerkraut Stuffing for Goose, 92
    Turkey or Chicken Liver, 92
Subrics, 294
Supper Scramble, 241
Supper Special, 220
Surprise Baked, 13
Surprise Barbecue, 251
Surprise Dumplings, 98
Sweet and Sour Fries, 33
Sweet Cream Pancakes, 105
Sweet Roll Dough, 160
Swedish Meat Balls, 284
Swiss Fries, 290

Tapioca Soufflé, 75
Tartar Mayonnaise, 154
Tempura, 25
Tender Pastry, 112
Toasted New Potatoes, 249
Tomato
    Casserole, 71
    Potage, 266
    Stew, 60
Toppings, Baked Potato, 8
Tuna
    Croquettes, 43
    Crunch Salad, 153
    Puff, 17
Turkey Liver Stuffing, 92
Turkey Pot Pie, 238
Turkish Potato Ragout, 287
Turnip Soup, 128
Turnip-Stuffed Potatoes, 18

Twice-Fried French Fries, 21

Veal Chops Grand'Mere, 236
Vegetable Stew, 59
Vegetable Stuffed Potatoes, 15
Vegetables with Mashed Potatoes, 39
Vichyssoise, 122
Vintner's Mashed Potatoes, 40
Vintner's Salad, 139

Waffles, 165
Waldorf Salad, 144
Whipped Potatoes, 37
White Bread, 156
White Cake de Luxe, 170

Yeast Starter, 162

Zucchini Salad, 146